THE FILM ADDICT'S ARCHIVE

AS HIMSELF

AS DON PABLO

AS THE RAJAH

AS AN AMERICAN

AS A TAXI-DRIVER

AS AN ARTIST

AS AN ACTOR

AS A COWBOY

IN LIGHTER MOOD DISGUISED AS "CHARLIE"

A MASTER OF FILM MAKE-UP

THE
FILM ADDICT'S
ARCHIVE

EDITED BY

PHILIP OAKES

ELM TREE BOOKS
HAMISH HAMILTON · LONDON

First published in Great Britain 1977
by Elm Tree Books/Hamish Hamilton Ltd
90 Great Russell Street, London WC1B 3PT

Copyright © 1977 by Philip Oakes

SBN 241 89384 4

Printed in Great Britain
by Ebenezer Baylis and Son Ltd
The Trinity Press, Worcester, and London

CONTENTS

Acknowledgements   vii

Introduction   ix

Prose:

DAVID STACTON
Dreamland   1

RUDYARD KIPLING
Mrs. Bathurst   7

NATHANAEL WEST
The Day of the Locust   23

F. SCOTT FITZGERALD
The Last Tycoon   34

CHRISTOPHER ISHERWOOD
Prater Violet   45

S. J. PERELMAN
Strictly From Hunger   59

JEFFREY DELL
Nobody Ordered Wolves   67

BUDD SCHULBERG
What Makes Sammy Run?   75

LARRY McMURTRY
The Last Picture Show   86

MAURICE DRUON
The Film of Memory   98

JIM KIRKWOOD
There Must Be A Pony   102

ALBERTO MORAVIA
The Film Test   112

GORE VIDAL
Myra Breckinridge   119

JAMES THURBER
The Man Who Hated Moonbaum   127

ALISON LURIE
  The Nowhere City   132
RONA JAFFE
  Guess Who This Is   141
JULIAN MACLAREN-ROSS
  Adventures in Film   148
JOHN O'HARA
  Can You Carry Me?   157
GAVIN LAMBERT
  The Closed Set   162
BARRY N. MALTZBERG
  Screen   206

Poetry:
JOHN HOLLANDER
  Movie-Going   82
JOHN COTTON
  Old Movies   94
A. S. J. TESSIMOND
  Chaplin   95
TOM RAWORTH
  Claudette Colbert by Billy Wilder   96
ROBERT LOWELL
  For Harpo Marx   97
HARRY BROWN
  This is Merely Part of the Studio Tour   123
KARL SHAPIRO
  Movie Actress   124
CHRISTOPHER LOGUE
  Film Star Poem   125
JOHN NORMANTON
  Stars in an Oldie   204
PHILIP OAKES
  The Midnight Movie   212

ACKNOWLEDGEMENTS

'Dreamland' by David Stacton is reprinted by permission of Elaine Greene, Ltd.; 'Mrs. Bathurst', from *Traffics and Discoveries* by Rudyard Kipling by permission of The Executors of the Estate of Mrs. Elsie Bambridge and The Macmillan Company of London & Basingstoke; the extracts from *The Day of the Locust* by Nathanael West (New Directions Publishing Corporation, New York, and Martin Secker & Warburg Ltd., London) by permission of Laurence Pollinger Ltd.; from *The Last Tycoon* by F. Scott Fitzgerald from *The Bodley Head Scott Fitzgerald* Vol. I by permission of The Bodley Head; from *Prater Violet* by Christopher Isherwood by permission of Methuen & Co. Ltd.; 'Strictly From Hunger', copyright © 1935, 1958 by S. J. Perelman as included in *The Most of S. J. Perelman*, reprinted by permission of Deborah Rogers Ltd., London; the extract from *Nobody Ordered Wolves* by Jeffrey Dell (Jonathan Cape Ltd.) is reprinted by permission of A. D. Peters & Co. Ltd.; from *What Makes Sammy Run?* by Budd Schulberg by permission of The Bodley Head; from *The Last Picture Show* by Larry McMurtry by permission of A. M. Heath & Co. Ltd.; from *The Film of Memory* by Maurice Druon by permission of A. D. Peters & Co. Ltd.; from *There Must Be A Pony* by Jim Kirkwood, copyright James Kirkwood, 1960, by permission of Elaine Greene Ltd.; 'The Film Test' from *Roman Tales* by Alberto Moravia (translated by Angus Davidson) is reprinted by permission of Martin Secker & Warburg Ltd.; the extract from *Myra Breckinridge* by Gore Vidal by permission of Blond & Briggs, London; 'The Man who Hated Moonbaum' from *Vintage Thurber* by James Thurber © 1963, by permission of Hamish Hamilton Ltd.; the extract from *The Nowhere City* by Alison Lurie by permission of William Heinemann Ltd.; 'Guess Who This Is' from *Mr. Right is Dead* by Rona Jaffe by permission of Jonathan Cape Ltd.; 'Adventures in Film' from *The Funny Bone* by Julian Maclaren-Ross by permission of Paul Elek Ltd.; 'Can You Carry Me?' from *Pipe Night* by John O'Hara by permission of Faber and Faber Ltd.; 'The Closed Set' from *The Slide Area* by Gavin Lambert by permission of A. D. Peters & Co. Ltd.; 'Movie-Going' from *Movie-Going And Other Poems* by John Hollander, Copyright ©

1961, 1962 by John Hollander, reprinted by permission of Atheneum Publishers, New York; 'Old Movies' © John Cotton from his collection *Old Movies and Other Poems*, Chatto & Windus; 'Chaplin' by A. S. J. Tessimond by permission of Hubert Nicholson; 'Claudette Colbert by Billy Wilder' from *Lion Lion* by Tom Raworth by permission of the Trigram Press Ltd.; 'For Harpo Marx' from *Notebook* by Robert Lowell by permission of Faber and Faber Ltd.; 'This is Merely Part of the Studio Tour' by Harry Brown by permission of A. M. Heath & Co. Ltd.; 'Movie Actress' from *V-Letter and Other Poems* by Karl Shapiro (Random House, Inc., New York and Martin Secker & Warburg Ltd., London) by permission of Laurence Pollinger Ltd.; Film Star poem from *New Numbers* © Christopher Logue (Jonathan Cape, 1969) by permission of Hope Leresche & Sayle; 'Stars in an Oldie' from *The Window Game* by John Normanton by permission of London Magazine Editions; 'The Midnight Movie' from *Married/Singular*, 1974, by Philip Oakes by permission of André Deutsch Ltd; the frontispiece drawing by Bert Thomas by permission of *Punch*.

Every effort has been made to trace the copyright holders of the material used in this volume. Should there be any omissions in this respect, we apologise and shall be pleased to make the appropriate acknowledgement in future editions.

INTRODUCTION

Social scientists may have exaggerated the ill effects of the screen on the adolescent mind and senses, but there is an inescapable hypnosis attached to the movie screen that can catch up from his plush seat a sane, balanced, even well-read, adult person, and emotionally implicate him in a novelette-in-action that, transposed into its literary equivalent, would be scorned by a 12-year-old schoolgirl. His mind may reject the film utterly, but he will be powerless to move while banality grips him.

RICHARD WINNINGTON
The Missing Element in the Cinema

I became a film addict at the age of four when my mother took me to see what was perhaps the last of the great silent westerns, James Cruze's *The Covered Wagon*. I suspect that she had been told it was a classic—a guarantee which made entertainment respectable. But, all unwittingly, she exposed me to a virus which, in the course of time, devoured my pocket money, ruined my school record and ruptured my eyeballs.

There were plenty of cinemas in my part of the world. I lived in the Potteries, a district celebrated in the novels of Arnold Bennett as the Five Towns—although local purists insisted that there were six—and each of them had one or two picture houses. There was the Regent, the Palladium, the Coliseum (a former theatre with pillars still intact which regulars knew how to avoid), the Roxy, the Globe, the Ritz and the Empire. All these were moderately respectable. But we chose the Palace and this was where the trouble began.

They had rats at the Palace, everyone knew that. Why else should they maintain a corps of cats—black, tabby, tortoiseshell and dirty white—to patrol the aisles, slinking under the tip-up seats, brushing our legs when the lights went down? They had other things too, some of them unmentionable. To our parents, the Palace was 'the flea-pit', 'the bug-hutch' where we soaked up trash, endangering both the body and the soul.

Week after week they warned us and week after week we ignored them. What they said was true enough. The Palace was a disgrace, a tatty, near-derelict cinema, where the projection jumped like a torch in the hand of a drunken man, where paper darts planed down from the gallery and where peanut shells detonated underfoot, popping like small-arms fire. It was every bit as bad as they said it was. And we loved it dearly.

At the Palace I saw *Flash Gordon on the Planet Mars*, a fifteen-part serial with Flash fighting intergalactic war lords, facing extinction at the fangs of bug-eyed monsters and guarding Dale, his scantily-clad companion, from a compendium of fates—all more titillating than instant death. Looking back I think this was where sex first reared its movie-going head. But its impact was strictly subliminal. The kicks I craved were all above the groin. I saw *The Haunted Mine* with Tim McCoy, the cowboy star (and real-life army colonel) whose white stetson curled like the lip of a buckskin aristocrat. I saw Tod Slaughter murdering his way to an inheritance by driving a tent peg through the skull of the rightful heir. I saw Laurel and Hardy and the Three Stooges and Rin-Tin-Tin the Wonder Dog and Charlie Chase and Shirley Temple tapping step for step with the great Bill Robinson and all for threepence admission, with a bag of boiled sweets, an apple and an orange thrown in on Saturday afternoons.

The queue began to form at one o'clock. The Palace was in a side street of a small mining village and after mid-day the pavements were thronged by colliers coming off the last shift. There were no pit-head baths. The men left work plastered in grime, their lips cherry-red, their eye-balls white as gob-stoppers that had been sucked for half an hour. Washing was done at home in a zinc tub in front of the kitchen fire. When the men were at the pit their tubs hung on the outhouse walls, as neatly arrayed as battle-shields in an armoury. I often thought of the miners themselves as members of an army. Their appearance was uniform. They swore mightily. Their sport was bloody (terriers were secretly pitted against each other in pub cellars). They were a race apart.

I remembered looking from them—helmeted, begrimed, smelling of coal and pit damp—to the heroes in the display of stills outside the cinema. There was no comparison. The worlds they encompassed were too distant to be linked by even a film-fired imagination. In the photographs fat comics and bronzed buckaroos grinned into the glare of a California sun. Outside the Palace rain soaked the roof-tops and carbon creatures hurried home towards soap and water.

At the end of the street the black pyramid of the tip—a man-made mountain of colliery waste—poked up like a sleeping volcano. Inside the cinema it was curious to think of it standing sentinel, a reminder that whatever the Palace offered by way of escape, work was still to be done. Not that I thought much along those lines. I did not belong to the village. The Palace was my sole reason for going there. But trying to sweep my memory clear of the dust of forty or so years, I know that the place itself—menacing, tarnished, melodramatic—sharpened my pleasure in movie-going.

It was like being on holiday from school, watching the blue swell of the sea from a cliff-top and saying luxuriously and preferably aloud, 'This time *last* week . . .' The Palace punctuated my life with holidays and with the prospect of better things to come. It was where I liked to be best, stowed away in the plush darkness, horsehair oozing from the seat and prickling my bare thighs, a Victory lozenge fuming in my mouth and on the screen Errol Flynn setting torch to the Spanish Main or Charlie Chan—the blandest of screen detectives—pointing out clues to his number one son, or Chester Morris driving his truck through an obstacle course of burning oil wells.

Later, in the throes of an education, I played truant to see Richard Whorf in *Blues in the Night* and Ingrid Bergman in *Adam Had Four Sons*. In the army I almost missed my troop-ship by extending my leave to catch a Bogart re-issue. In Cairo I saw a local bookie clean up by taking bets on the chariot race in *Ben Hur* (the 1926 version). And with an audience of German prisoners-of-war I watched Leni Riefenstahl's film of the Olympiad, since when nostalgia has never seemed to me entirely innocent.

For me, movie-going has always been so perfectly fused with life itself that I remember signal events—falling in or out of love, changing a job, publishing a book—by recalling the film that marked the moment. Even fifteen years spent as a film critic—a sentence gruelling enough to dull most sensibilities—has done nothing to blur or diminish the images received from a thousand screens. One part of my brain is equipped as a projection room where the programme is continuous, where Marilyn eternally moistens her lips, where Rita Hayworth (a goddess in *Gilda*) strips off her black silk gloves, where John Wayne prowls pigeon-toed to meet the gun-hands in *Rio Bravo*, where Gene Kelly dances in an MGM deluge and Fred Astaire mows down the chorus line with a cane turned tommy-gun in *Top Hat*. James Cagney's there too, blowing himself to eternity in *White Heat* and Jack Lemmon shearing the blooms from his bouquet between the fast-closing doors of an elevator in *Days of Wine and Roses*. W. C. Fields puts in a frequent appearance (most often steering the pesky blind customer into a street teeming with traffic) and Buster Keaton survives again and again as the building collapses, leaving him dusty but still standing in the slot of an open window.

It's the greatest free show in the world. But what the images also preserve is a mood, a fragment of one's self where the flesh has been candied by fantasy which melts in the mind reconstituting what's gone. Not all of it is happy. Not all of it is drawn to scale. But even the pangs and the lack of perspective are part of movie-going. Movies are something we live with (if not by). They entertain us. They divert us. But they also help to make us what we are. They are both mirrors and moulds, commentaries and catalysts. They are part of our experience.

Most writers that I know have what's best described in 1950s Warner Brothers' style as 'a love-hate relationship' with the movies. Actors likewise. But actors—with few exceptions—rarely retain enough objectivity to tell the tale. This anthology attempts to do that—and more. It is, hopefully, a feature in which the reader can be the audience, the star, or any one of a cast of thousands.

PHILIP OAKES

DAVID STACTON

(1925–1965)

The settings of David Stacton's novels—he published thirteen under his own name and many more under pseudonyms—range from ancient Egypt (On A Balcony) to modern Hollywood (Dolores). He died in 1965, leaving among his papers an uncompleted million-word novel entitled Restless Sleep. *'Dreamland', one of a number of uncollected stories, first appeared in* World Review.

Dreamland

WHEN ABEL died in 1933, Miss Winnie inherited the estate. She was a very distant relative. The estate was Dreamland, and Dreamland was a third-run motion picture palace way down in the slums. She'd never even heard of it, and even now that she owned it, she did not go inside. She was sure she was very grateful to Abel; not that he had any other kin, but she didn't like the look of it. When she thought about it, she just pursed her lips.

She was a retired schoolteacher. She did not smoke; she did not drink, and she never spoke to Abel, for he wasn't respectable. She lived alone in a small apartment in downtown Los Angeles, in a dingy building whose hallways always smelt of cooking. In the largest window, which looked out on to an alley, she kept her cage of canaries. It was a small world, and it was air-tight: nobody went into Miss Winnie's rooms but Miss Winnie. She and the canaries understood each other very well.

The inheritance scarcely changed her life at all. She bought a larger cage for the canaries and let the doorman manage everything. It wasn't that she trusted him. She didn't trust anybody any more. It was because he was an old man and she was an old woman, and she didn't want to be bothered about things.

There were two days in the year that Miss Winnie dreaded. They were the two days in the year when she felt old and lonely, and when she caught sight of herself in shop windows, while she talked to herself.

She enjoyed talking to herself, but on those two days of the year she knew she did it because she didn't have anybody else to talk to but the canaries, who didn't count. The two days were Christmas Eve and her birthday. She was afraid to be alone on those days. She would walk along Sunset Boulevard until midnight. New Year's Day gave her hope. On New Year's Day she drank sherry out of a small stem glass all morning long. In the afternoon she re-read *The Rosary*, which was a very, very great and deeply-moving book that reminded her of her mother.

Her birthday was on the twenty-fifth of October. When she woke up, her rooms were damp and the canaries were not happy. She decided to go out, dressed as she was, in her best black dress, as though she expected to meet somebody.

It was only by chance that she went by the theatre. She went round the block twice, and then, because it was raining, and for no other reason, she crept into the theatre. It was very dark inside.

She felt bewildered, but she also felt excited, as though she really was going to meet somebody. It was very strange. The theatre was small, and all she could see was a line of light from the projection booth to the screen. She sat down, and little by little she began to relax. She sat there for a long time. It did not seem unreal and it did not seem wicked. Some men were chasing other men through a forest, and she forgot about the time. She saw it again. At last, when the lights came on, she did not notice how shabby the theatre was, and when she left the building, the world seemed unreal to her. It seemed hostile and strange. When she got home, the canaries began to sing to her. She chopped them some groundsel, which she collected in vacant lots, and gave it to them. She felt almost happy.

But the apartment seemed still and empty now. She stood it for a week before going back shamefacedly to the theatre. Once inside she felt alive again. She leaned back in her seat and began to dream about just how it had been to walk down a flowery hillside as a young girl, and, for the first time in many years, she remembered how it did feel, and it felt delicious. While she sat there, the long flat figures moved and talked and came and went away from each other, in the most beautiful coloured world she had ever seen in her life. There was a woman her own age up there, and how nice she did look, with silver hair and such kind eyes. But Miss Winnie preferred it when she was young and walking through the flowered fields, beside a young man from Ohio. She could smell the warm Ohio summer in the air and could see the way the fields shimmered in the heat.

She did not want to leave the theatre any more. She now went two or three times a week. It was a life she had always known she could live, and at last she was living it, as she had always known she would. She told her canaries about her life in the theatre and about Robert Taylor, who was quite a nice young man who loved Camille very much.

It was at this time that she began to notice the trailers. They were very exciting. They told you what came next. She had to know who married Merle Oberon, so she went right down to the theatre as soon as the film came in. It was packed in a set of big aluminium tins which she held wistfully in her hands.

'Do you suppose I dare see them?' she asked the projection man.

'It's your theatre,' he said, and shrugged.

It was true. It was her world and the most wonderful things happened in it. She sat down and he ran it off for her. She somehow missed a bit, so he ran it off again. It was exciting. She went and told Charlie to cancel the run of what was playing, which had another three days to go, and put this on instead. She knew everyone would want to see it.

For she wasn't selfish. She liked it when people came into her world, because then she wasn't lonely any more. Of course they could never feel at home the way she did. They were only visitors.

One night she said goodbye to the canaries and took the trolley to the theatre. It was a sophisticated picture, but you could tell that Merle Oberon really did love those men, and she looked so lovable herself. Part of it was about Maine, and she had been to Maine when she was a little girl. At the theatre they told her that Charlie, the doorman, was dead. It did not mean much. He was not real. He wasn't real the way Joseph Cotten was real. Joseph Cotten was sturdy and reliable. She trusted him. She trusted him as she had never trusted Charlie.

But when she went home, one of the canaries was dead. It was lying on the bottom of the cage, with its feet in the air, and the others were huddled silently in one corner near the top of the cage. She felt guilty. She should never have left them in the apartment. She looked around the apartment, seeing how shabby and mean and unreal it was, and took the dead canary in her hand. It was Pete. She thought that the other canaries seemed to reproach her. She made up her mind right then. She put Pete in a box, put the box in her purse, and picking up the canary cage, went out into the street and called a cab. She went down to the theatre and put the cage of canaries in the projection booth, where it was always warm, and gave the birds some groundsel. Then she took the box with Pete in it, and going out the side exit, she buried it in the area way, just like Grauman's Chinese Theatre.

The next day she put a camp cot in the manager's office and moved in.

3

She could take her meals there, and she need never go out into the unreal world again.

She was happy. She wasn't even afraid of her birthday any more. On Christmas Eve they had such jolly shows, really friendly and everyone together, singing songs with the screen. There was even a real Christmas tree in the lobby, and she gave away door prizes. She did the same thing at New Year, and all her friends came. On New Year's morning she always treated herself to something expensive that wasn't supposed to be shown until next year, and that was thrilling too, because she could know what was going to come next year, which made her feel more sure of herself. It gave you something to look forward to. On New Year's Eve, and the whole week before, she ran all sorts of coming attraction trailers, so everyone else would also know what was coming. And when she took down the tree on New Year's Day, she didn't feel blue, because she knew there would be another next year. On New Year's Day she let children in free. She didn't want to shut them out of her wonderful world. They had a right to grow up in it and be happy.

Even her birthdays didn't frighten her any more. When she sat watching the screen, the people up there were never any older, and she was never any older either. She felt as young as ever she had, and she could remember as clearly as if it had been yesterday her twenty-first birthday, when the world had been so crisp and new. And it went on for ever, up there.

The canaries liked the theatre. Sometimes she would bring the cage down, if the theatre was almost empty, and let the birds watch with her, but what they liked best was to watch through the little square holes in the projection booth, so she had a cage built into the wall for them. They always sang during the sad parts, to cheer her up. She knew they were happy. Even the detective movies ended happily for the good people in them. Good people were always happy. They might have to suffer for a reel or two, but it all came out right in the end, just as her own life had.

She spent her mornings in the office, poring over the catalogues, announcements, publicity releases, and movie magazines, until she knew more about those people up there than anybody else. It was just like being right in their own homes, only better. When some of them separated, she couldn't have been happier when they saw they had been hasty and foolish and made it up. And if they were divorced, she always felt sorry for the poor little things, who never would seem to learn that there were bad men in the world. She was very happy.

But sometimes she felt tired in the mornings, particularly lately. She wished she were allowed to work the projector, for in the mornings there

4

was nothing to do at all, except to feed the canaries and water the plants in the lobby, or see that the candy bar was stocked properly. The shows didn't begin until eleven thirty, and since she always woke up at six, it was such a long wait. She began to be afraid of those hours. It was the only part of the day, any more, that she was afraid of. Even the radio didn't help much. It wasn't something you could touch or see. It was in the mornings she had to be careful.

One morning there was mail. Not just the usual announcements, but a real letter, and when she opened it, she could not breathe, her heart pounded so. It was what she had always prayed for, but she couldn't believe it. It was such a nice letter and it was really true. It was about the preview. There was really going to be one, and they wouldn't tell her what the picture was. It was two whole weeks to wait. She went up and fed the canaries, lost in her own dreams. It was a surprise, and since it would be the week of her birthday, it would be a birthday present. On her birthdays she always did order one or two pictures, just for herself. It was like getting gifts. You never knew what would be in them. But this was something else. This was something golden.

She was so happy, she went and told the cashier, who smiled and said she was happy too. Miss Winnie thought it was the most wonderful thing that had ever happened to her. It was so good it made her heart burst. It showed you how good these people really were. And besides, she might be in it.

For she was in some pictures. She knew it. Sometimes she thought she was in all of them, but that was only vanity.

She had not caught a glimpse of herself at first. And then, one day, when she was watching *The Magnificent Ambersons*, it seemed to her that she saw herself in a crowd. It was only logical. She had known the Ambersons well. She had had the picture run off for her the next morning, to make sure, and this time she was certain. After that she began to watch carefully. It was Robert Taylor who helped her. He came right into her room one morning and stood beside her cot and told her to be sure not to miss his next picture. He wouldn't tell her why, but he was definite about it, and she had known what he meant. Yes, there she was. She was the housekeeper who loved to tidy up after him, and she had never trusted that wicked little snip he was so fond of. She was right, and since he was intelligent, he saw it for himself in time, and married the good girl, the one who had talked it all over with her in the kitchen.

It was her secret that she was up there. She was her real self up there, the one she had always had to keep hidden. Sometimes in the older

5

pictures she saw herself as she had been as a girl. It was like going through a photographic album, and you never did know what you would find. There was a very sweet picture called *Meet Me in St. Louis*, and she was a little girl in that. And how they had ever found out all that about her she never would know, but it was wonderful to live through those years again.

Tonight, with the preview coming, she hoped that she would be able to see herself again. These days she was very seldom disappointed. She was in almost everything now. That was because they knew how good she was with children. She sat down expectantly to wait. She didn't doubt she was in the preview, too.

But something was wrong. She did not know what it was, but the canaries knew. She could hear them singing behind her. And it was different. Tonight the screen was all around her. She was part of it. At first they did not seem to know her. They spoke over and around her. But then Joseph Cotten, who always had been her dear friend, introduced her, and everyone was very friendly, knowing who she was. She had a wonderful time. It was such a comfortable house, in such a respectable, really nice street. They were old friends. She knew all about them, and she tried to help them as much as she could. There was a strange gentleman she'd never seen before, though. Pretty soon now he would try to shoot Carol. He always did, and now she was really part of it, now that she was really there, at last, and everyone had been so good to her, she couldn't let that happen. Not to a nice girl like that. She rushed forward, to prevent it, and felt a sharp pain right over her heart. She was falling fast, and all their voices, so kind and safe, flew around her, and it was dark. It was very dark, but she could hear the canaries singing, and so everything would be all right, and the lovers would be reunited.

She was right up there with them, right in the stars' own homes, and the canaries knew it. Nothing mattered. The pain did not hurt. There was no pain. They were always young and happy up there together, all of them. She wished Pete was there to see her. She felt proud as could be.

But she was very tired. She looked down from the screen. It was a long picture and she was tired. She could hear the canaries singing, so she knew she was up there at last. She was home. She was home in Ohio, years and years ago, with her mother and father and Joseph Cotten and all of them, but it had been a long journey and she was tired. Everyone was fond of her, and she thought she'd just go upstairs, leaving the united lovers, and take a little nap in her own room.

6

RUDYARD KIPLING

(1865–1936)

*As far as I can ascertain, Rudyard Kipling's story, 'Mrs. Bathurst',
written in 1904, is the first reference in all fiction to the cinema—or
Biograph, as it was known then. It may strike you as an untypical tale for
the buoyantly Imperialist Kipling to have written (its starting point, he
said, was a petty officer's remarks overheard in a train near Durban). But,
as he proved elsewhere, Kipling was fascinated by the insidious power of one
person (or one medium) over another. The Biograph clearly had it.
Incidentally, 'Mrs. Bathurst' is a good piece to test the supposed infallibility
of your film-addict friends. The omniscient Philip French first pointed out
the story to me, since when I have scored conversational points by challenging
all comers to name the first-ever piece of movie fiction. The only person to
come up with the right answer was Gore Vidal, a man who knows his movies.*

Mrs. Bathurst

THE DAY that I chose to visit H.M.S. *Peridot* in Simon's Bay was the
day that the Admiral had chosen to send her up the coast. She was just
steaming out to sea as my train came in, and since the rest of the Fleet
were either coaling or busy at the rifle-ranges a thousand feet up the hill,
I found myself stranded, lunchless, on the sea-front with no hope of
return to Cape Town before 5 p.m. At this crisis I had the luck to come
across my friend Inspector Hooper, Cape Government Railways, in
command of an engine and a brake-van chalked for repair.

'If you get something to eat.' he said, 'I'll run you down to Glengariff
siding till the goods comes along. It's cooler there than here, you
see.'

I got food and drink from the Greeks who sell all things at a price, and
the engine trotted us a couple of miles up the line to a bay of drifted sand
and a plank-platform half buried in sand not a hundred yards from the
edge of the surf. Moulded dunes, whiter than any snow, rolled far inland
up a brown and purple valley of splintered rocks and dry scrub. A crowd
of Malays hauled at a net beside two blue and green boats on the beach;

a picnic party danced and shouted bare-foot where a tiny river trickled across the flat, and a circle of dry hills, whose feet were set in sands of silver, locked us in against a seven-coloured sea. At either horn of the bay the railway line, just above high-water mark, ran round a shoulder of piled rocks, and disappeared.

'You see, there's always a breeze here,' said Hooper, opening the door as the engine left us in the siding on the sand, and the strong south-easter buffeting under Elsie's Peak dusted sand into our tickey beer. Presently he sat down to a file full of spiked documents. He had returned from a long trip up-country, where he had been reporting on damaged rolling-stock, as far away as Rhodesia. The weight of the bland wind on my eyelids; the song of it under the car-roof, and high up among the rocks; the drift of fine grains chasing each other musically ashore; the tramp of the surf; the voices of the picnickers; the rustle of Hooper's file, and the presence of the assured sun, joined with the beer to cast me into magical slumber. The hills of False Bay were just dissolving into those of fairyland when I heard footsteps on the sand outside, and the clink of our couplings.

'Stop that!' snapped Hooper, without raising his head from his work. 'It's those dirty little Malay boys, you see: they're always playing with the trucks . . .'

'Don't be hard on 'em. The railway's a general refuge in Africa,' I replied.

' 'Tis—up-country at any rate. That reminds me,' he felt in his waistcoat-pocket, 'I've got a curiosity for you from Wankies—beyond Bulawayo. It's more of a souvenir perhaps than—'

'The old hotel's inhabited,' cried a voice. 'White men, from the language. Marines to the front! Come on, Pritch. Here's your Belmont. Wha—i—i!'

The last word dragged like a rope as Mr. Pyecroft ran round to the open door, and stood looking up into my face. Behind him an enormous Sergeant of Marines trailed a stalk of dried seaweed, and dusted the sand nervously from his fingers.

'What are you doing here?' I asked. 'I thought the *Hierophant* was down the coast?'

'We came in last Tuesday—from Tristan da Cunha—for overhaul, and we shall be in dockyard 'ands for two months, with boiler-seatings.'

'Come and sit down.' Hooper put away the file.

'This is Mr. Hooper of the Railway,' I explained, as Pyecroft turned to haul up the black-moustached sergeant.

'This is Sergeant Pritchard, of the *Agaric*, and old shipmate,' said he.

'We were strollin' on the beach.' The monster blushed and nodded. He filled up one side of the van when he sat down.

'And this is my friend, Mr. Pyecroft,' I added to Hooper, already busy with the extra beer which my prophetic soul had bought from the Greeks.

'*Moi aussi*,' quoth Pyecroft, and drew out beneath his coat a labelled quart bottle.

'Why, it's Bass!' cried Hooper.

'It was Pritchard,' said Pyecroft. 'They can't resist him.'

'That's not so,' said Pritchard mildly.

'Not *verbatim* per'aps, but the look in the eye came to the same thing.'

'Where was it?' I demanded.

'Just on beyond here—at Kalk Bay. She was slappin' a rug in a back verandah. Pritch 'adn't more than brought his batteries to bear, before she stepped indoors an' sent it flyin' over the wall.'

Pyecroft patted the warm bottle.

'It was all a mistake,' said Pritchard. 'I shouldn't wonder if she mistook me for Maclean. We're about of a size.'

I had heard householders of Muizenberg, St. James, and Kalk Bay complain of the difficulty of keeping beer or good servants at the seaside, and I began to see the reason. None the less, it was excellent Bass, and I too drank to the health of the large-minded maid.

'It's the uniform that fetches 'em, an' they fetch it,' said Pyecroft. 'My simple navy blue is respectable, but not fascinatin'. Now Pritch in 'is Number One rig is always "purr Mary, on the terrace"—*ex officio* as you might say.'

'She took me for Maclean, I tell you,' Pritchard insisted. 'Why—why —to listen to him you wouldn't think that only yesterday—'

'Pritch,' said Pyecroft, 'be warned in time. If we begin tellin' what we know about each other we'll be turned out of the pub. Not to mention aggravated desertion on several occasions—'

'Never anything more than absence without leaf—I defy you to prove it,' said the Sergeant hotly. 'An' if it comes to that, how about Vancouver in '87?'

'How about it? Who pulled bow in the gig going ashore? Who told Boy Niven . . .?'

'Surely you were court-martialled for that?' I said. The story of Boy Niven who lured seven or eight able-bodied seamen and marines into the woods of British Columbia used to be a legend of the Fleet.

'Yes, we were court-martialled to rights,' said Pritchard, 'but we should have been tried for murder if Boy Niven 'adn't been unusually tough. He told us he had an uncle 'oo'd give us land to farm. 'E said he was born at the back o' Vancouver Island, and *all* the time the beggar was a balmy Barnardo Orphan!'

'*But* we believed him,' said Pyecroft. 'I did—you did— Paterson did —an' 'oo was the Marine that married the coconut woman afterwards —him with the mouth?'

'Oh, Jones, Spit-Kid Jones. I 'aven't thought of 'im in years,' said Pritchard. 'Yes, Spit-Kid believed it, an' George Anstey and Moon. We were very young an' very curious.'

'*But* lovin' an' trustful to a degree,' said Pyecroft.

'Remember when 'e told us to walk in single file for fear o' bears? Remember, Pye, when 'e 'opped about in that bog full o' ferns an' sniffed an' said 'e could smell the smoke of 'is uncle's farm? An' *all* the time it was a dirty little outlyin' uninhabited island. We walked round it in a day, an' come back to our boat lyin' on the beach. A whole day Boy Niven kept us walkin' in circles lookin' for 'is uncle's farm! He said his uncle was compelled by the law of the land to give us a farm!'

'Don't get hot, Pritch. We believed,' said Pyecroft.

'He'd been readin' books. He only did it to get a run ashore an' have himself talked of. A day an' a night—eight of us— followin' Boy Niven round an uninhabited island in the Vancouver archipelago! Then the picket came for us an' a nice pack o' idiots we looked!'

'What did you get for it?' Hooper asked.

'Heavy thunder with continuous lightning for two hours. Thereafter sleet-squalls, a confused sea, and cold, unfriendly weather till conclusion o' cruise,' said Pyecroft. 'It was only what we expected, but what we felt —an' I assure you, Mr. Hooper, even a sailor-man has a heart to break— was bein' told that we able seamen an' promisin' marines 'ad misled Boy Niven. Yes, we poor back-to-the-landers was supposed to 'ave misled him! He rounded on us, o' course, an' got off easy.'

'Excep' for what we gave him in the steerin'-flat when we came out o' cells. 'Eard anything of 'im lately, Pye?'

'Signal Boatswain in the Channel Fleet, I believe—Mr. L. L. Niven is.'

'An' Anstey died o' fever in Benin,' Pritchard mused. 'What come to Moon? Spit-Kid we know about.'

'Moon—Moon! Now where did I last . . . ? Oh yes, when I was in the *Palladium*. I met Quigley at Buncrana Station. He told me Moon 'ad run when the *Astrild* sloop was cruising among the South Seas three years back. He always showed signs o' bein' a Mormonastic beggar. Yes, he slipped off quietly an' they 'adn't time to chase 'im round the islands even if the navigatin' officer 'ad been equal to the job.'

'Wasn't he?' said Hooper.

'Not so. Accordin' to Quigley the *Astrild* spent half her commission rompin' up the beach like a she-turtle, an' the other half hatching turtles' eggs on the top o' numerous reefs. When she was docked at Sydney her copper looked like Aunt Maria's washing on the line—an' her 'midship frames was sprung. The commander swore the dockyard 'ad done it haulin' the pore thing on to the slips. They *do* do strange things at sea, Mr. Hooper.'

'Ah! I'm not a taxpayer,' said Hooper, and opened a fresh bottle. The Sergeant seemed to be one who had a difficulty in dropping subjects.

'How it all comes back, don't it?' he said. 'Why, Moon must 'ave 'ad sixteen years' service before he ran.'

'It takes 'em at all ages. Look at—you know,' said Pyecroft.

'Who?' I asked.

'A service man within eighteen months of his pension is the party you're thinkin' of,' said Pritchard. 'A warrant 'oo's name begins with a V, isn't it?'

'But, in a way o' puttin' it, we can't say that he actually did desert,' Pyecroft suggested.

'Oh no,' said Pritchard. 'It was only permanent absence up-country without leaf. That was all.'

'Up-country?' said Hooper. 'Did they circulate his description?'

'What for?' said Pritchard, most impolitely.

'Because deserters are like columns in the war. They don't move away from the line, you see. I've known a chap caught at Salisbury that way tryin' to get to Nyassa. They tell me, but o' course I don't know, that they don't ask questions on the Nyassa Lake Flotilla up there. I've heard of a P. and O. quartermaster in full command of an armed launch there.'

'Do you think Click 'ud ha' gone up that way?' Pritchard asked.

'There's no saying. He was sent up to Bloemfontein to take over some Navy ammunition left in the fort. We know he took it over and saw it into the trucks. Then there was no more Click—then or thereafter. Four months ago it transpired, and thus the *casus belli* stands at present,' said Pyecroft.

'What were his marks?' said Hooper again.

'Does the Railway get a reward for returnin' 'em, then?' said Pritchard.

'If I did d'you suppose I'd talk about it?' Hooper retorted angrily.

'You seemed so very interested,' said Pritchard with equal crispness.

'Why was he called Click?' I asked, to tide over an uneasy little break in the conversation. The two men were staring at each other very fixedly.

'Because of an ammunition hoist carryin' away,' said Pyecroft. 'And it carried away four of 'is teeth—on the lower port side, wasn't it, Pritch? The substitutes which he bought weren't screwed home, in a manner o' sayin'. When he talked fast they used to lift a little on the bedplate. 'Ence, "Click". They called 'im a superior man, which is what we'd call a long, black-'aired, genteelly-speakin', 'alf-bred beggar on the lower deck.'

'Four false teeth in the lower left jaw,' said Hooper, his hand in his waistcoat-pocket. 'What tattoo marks?'

'Look here,' began Pritchard, half rising. 'I'm sure we're very grateful to you as a gentleman for your 'orspitality, but per'aps we may 'ave made an error in—'

I looked at Pyecroft for aid—Hooper was crimsoning rapidly.

'If the fat marine now occupying the foc'-sle will kindly bring 'is *status quo* to an anchor yet once more, we may be able to talk like gentlemen—not to say friends,' said Pyecroft. 'He regards you, Mr. Hooper, as a emissary of the Law.'

'I only wish to observe that when a gentleman exhibits such a peculiar, or I should rather say, such a *bloomin'* curiosity in identification marks as our friend here—'

'Mr. Pritchard,' I interposed, 'I'll take all the responsibility for Mr. Hooper.'

'An' *you'll* apologise all round,' said Pyecroft. 'You're a rude little man, Pritch.'

'But how was I—' he began, wavering.

'I don't know an' I don't care. Apologise!'

The giant looked round bewildered and took our little hands into his vast grip, one by one.

'I was wrong,' he said meekly as a sheep. 'My suspicions was unfounded. Mr. Hooper, I apologise.'

'You did quite right to look out for your own end o' the line,' said Hooper. 'I'd ha' done the same with a gentleman I didn't know, you see. If you don't mind I'd like to hear a little more o' your Mr. Vickery. It's safe with me, you see.'

'Why did Vickery run?' I began, but Pyecroft's smile made me turn my question to 'Who was she?'

'She kep' a little hotel at Hauraki—near Auckland,' said Pyecroft.

'By Gawd!' roared Pritchard, slapping his hand on his leg. 'Not Mrs. Bathurst!'

Pyecroft nodded slowly, and the Sergeant called all the powers of darkness to witness his bewilderment.

'So far as I could get at it, Mrs. B. was the lady in question.'

'But Click was married,' cried Pritchard.

'An' 'ad a fifteen-year-old daughter. 'E's shown me her photograph. Settin' that aside, so to say, 'ave you ever found these little things make —much difference? Because I haven't.'

'Good Lord Alive an' Watchin'! . . . Mrs. Bathurst . . .' Then with another roar: 'You can say what you please, Pye, but you don't make me believe it was any of 'er fault. She wasn't *that*!'

'If I was going to say what I please, I'd begin by callin' you a silly ox an' work up to the higher pressures at leisure. I'm trying to say solely what transpired. M'rover, for once you're right. It wasn't her fault.'

'You couldn't 'aven't made me believe it if it 'ad been,' was the answer.

Such faith in a Sergeant of Marines interested me greatly. 'Never mind about that,' I cried. 'Tell me what she was like.'

'She was a widow,' said Pyecroft. 'Left so very young and never re-spliced. She kep' a little hotel for warrants and non-coms close to Auckland, an' she always wore black silk, and 'er neck—'

'You ask what she was like,' Pritchard broke in. 'Let me give you an instance. I was at Auckland first in '97, at the end o' the *Marroquin*'s commission, an' as I'd been promoted I went up with the others. She used to look after us all, an' she never lost by it—not a penny! "Pay me now," she'd say, "or settle later. I know you won't let me suffer. Send the money from home if you like." Why, gentlemen all, I tell you I've see that lady take her own gold watch an' chain off her neck in the bar an' pass it to a bosun 'oo'd come ashore without 'is ticker an' 'ad to catch the last boat. "I don't know your name," she said, "but when you've done with it, you'll find plenty that know me on the front. Send it back by one o' them." And it was worth thirty pounds if it was worth 'arf-a-crown. The little gold watch, Pye, with the blue monogram at the back. But, as was sayin', in those days she kep' a beer that agreed with me—Slits it was called. One way an' another I must 'ave punished a good few bottles of it while we was in the bay—comin' ashore every night or so. Chaffin' across the bar like, once when we were alone, "Mrs. B.," I said, "when next I call I want you to remember that this is my particular—just as you're my particular." (She'd let you go *that* far!) "Just as you're my particular," I said. "Oh, thank you, Sergeant Pritchard," she says, an'

13

put 'er hand up to the curl be'ind 'er ear. Remember that way she had, Pye?'

'I think so,' said the sailor.

'Yes, "Thank you, Sergeant Pritchard," she says. "The least I can do is to mark it for you in case you change your mind. There's no great demand for it in the Fleet," she says, "but to make sure I'll put it at the back o' the shelf," an' she snipped off a piece of her hair ribbon with that old dolphin cigar-cutter on the bar—remember it, Pye?—an' she tied a bow round what was left—just four bottles. That was '97 no, '96. In '98 I was in the *Resilient*—China Station—full commission. In Nineteen One, mark you, I was in the *Carthusian*, back in Auckland Bay again. Of course I went up to Mrs. B.'s with the rest of us to see how things were goin'. They were the same as ever. (Remember the big tree on the pavement by the side-bar, Pye?) I never said anythin' in special (there was too many of us talkin' to her), but she saw me at once.'

'That wasn't difficult?' I ventured.

'Ah, but wait. I was comin' up to the bar, when ,"Ada," she says to her niece, "get me Sergeant Pritchard's particular," and, gentlemen all, I tell you before I could shake 'ands with the lady, there were those four bottles o' Slits, with 'er 'air-ribbon in a bow round each o' their necks, set down in front o' me, an' as she drew the cork she looked at me under her eyebrows in that blindish way she had o' lookin', an', "Sergeant Pritchard," she says, "I do 'ope you 'aven't changed your mind about your particulars." That's the kind o' woman she was—after five years!'

'I don't *see* her yet somehow,' said Hooper, but with sympathy.

'She—she never scrupled to feed a lame duck or set 'er foot on a scorpion at any time of 'er life,' Pritchard added valiantly.

'That don't help me either. My mother's like that for one.'

The giant heaved inside his uniform and rolled his eyes at the car-roof. Said Pyecroft suddenly:

'How many women have you been intimate with all over the world, Pritch?'

Pritchard blushed plum-colour to the short hairs of his seventeen-inch neck.

' 'Undreds,' said Pyecroft. 'So've I. How many of 'em can you remember in your own mind, settin' aside the first—an' per'aps the last —*and one more?*'

'Few, wonderful few, now I tax myself,' said Sergeant Pritchard relievedly. 'An' how many times might you 'ave been at Auckland?'

'One—two,' he began—'why, I can't make it more than three times in ten years. But I can remember every time that I ever saw Mrs. B.'

'So can I—an' I've only been to Auckland twice—how she stood an' what she was sayin' an' what she looked like. That's the secret. 'Tisn't beauty, so to speak, nor good talk necessarily. It's just It. Some women'll stay in a man's memory if they once walk down a street, but most of 'em you can live with a month on end, an' next commission you'd be put to it to certify whether they talked in their sleep or not, as one might say.'

'Ah!' said Hopper. 'That's more the idea. I've known just two women of that nature.'

'An' it was no fault o' theirs?' asked Pritchard.

'None whatever. I know *that*!'

'An' if a man gets struck with that kind o' woman, Mr. Hooper?' Pritchard went on.

'He goes crazy—or just saves himself,' was the slow answer.

'You've hit it,' said the Sergeant. 'You've seen an' known somethin' in the course o' your life, Mr. Hooper. I'm lookin' at you!' He set down his bottle.

'And how often had Vickery seen her?' I asked.

'That's the dark an' bloody mystery,' Pyecroft answered. 'I'd never come across him till I come out in the *Hierophant* just now, an' there wasn't any one in the ship who knew much about him. You see, he was what you call a superior man. 'E spoke to me once or twice about Auckland and Mrs. B. on the voyage out. I called that to mind subsequently. There must 'ave been a good deal between 'em, to my way o' thinkin'. Mind you, I'm only giving you my *résumé* of it all, because all I know is second-hand so to speak, or rather I should say more than second-'and.'

'How?' said Hooper peremptorily. 'You must have seen it or heard it'.

'Ye-es,' said Pyecroft. 'I used to think seein' and hearin' was the only regulation aids to ascertainin' facts, but as we get older we get more accommodatin'. The cylinders work easier, I suppose. . . . Were you in Cape Town last December when Phyllis's Circus came?'

'No—up-country,' said Hooper, a little nettled at the change of venue.

'I ask because they had a new turn of a scientific nature called "Home and Friends for a Tickey".'

'Oh, you mean the cinematograph—the pictures of prize-fights and steamers. I've seen 'em up-country.'

'Biograph or cinematograph was what I was alludin' to. London Bridge with the omnibuses—a troopship goin' to the war—marines on parade at Portsmouth, an' the Plymouth Express arrivin' at Paddin'ton.'

'Seen 'em all. Seen 'em all,' said Hooper impatiently.

'We *Heirophants* came in just before Christmas week an' leaf was easy.'

'I think a man gets fed up with Cape Town quicker than anywhere else on the station. Why, even Durban's more like Nature. We was there for Christmas,' Pritchard put in.

'Not bein' a devotee of Indian *peeris*, as our Doctor said to the Pusser, I can't exactly say. Phyllis's was good enough after musketry practice at Mozambique. I couldn't get off the first two or three nights on account of what you might call an imbroglio with our Torpedo Lieutenant in the submerged flat, where some pride of the West Country had sugared up a gyroscope; but I remember Vickery went ashore with our Carpenter Rigdon—old Crocus we called him. As a general rule Crocus never left 'is ship unless an' until he was 'oisted out with a winch, but *when* 'e went 'e would return noddin' like a lily gemmed with dew. We smothered him down below that night, but the things 'e said about Vickery as a fittin' playmate for a Warrant Officer of 'is cubic capacity, before we got him quiet, was what I should call pointed.'

'I've been with Crocus—in the *Redoubtable*,' said the Sergeant. 'He's a character if there is one.'

'Next night I went into Cape Town with Dawson and Pratt; but just at the door of the Circus I came across Vickery. "Oh!" he says, "you're the man I'm looking for. Come and sit next me. This way to the shillin' places!" I went astern at once, protestin' because tickey seats better suited my so-called finances. "Come on," says Vickery, "I'm payin'." Naturally I abandoned Pratt and Dawson in anticipation o' drinks to match the seats. "No," he says, when this was 'inted—"not now. Not now. As many as you please afterwards, but I want you sober for the occasion." I caught 'is face under a lamp just then, an' the appearance of it quite cured me of my thirst. Don't mistake. It didn't frighten me. It made me anxious. I can't tell you what it was like, but that was the effect which it 'ad on me. If you want to know, it reminded me of those things in bottles in those herbalistic shops at Plymouth—preserved in spirits of wine. White an' crumply things—previous to birth as you might say.'

'You 'ave a bestial mind, Pye,' said the Sergeant, relighting his pipe.

'Perhaps. We were in the front row, an' "Home an' Friends" came on early. Vickery touched me on the knee when the number went up. "If you see anything that strikes you," he says, "drop me a hint"; then he went on clicking. We saw London Bridge an' so forth an' so on, an' it was most interestin'. I'd never seen it before. You 'eard a little dynamo like buzzin', but the pictures were the real thing—alive an' movin'.'

'I've seen 'em,' said Hooper. 'Of course they are taken from the very thing itself—you see.'

'Then the Western Mail came in to Paddin'ton on the big magic-lantern sheet. First we saw the platform empty an' the porters standin' by. Then the engine come in, head on, an' the women in the front row jumped: she headed so straight. Then the doors opened and the passengers came out and the porters got the luggage—just like life. Only —only when any one came down too far towards us that was watchin', they walked right out o' the picture, so to speak. I was 'ighly interested, I can tell you. So were all of us. I watched an old man with a rug 'oo'd dropped a book an' was tryin' to pick it up, when quite slowly, from be'ind two porters—carryin' a little reticule an' lookin' from side to side —comes our Mrs. Bathurst. There was no mistakin' the walk in a hundred thousand. She come forward—right forward—she looked out straight at us with that blindish look which Pritch alluded to. She walked on and on till she melted out of the picture—like—like a shadow jumpin' over a candle, an' as she went I 'eard Dawson in the tickey seats be'ind sing out: "Christ! there's Mrs. B.!"'

Hooper swallowed his spittle and leaned forward intently.

'Vickery touched me on the knee again. He was clickin' his four false teeth with his jaw down like an enteric at the last kick. "Are you sure?" says he. "Sure," I says, "didn't you 'ear Dawson give tongue? Why, it's the woman herself." "I was sure before," he says, "but I brought you to make sure. Will you come again with me tomorrow?"'

' "Willingly," I says, "it's like meetin' old friends."'

' "Yes," he says, openin' his watch, "very like. It will be four-and-twenty hours less four minutes before I see her again. Come and have a drink," he says. "It may amuse you, but it's no sort of earthly use to me." He went out shaking his head an' stumblin' over people's feet as if he was drunk already. I anticipated a swift drink an' a speedy return, because I wanted to see the performin' elephants. Instead o' which Vickery began to navigate the town at the rate o' lookin' in at a bar every three minutes approximate Greenwich time. I'm not a drinkin' man, though there are those present'—he cocked his unforgettable eye at me —'who may have seen me more or less imbued with the fragrant spirit. None the less when I drink I like to do it at anchor an' not at an average speed of eighteen knots on the measured mile. There's a tank as you might say at the back o' that big hotel up the hill—what do they call it?'

'The Molteno Reservoir,' I suggested, and Hooper nodded.

17

'That was his limit o' drift' We walked there an' we come down through the Gardens—there was a South-Easter blowin'—an' we finished up by the Docks. Then we bore up the road to Salt River, and wherever there was a pub Vickery put in sweatin'. He didn't look at what he drunk—he didn't look at the change. He walked an' he drunk an' he perspired rivers. I understood why old Crocus 'ad come back in the condition 'e did, because Vickery an' I 'ad two an' a half hours o' this gipsy manœuvre, an' when we got back to the station there wasn't a dry atom on or in me.'

'Did he say anything?' Pritchard asked.

'The sum total of 'is conversation from 7.45 p.m. till 11.15 p.m. was "Let's have another". Thus the mornin' an' the evenin' were the first day, as Scripture says. . . . To abbreviate a lengthy narrative, I went into Cape Town for five consecutive nights with Master Vickery, and in that time I must 'ave logged about fifty knots over the ground an' taken in two gallon o' all the worst spirits south the Equator. The evolution never varied. Two shilling seats for us two; five minutes o' the pictures, an' perhaps forty-five seconds o' Mrs. B. walking down towards us with that blindish look in her eyes an' the reticule in her hand. Then out—walk— and drink till train time.'

'What did you think?' said Hooper, his hand fingering his waistcoat-pocket.

'Several things,' said Pyecroft. 'To tell you the truth, I aren't quite done thinkin' about it yet. Mad? The man was a dumb lunatic—must 'ave been for months—years p'raps. I know somethin' o' maniacs, as every man in the Service must. I've been shipmates with a mad skipper —an' a lunatic Number One, but never both together, I thank 'Eaven. I could give you the names o' three captains now 'oo ought to be in an asylum, but you don't find me interferin' with the mentally afflicted till they begin to lay about 'em with rammers an' winch-handles. Only once I crept up a little into the wind towards Master Vickery. "I wonder what she's doin' in England," I says. "Don't it seem to you she's lookin' for somebody?" That was in the Gardens again. with the South-Easter blowin' as we were makin' our desperate round. "She's lookin' for me," he says, stoppin' dead under a lamp an' clickin'. When he wasn't drinkin', in which case all 'is teeth clicked on the glass, 'e was clickin' 'is four false teeth like a Marconi ticker. "Yes! lookin' for me," he said, an' he went on very softly an' as you might say affectionately. "*But*," he went on, "in future, Mr. Pyecroft, I should take it kindly of you if you'd confine your remarks to the drinks set before you. Otherwise," he says, "with the best will in the world towards you, I may find myself guilty of murder! Do you understand?" he says. "Perfectly," I says, "but would it at all soothe you to know that in such a case the chances o' your being killed are precisely equivalent to the chances o' me being outed." "Why, no," he said, "I'm almost afraid that 'ud be a temptation." Then I said—we was right under the lamp by that arch at the end o' the Gardens where the trams come round—"Assumin' murder was done—or attempted murder—I put it to you that you would still be left so badly crippled, as one might say, that your subsequent capture by the police—to 'oom you would 'ave to explain—would be largely inevitable." "That's better," 'e says, passin' 'is hands over his forehead. "That's much better, because," he says, "do you know, as I am now, Pye, I'm not so sure if I could explain anything much." Those were the only particular words I had with 'im in our walks as I remember.'

'What walks!' said Hooper. 'Oh my soul, what walks!'

'They were chronic,' said Pyecroft gravely, 'but I didn't anticipate any danger till the Circus left. Then I anticipated that, bein' deprived of 'is stimulant, he might react on me, so to say, with a hatchet. Consequently, after the final performance an' the ensuin' wet walk, I kep' myself aloof from my superior officer on board in the execution of 'is duty, as you might put it. Consequently, I was interested when the sentry informs me while I was passin' on my lawful occasions that Click had asked to see the captain. As a general rule warrant-officers don't dissipate much of the owner's time, but Click put in an hour and more be'ind that door. My duties kep' me within eyeshot of it. Vickery came out first, an' 'e actually nodded at me an' smiled. This knocked me out o' the boat, because, havin' seen 'is face for five consecutive nights, I didn't anticipate any change there more than a condenser in hell, so to speak. The owner emerged later. His face didn't read off at all, so I fell back on his cox, 'oo'd been eight years with him and knew him better than boat signals. Lamson—that was the cox's name—crossed 'is bows once or twice at low speeds an' dropped down to me visibly concerned. "He's shipped 'is court-martial face," says Lamson. "Some one's goin' to be 'ung. I've never seen that look but once before, when they chucked the gun-sights overboard in the *Fantastic*." Throwin' gun-sights overboards, Mr. Hooper, is the equivalent for mutiny in these degenerate days. It's done to attract the notice of the authorities an' the *Western Mornin' News*—generally by a stoker. Naturally, word went round the lower deck an' we had a private over'aul of our little consciences. But, barrin' a shirt which a second-class stoker said 'ad walked into 'is bag from the marines' flat by itself, nothin' vital transpired. The owner went about flyin' the signal for "attend public execution", so to say, but there was no corpse at the yard-arm. 'E lunched on the beach an' 'e returned with 'is regulation harbour-routine face about 3 p.m. Thus Lamson lost prestige for raising false alarms. The only person 'oo might 'ave connected the epicycloidal gears correctly was one Pyecroft, when he was told that Mr. Vickery would go up-country that same evening to take over certain naval ammunition left after the war in Bloemfontein Fort. No details was ordered to accompany Master Vickery. He was told off first person singular—as a unit—by himself.'

The marine whistled penetratingly.

'That's what I thought,' said Pyecroft. 'I went ashore with him in the cutter an' 'e asked me to walk through the station. He was clickin' audibly, but otherwise seemed happy-ish.

' "You might like to know," he says, stoppin' just opposite the Admiral's front gate, "that Phyllis's Circus will be performin' at Worcester tomorrow night. So I shall see 'er yet once again. You've been very patient with me," he says.

' "Look here, Vickery," I said, "this thing's come to be just as much as I can stand. Consume your own smoke. I don't want to know any more."

' "You!" he said. "What have you got to complain of?—you've only 'ad to watch. I'm *it*," he says, "but that's neither here nor there," he says. "I've one thing to say before shakin' 'ands. Remember," 'e says— we were just by the Admiral's garden-gate then—"remember that I am *not* a murderer, because my lawful wife died in childbed six weeks after I came out. That much at least I am clear of," 'e says.

' "Then what have you done that signifies?" I said. "What's the rest of it?"

' "The rest," 'e says, "is silence," an' he shook 'ands and went clickin' into Simonstown station.'

'Did he stop to see Mrs. Bathurst at Worcester?' I asked.

'It's not known. He reported at Bloemfontein, saw the ammunition into the trucks, and then 'e disappeared. Went out—deserted, if you care to put it so—within eighteen months of his pension, an' if what 'e said about 'is wife was true he was a free man as 'e then stood. How do you read it off?'

'Poor devil!' said Hooper. 'To see her that way every night! I wonder what it was.'

'I've made my 'ead ache in that direction many a long night.'

'But I'll swear Mrs. B. 'ad no 'and in it,' said the Sergeant, unshaken.

'No. Whatever the wrong or deceit was, he did it, I'm sure o' that. I 'ad to look at 'is face for five consecutive nights. I'm not so fond o' navigatin' about Cape Town with a South-Easter blowin' these days. I can hear those teeth click, so to say.'

'Ah, those teeth,' said Hooper, and his hand went to his waistcoat-pocket once more. 'Permanent things false teeth are. You read about 'em in all the murder trials.'

'What d'you suppose the captain knew—or did?' I asked.

'I've never turned my searchlight that way.' Pyecroft answered unblushingly.

We all reflected together, and drummed on empty beer bottles as the picnic-party, sunburned, wet, and sandy, passed our door singing 'The Honeysuckle and the Bee'.

'Pretty girl under that kapje,' said Pyecroft.

'They never circulated his description?' said Pritchard.

'I was askin' you before these gentlemen came,' said Hooper to me, 'whether you knew Wankies—on the way to the Zambesi—beyond Bulawayo?'

'Would he pass there—tryin' get to that Lake what's 'is name?' said Pritchard.

Hooper shook his head and went on: 'There's a curious bit o' line there, you see. It runs through solid teak forest—a sort o' mahogany really—seventy-two miles without a curve. I've had a train derailed there twenty-three times in forty miles. I was up there a month ago relievin' a sick inspector, you see. He told me to look out for a couple of tramps in the teak.'

'Two?' Pyecroft said. 'I don't envy that other man if—'

'We get heaps of tramps up there since the war. The inspector told me I'd find 'em at M'Bindwe siding waiting to go North. He'd given 'em some grub and quinine, you see. I went up on a construction train. I looked out for 'em. I saw them miles ahead along the straight, waiting in the teak. One of 'em was standin' up by the dead-end of the siding an' the other was squattin' down lookin' up at 'im, you see.'

'What did you do for 'em?' said Pritchard.

'There wasn't much I could do, except bury 'em. There'd been a bit of a thunderstorm in the teak, you see, and they were both stone dead and as black as charcoal. That's what they really were, you see— charcoal. They fell to bits when we tried to shift 'em. The man who was standin' up had the false teeth. I saw 'em shinin' against the black. Fell to bits he did too, like his mate squatting down an' watchin' him, both of 'em all wet in the rain. Both burned to charcoal, you see. And—that's what made me ask about marks just now—the false-toother was

21

tattooed on the arms and chest—a crown and foul anchor with M. V. above.'

'I've seen that,' said Pyecroft quickly. 'It was so.'

'But if he was all charcoal-like?' said Pritchard, shuddering.

'You know how writing shows up white on a burned letter? Well, it was like that, you see. We buried 'em in the teak and I kept. . . . But he was a friend of you two gentlemen, you see.'

Mr. Hooper brought his hand away from his waistcoat-pocket—empty.

Pritchard covered his face with his hands for a moment, like a child shutting out an ugliness.

'And to think of her at Hauraki!' he murmured—'with 'er 'air-ribbon on my beer. "Ada," she said to her niece. . . . Oh, my Gawd!' . . .

'On a summer afternoon, when the honeysuckle blooms,
    And all Nature seems at rest,
Underneath the bower, 'mid the perfume of the flower,
    Sat a maiden with the one she loves the best—'

sang the picnic-party waiting for their train at Glengariff.

'Well, I don't know how you feel about it,' said Pyecroft, 'but 'avin' seen 'is face for five consecutive nights on end, I'm inclined to finish what's left of the beer an' thank Gawd he's dead!'

NATHANAEL WEST

(1903–1940)

F. SCOTT FITZGERALD

(1896–1940)

The two great Hollywood novels are unquestionably Nathanael West's The Day of the Locust *(1939) and F. Scott Fitzgerald's* The Last Tycoon *(1941), an uncompleted study of a master producer, based on MGM's golden boy, Irving Thalberg. Both authors died young: West in a car crash, with only four books behind him; Fitzgerald of a heart attack, after years of undeserved neglect by an industry which had helped to debauch his talent. 'Poor son of a bitch,' said Dorothy Parker as his casket was displayed in a Los Angeles mortuary—the same epitaph which Fitzgerald had provided for one of his own fictional heroes, Jay Gatsby. Both books brilliantly record the romance and the miseries of making movies. Both are inside jobs (West and Fitzgerald worked for a time as screen-writers) which burrow beneath the industry's cosmetic tan and find disenchantment.*

The Day of the Locust

CHAPTER I

AROUND QUITTING time, Tod Hackett heard a great din on the road outside his office. The groan of leather mingled with the jangle of iron and over all beat the tattoo of a thousand hooves. He hurried to the window.

An army of cavalry and foot was passing. It moved like a mob; its lines broken, as though fleeing from some terrible defeat. The dolmans of the hussars, the heavy shakos of the guards, Hanoverian light horse, with their flat leather caps and flowing red plumes, were all jumbled together in bobbing disorder. Behind the cavalry came the infantry, a wild sea of waving sabretaches, sloped muskets, crossed shoulder belts and swinging cartridge boxes. Tod recognised the scarlet infantry of

23

England with their white shoulder pads, the black infantry of the Duke of Brunswick, the French grenadiers with their enormous white gaiters, the Scotch with bare knees under plaid skirts.

While he watched, a little fat man, wearing a cork sun-helmet, polo shirt and knickers, darted around the corner of the building in pursuit of the army.

'Stage Nine—you bastards—Stage Nine!' he screamed through a small megaphone.

The cavalry put spur to their horses and the infantry broke into a dogtrot. The little man in the cork hat ran after them, shaking his fist and cursing.

Tod watched until they had disappeared behind half a Mississippi steamboat, then put away his pencils and drawing board, and left the office. On the sidewalk outside the studio he stood for a moment trying to decide whether to walk home or take a streetcar. He had been in Hollywood less than three months and still found it a very exciting place, but he was lazy and didn't like to walk. He decided to take the streetcar as far as Vine Street and walk the rest of the way.

A talent scout for National Films had brought Tod to the Coast after seeing some of his drawings in an exhibit of undergraduate work at the Yale School of Fine Arts. He had been hired by telegram. If the scout had met Tod, he probably wouldn't have sent him to Hollywood to learn set and costume designing. His large, sprawling body, his slow blue eyes and sloppy grin made him seem completely without talent, almost doltish in fact.

Yes, despite his appearance, he was really a very complicated young man with a whole set of personalities, one inside the other like a nest of Chinese boxes. And 'The Burning of Los Angeles,' a picture he was soon to paint, definitely proved he had talent.

He left the car at Vine Street. As he walked along, he examined the evening crowd. A great many of the people wore sports clothes which were not really sports clothes. Their sweaters, knickers, slacks, blue flannel jackets with brass buttons were fancy dress. The fat lady in the yachting cap was going shopping, not boating; the man in the Norfolk jacket and Tyrolean hat was returning, not, from a mountain, but an insurance office; and the girl in slacks and sneaks with a bandanna around her head had just left a switchboard, not a tennis court.

Scattered among these masquerades were people of a different type. Their clothing was sombre and badly cut, bought from mail-order houses. While the others moved rapidly, darting into stores and cocktail bars, they loitered on the corners or stood with their backs to the shop

24

windows and stared at everyone who passed. When their stare was returned, their eyes filled with hatred. At this time Tod knew very little about them except that they had come to California to die.

He was determined to learn much more. They were the people he felt he must paint. He would never again do a fat red barn, old stone wall or sturdy Nantucket fisherman. From the moment he had seen them, he had known that, despite his race, training and heritage, neither Winslow Homer nor Thomas Ryder could be his masters and he turned to Goya and Daumier.

He had learned this just in time. During his last year in art school, he had begun to think that he might give up painting completely. The pleasures he received from the problems of composition and colour had decreased as his facility had increased and he had realised that he was going the way of all his classmates, towards illustration or mere hand-someness. When the Hollywood job had come along, he had grabbed it despite the arguments of his friends who were certain that he was selling out and would never paint again.

He reached the end of Vine Street and began the climb into Pinyon Canyon. Night had started to fall.

The edges of the trees burned with a pale violet light and their centres gradually turned from deep purple to black. The same violet piping, like a Neon tube, outlined the tops of the ugly, hump-backed hills and they were almost beautiful.

But not even the soft wash of dusk could help the houses. Only dynamite would be of any use against the Mexican ranch houses, Samoan huts, Mediterranean villas, Egyptian and Japanese temples, Swiss chalets, Tudor cottages, and every possible combination of these styles that lined the slopes of the canyon.

When he noticed that they were all of plaster, lath and paper, he was charitable and blamed their shape on the materials used. Steel, stone and brick curb a builder's fancy a little, forcing him to distribute his stresses and weights and to keep his corners plumb, but plaster and paper know no law, not even that of gravity.

On the corner of La Huerta Road was a miniature Rhine castle with tarpaper turrets pierced for archers. Next to it was a little highly coloured shack with domes and minarets out of the *Arabian Nights*. Again he was charitable. Both houses were comic, but he didn't laugh. Their desire to startle was so eager and guileless.

It is hard to laugh at the need for beauty and romance, no matter how tasteless, even horrible, the results of that need are. But it is easy to sigh. Few things are sadder than the truly monstrous.

Tod had fallen asleep. When he woke again, it was after eight o'clock. He took a bath and shaved, then dressed in front of the bureau mirror. He tried to watch his fingers as he fixed his collar and tie, but his eyes kept straying to the photograph that was pushed into the upper corner of the frame.

It was a picture of Faye Greener, a still from a two-reel farce in which she had worked as an extra. She had given him the photograph willingly enough, had even autographed it in a large, wild hand, 'Affectionately yours, Faye Greener,' but she refused his friendship, or, rather, insisted on keeping it impersonal. She had told him why. He had nothing to offer her, neither money nor looks, and she could only love a handsome man and would only let a wealthy man love her. Tod was a 'good-hearted man', and she liked 'good-hearted men', but only as friends. She wasn't hard-boiled. It was just that she put love on a special plane, where a man without money or looks couldn't move.

Tod grunted with annoyance as he turned to the photograph. In it she was wearing a harem costume, full Turkish trousers, breastplates and a monkey jacket, and lay stretched out on a silken divan. One hand held a beer bottle and the other a pewter stein.

He had gone all the way to Glendale to see her in that movie. It was about an American drummer who gets lost in the seraglio of a Damascus merchant and has a lot of fun with the female inmates. Faye played one of the dancing girls. She had only one line to speak, 'Oh, Mr. Smith!' and spoke it badly.

She was a tall girl with wide, straight shoulders and long, swordlike legs. Her neck was long, too, and columnar. Her face was much fuller than the rest of her body would lead you to expect and much larger. It was a moon face, wide at the cheek bones and narrow at chin and brow. She wore her 'platinum' hair long, letting it fall almost to her shoulders at the back, but kept it away from her face and ears with a narrow blue ribbon that went under it and was tied on top of her head with a little bow.

She was supposed to look drunk and she did, but not with alcohol. She lay stretched out on the divan with her arms and legs spread, as though welcoming a lover, and her lips were parted in a heavy, sullen smile. She was supposed to look inviting, but the invitation wasn't to pleasure.

Tod lit a cigarette and inhaled with a nervous gasp. He started to fool with his tie again, but had to go back to the photograph.

Her invitation wasn't to pleasure, but to struggle, hard and sharp, closer to murder than to love. If you threw yourself on her, it would be like throwing yourself from the parapet of a skyscraper. You would do it with a scream. You couldn't expect to rise again. Your teeth would be driven into your skull like nails into a pine board and your back would be broken. You wouldn't even have time to sweat or close your eyes.

He managed to laugh at his language, but it wasn't a real laugh and nothing was destroyed by it.

If she would only let him, he would be glad to throw himself, no matter what the cost. But she wouldn't have him. She didn't love him and he couldn't further her career. She wasn't sentimental and she had no need for tenderness, even if he were capable of it.

When he had finished dressing, he hurried out of the room. He had promised to go to a party at Claude Estee's.

CHAPTER 4

Claude was a successful screen writer who lived in a big house that was an exact reproduction of the old Dupuy mansion near Biloxi, Mississippi. When Tod came up the walk between the boxwood hedges, he greeted him from the enormous, two-storey porch by doing the impersonation that went with the Southern colonial architecture. He teetered back and forth on his heels like a Civil War colonel and made believe he had a large belly.

He had no belly at all. He was a dried-up little man with the rubbed features and stooped shoulders of a postal clerk. The shiny mohair coat and nondescript trousers of that official would have become him, but he was dressed, as always, elaborately. In the buttonhole of his brown jacket was a lemon flower. His trousers were of reddish Harris tweed with a hound tooth check and on his feet were a pair of magnificent, rust-coloured blüchers. His shirt was ivory flannel and his knitted tie a red that was almost black.

While Tod mounted the steps to reach his outstretched hand, he shouted to the butler.

'Here, you black rascal! A mint julep.'

A Chinese servant came running with a Scotch and soda.

After talking to Tod for a moment, Claude started him in the direction of Alice, his wife, who was at the other end of the porch.

'Don't run off,' he whispered. 'We're going to a sporting house.'

Alice was sitting in a wicker swing with a woman named Mrs. Joan Schwartzen. When she asked him if he was playing any tennis, Mrs. Schwartzen interrupted her.

'How silly, batting an inoffensive ball across something that ought to be used to catch fish on account of millions are starving for a bite of herring.'

'Joan's a female tennis champ,' Alice explained.

Mrs. Schwartzen was a big girl with large hands and feet and square, bony shoulders. She had a pretty, eighteen-year-old face and a thirty-five-year-old neck that was veined and sinewy. Her deep sunburn, ruby coloured with a slight blue tint, kept the contrast between her face and neck from being too startling.

'Well, I wish we were going to a brothel this minute,' she said. 'I adore them.'

She turned to Tod and fluttered her eyelids.

'Don't you, Mr. Hackett?'

'That's right, Joan darling,' Alice answered for him. 'Nothing like a bagnio to set a fellow up. Hair of the dog that bit you.'

'How dare you insult me!'

She stood up and took Tod's arm.

'Convoy me over there.'

She pointed to the group of men with whom Claude was standing.

'For God's sake, convoy her,' Alice said. 'She thinks they're telling dirty stories.'

Mrs. Schwartzen pushed right among them, dragging Tod after her.

'Are you talking smut?' she asked 'I adore smut.'

They all laughed politely.

'No, shop,' said someone.

'I don't believe it. I can tell from the beast in your voices. Go ahead, do say something obscene.'

This time no one laughed.

Tod tried to disengage her arm, but she kept a firm grip on it. There was a moment of awkward silence, then the man she had interrupted tried to make a fresh start.

'The picture business is too humble,' he said. 'We ought to resent people like Coombes.'

'That's right,' said another man. 'Guys like that come out here, make a lot of money, grouse all the time about the place, flop on their assignments, then go back East and tell dialect stories about producers they've never met.'

'My God,' Mrs. Schwartzen said to Tod in a loud, stagey whisper, 'they *are* talking shop.'

'Let's look for the man with the drinks,' Tod said.

'No. Take me into the garden. Have you seen what's in the swimming pool?'

She pulled him along.

The air of the garden was heavy with the odour of mimosa and honeysuckle. Through a slit in the blue serge sky poked a grained moon that looked like an enormous bone button. A little flagstone path, made narrow by its border of oleander, led to the edge of the sunken pool. On the bottom, near the deep end, he could see a heavy, black mass of some kind.

'What is it?' he asked.

She kicked a switch that was hidden at the base of a shrub and a row of submerged floodlights illuminated the green water. The thing was a dead horse, or, rather, a lifesize, realistic reproduction of one. Its legs stuck up stiff and straight and it had an enormous, distended belly. Its hammerhead lay twisted to one side and from its mouth, which was set in an agonised grin, hung a heavy, black tongue.

'Isn't it marvellous!' exclaimed Mrs. Schwartzen, clapping her hands and jumping up and down excitedly like a little girl.

'What's it made of?'

'Then you weren't fooled? How impolite! It's rubber, of course. It cost lots of money.'

'But why?'

'To amuse. We were looking at the pool one day and somebody, Jerry Appis, I think, said that it needed a dead horse on the bottom, so Alice got one. Don't you think it looks cute?'

'Very.'

'You're just an old meanie. Think how happy the Estees must feel, showing it to people and listening to their merriment and their oh's and ah's of unconfined delight.'

She stood on the edge of the pool and 'ohed and ahed' rapidly several times in succession.

'Is it still there?' someone called.

Tod turned and saw two women and a man coming down the path.

'I think its belly's going to burst,' Mrs. Schwartzen shouted to them gleefully.

'Goody,' said the man, hurrying to look.

'But it's only full of air,' said one of the women.

Mrs. Schwartzen made believe she was going to cry.

'You're just like that mean Mr. Hackett. You just won't let me cherish my illusions.'

Tod was halfway to the house when she called after him. He waved but kept going.

The men with Claude were still talking shop.

'But how are you going to get rid of the illiterate mockies that run it? They've got a strangle hold on the industry. Maybe they're intellectual stumblebums, but they're damn good businessmen. Or at least they know how to go into receivership and come up with a gold watch in their teeth.'

'They ought to put some of the millions they make back into the business again. Like Rockefeller does with his Foundation. People used to hate the Rockefellers, but now instead of hollering about their ill-gotten oil dough, everybody praises them for what the Foundation does. It's a swell stunt and pictures could do the same thing. Have a Cinema Foundation and make contributions to Science and Art. You know, give the racket a front.'

Tod took Claude to one side to say good night, but he wouldn't let him go. He led him into the library and mixed two double Scotches. They sat down on the couch facing the fireplace.

'You haven't been to Audrey Jenning's place?' Claude asked.

'No, but I've heard tell of it.'

'Then you've got to come along.'

'I don't like pro-sport.'

'We won't indulge in any. We're just going to see a movie.'

'I get depressed.'

'Not at Jenning's you won't. She makes vice attractive by skilful packaging. Her dive's a triumph of industrial design.'

Tod liked to hear him talk. He was master of an involved comic rhetoric that permitted him to express his moral indignation and still keep his reputation for worldliness and wit.

Tod fed him another lead. 'I don't care how much cellophane she wraps it in,' he said—'nautch joints are depressing, like all places for deposit, banks, mail boxes, tombs, vending machines.'

'Love is like a vending machine, eh? Not bad. You insert a coin and press home the lever. There's some mechanical activity inside the bowels of the device. You receive a small sweet, frown at yourself in the dirty mirror, adjust your hat, take a firm grip on your umbrella and walk away, trying to look as though nothing had happened. It's good, but it's not for pictures.'

Tod played straight again.

'That's not it. I've been chasing a girl and it's like carrying something a little too large to conceal in your pocket, like a briefcase or a small valise. It's uncomfortable.'

'I know, I know. It's always uncomfortable. First your right hand gets tired, then your left. You put the valise down and sit on it, but people are surprised and stop to stare at you, so you move on. You hide it behind a tree and hurry away, but someone finds it and runs after you to return it. It's a small valise when you leave home in the morning, cheap and with a bad handle, but by evening it's a trunk with brass corners and many foreign labels. I know. It's good, but it won't film. You've got to remember your audience. What about the barber in Purdue? He's been cutting hair all day and he's tired. He doesn't want to see some dope carrying a valise or fooling with a nickel machine. What the barber wants is amour and glamour.'

The last part was for himself and he sighed heavily. He was about to begin again when the Chinese servant came in and said that the others were ready to leave for Mrs. Jenning's.

CHAPTER 5

They started out in several cars. Tod rode in the front of the one Claude drove and as they went down Sunset Boulevard he described Mrs. Jenning for him. She had been a fairly prominent actress in the days of silent films, but sound made it impossible for her to get work. Instead of becoming an extra or a bit player like many other old stars, she had shown excellent business sense and had opened a callhouse. She wasn't vicious. Far from it. She ran her business just as other women run lending libraries, shrewdly and with taste.

None of the girls lived on the premises. You telephoned and she sent a girl over. The charge was thirty dollars for a single night of sport and Mrs. Jenning kept fifteen of it. Some people might think that fifty per cent is a high brokerage fee, but she really earned every cent of it. There was a big overhead. She maintained a beautiful house for the girls to wait in and a car and a chauffeur to deliver them to the clients.

Then, too, she had to move in the kind of society where she could make the right contacts. After all, not every man can afford thirty dollars. She permitted her girls to service only men of wealth and position, not to say taste and discretion. She was so particular that she insisted on meeting the prospective sportsman before servicing him.

31

She had often said, and truthfully, that she would not let a girl of hers go to a man with whom she herself would not be willing to sleep.

And she was really cultured. All the most distinguished visitors considered it quite a lark to meet her. They were disappointed, however, when they discovered how refined she was. They wanted to talk about certain lively matters of universal interest, but she insisted on discussing Gertrude Stein and Juan Gris. No matter how hard the distinguished visitor tried, and some had been known to go to really great lengths, he could never find a flaw in her refinement or make a breach in her culture.

Claude was still using his peculiar rhetoric on Mrs. Jenning when she came to the door of her house to greet them.

'It's so nice to see you again,' she said. 'I was telling Mrs. Prince at tea only yesterday—the Estees are my favourite couple.'

She was a handsome woman, smooth and buttery, with fair hair and a red complexion.

She led them into a small drawing room whose colour scheme was violet, grey and rose. The Venetian blinds were rose, as was the ceiling, and the walls were covered with a pale grey paper that had a tiny, widely spaced flower design in violet. On one wall hung a silver screen, the kind that rolls up, and against the opposite wall, on each side of a cherrywood table, was a row of chairs covered with rose and grey, glazed chintz bound in violet piping. There was a small projection machine on the table and a young man in evening dress was fumbling with it.

She waved them to their seats. A waiter then came in and asked what they wanted to drink. When their orders had been taken and filled, she flipped the light switch and the young man started his machine. It whirred merrily, but he had trouble in getting it focused.

'What are we going to see first?' Mrs. Schwartzen asked.

'*Le Predicament de Marie.*'

'That sounds ducky.'

'It's charming, utterly charming,' said Mrs. Jenning.

'Yes,' said the cameraman, who was still having trouble. 'I love *Le Predicament de Marie*. It has a marvellous quality that is too exciting.'

There was a long delay, during which he fussed desperately with his machine. Mrs. Schwartzen started to whistle and stamp her feet and the others joined in. They imitated a rowdy audience in the days of the nickelodeon.

'Get a move on, slow poke.'

'What's your hurry? Here's your hat.'

'Get a horse!'

'Get out and get under!'

The young man finally found the screen with his light beam and the film began.

LE PREDICAMENT DE MARIE

ou

LA BONNE DISTRAITE

Marie, the 'bonne,' was a buxom young girl in a tight-fitting black silk uniform with very short skirts. On her head was a tiny lace cap. In the first scene, she was shown serving dinner to a middle-class family in an oak-panelled dining room full of heavy, carved furniture. The family was very respectable and consisted of a bearded, frock-coated father, a mother with a whalebone collar and a cameo brooch, a tall, thin son with a long moustache and almost no chin and a little girl wearing a large bow in her hair and a crucifix on a gold chain around her neck.

After some low comedy with father's beard and the soup, the actors settled down seriously to their theme. It was evident that while the whole family desired Marie, she only desired the young girl. Using his napkin to hide his activities, the old man pinched Marie, the son tried to look down the neck of her dress and the mother patted her knee. Marie, for her part, surreptitiously fondled the child.

The scene changed to Marie's room. She undressed and got into a chiffon negligee, leaving on only her black silk stockings and high-heeled shoes. She was making an elaborate night toilet when the child entered. Marie took her on her lap and started to kiss her. There was a knock on the door. Consternation. She hid the child in the closet and let in the bearded father. He was suspicious and she had to accept his advances. He was embracing her when there was another knock. Again consternation and tableau. This time it was the moustachioed son. Marie hid the father under the bed. No sooner had the son begun to grow warm than there was another knock. Marie made him climb into a large blanket chest. The new caller was the lady of the house. She, too, was just settling to work when there was another knock.

Who could it be? A telegram? A policeman? Frantically Marie counted the different hiding places. The whole family was present. She tiptoed to the door and listened.

'Who can it be that wishes to enter now?' read the title card.

And there the machine stuck. The young man in evening dress became as frantic as Marie. When he got it running again, there was a flash of light and the film whizzed through the apparatus until it had all run out.

'I'm sorry, extremely,' he said. 'I'll have to rewind.'

33

'It's a frameup,' someone yelled.

'Fake!'

'Cheat!'

'The old teaser routine!'

They stamped their feet and whistled.

Under cover of the mock riot, Tod sneaked out. He wanted to get some fresh air. The waiter, whom he found loitering in the hall, showed him to the patio at the back of the house.

On his return, he peeked into the different rooms. In one of them he found a large number of miniature dogs in a curio cabinet. There were glass pointers, silver beagles, porcelain schnauzers, stone dachshunds, aluminium bulldogs, onyx whippets, china bassets, wooden spaniels. Every recognised breed was represented and almost every material that could be sculptured, cast or carved.

While he was admiring the little figures, he heard a girl singing. He thought he recognised her voice and peeked into the hall. It was Mary Dove, one of Faye Greener's best friends.

Perhaps Faye also worked for Mrs. Jenning. If so, for thirty dollars . . . He went back to see the rest of the film.

The Last Tycoon

CHAPTER 2

IT WAS nine o'clock of a July night and there were still some extras in the drug-store across from the studio—I could see them bent over the pin-games inside—as I parked my car. 'Old' Johnny Swanson stood on the corner in his semi-cowboy clothes, staring gloomily past the moon. Once he had been as big in pictures as Tom Mix or Bill Hart—now it was too sad to speak to him, and I hurried across the street and through the front gate.

There is never a time when a studio is absolutely quiet. There is always a night shift of technicians in the laboratories and dubbing rooms and people on the maintenance staff dropping in at the commissary. But the sounds are all different—the padded hush of tyres, the quiet tick of a motor running idle, the naked cry of a soprano singing into a nightbound microphone. Around a corner I came upon a man in rubber boots washing down a car in a wonderful white light—a fountain among the dead industrial shadows. I slowed up as I saw Mr. Marcus being hoisted into his car in front of the administration building, because he took so long to say anything, even good night—and while I waited I realised that the soprano was singing, *Come, come, I love you only* over and over; I remember this because she kept singing the same line during the earthquake. That didn't come for five minutes yet.

Father's offices were in the old building with the long balconies and iron rails with their suggestion of a perpetual tightrope. Father was on the second floor, with Stahr on one side and Mr. Marcus on the other—this evening there were lights all along the row. My stomach dipped a little at the proximity to Stahr, but that was in pretty good control now —I'd seen him only once in the month I'd been home.

There were a lot of strange things about Father's office, but I'll make it brief. In the outer part were three poker-faced secretaries who had sat there like witches ever since I could remember—Birdy Peters, Maude something, and Rosemary Schmiel; I don't know whether this was her name, but she was the dean of the trio, so to speak, and under her desk was the kick-lock that admitted you to Father's throne room. All three of the secretaries were passionate capitalists, and Birdy had invented the rule that if typists were seen eating together more than once in a single week, they were hauled up on the carpet. At that time the studios feared mob rule.

I went on in. Nowadays all chief executives have huge drawing rooms, but my father's was the first. It was also the first to have one-way glass in the big French windows, and I've heard a story about a trap in the floor that would drop unpleasant visitors to an oubliette below, but believe it to be an invention. There was a big painting of Will Rogers, hung conspicuously and intended, I think, to suggest Father's essential kinship with Hollywood's St. Francis; there was a signed photograph of Minna Davis, Stahr's dead wife, and photos of other studio celebrities and big chalk drawings of mother and me. Tonight the one-way French windows were open and a big moon, rosy-gold with a haze around, was wedged helpless in one of them. Father and Jacques La Borwitz and Rosemary Schmiel were down at the end around a big circular desk.

What did Father look like? I couldn't describe him except for once in New York when I met him where I didn't expect to; I was aware of a bulky, middle-aged man who looked a little ashamed of himself, and I wished he'd move on—and then I saw he was Father. Afterwards I was shocked at my impression. Father can be very magnetic—he had a tough jaw and an Irish smile.

But as for Jacques La Borwitz, I shall spare you. Let me just say he was an assistant producer, which is something like a commissar, and let it go at that. Where Stahr picked up such mental cadavers or had them forced upon him—or especially how he got any use out of them—has always amazed me, as it amazed everyone fresh from the East who slapped up against them. Jacques La Borwitz had his points, no doubt, but so have the sub-microscopic protozoa, so has a dog prowling for a bitch and a bone. Jacques La—oh my!

From their expressions I was sure they had been talking about Stahr. Stahr had ordered something or forbidden something, or defied Father or junked one of La Borwitz' pictures or something catastrophic, and they were sitting there in protest at night in a community of rebellion and helplessness. Rosemary Schmiel sat pad in hand, as if ready to write down their dejection.

'I'm to drive you home dead or alive,' I told Father. 'All those birthday presents rotting away in their packages!'

'A birthday!' cried Jacques in a flurry of apology. 'How old? I didn't know.'

'Forty-three,' said Father distinctly.

He was older than that—four years—and Jacques knew it; I saw him note it down in his account book to use some time. Out here these account books are carried open in the hand. One can see the entries being made without recourse to lip-reading, and Rosemary Schmiel was compelled in emulation to make a mark on her pad. As she rubbed it out, the earth quaked under us.

We didn't get the full shock like at Long Beach, where the upper storeys of shops were spewed into the streets and small hotels drifted out to sea—but for a full minute our bowels were one with the bowels of the earth—like some nightmare attempt to attach our navel cords again and jerk us back to the womb of creation.

Mother's picture fell off the wall, revealing a small safe—Rosemary and I grabbed frantically for each other and did a strange screaming waltz across the room. Jacques fainted or at least disappeared, and Father clung to his desk and shouted, 'Are you all right?' Outside the window the singer came to the climax of *I love you only*, held it a moment and then, I swear, started it all over. Or maybe they were playing it back to her from the recording machine.

The room stood still, shimmying a little. We made our way to the door, suddenly including Jacques, who had reappeared, and tottered out dizzily through the anteroom on to the iron balcony. Almost all the lights were out, and from here and there we could hear cries and calls. Momentarily we stood waiting for a second shock—then, as with a common impulse, we went into Stahr's entry and through to his office.

The office was big, but not as big as Father's. Stahr sat on the side of

36

his couch rubbing his eyes. When the quake came he had been asleep, and he wasn't sure yet whether he had dreamed it. When we convinced him he thought it was all rather funny—until the telephones began to ring. I watched him as unobtrusively as possible. He was grey with fatigue while he listened to the phone and dictagraph; but as the reports came in, his eyes began to pick up shine.

'A couple of water mains have burst,' he said to Father, '—they're heading into the back lot.'

'Gray's shooting in the French Village,' said Father.

'It's flooded around the Station, too, and in the Jungle and the City Corner. What the hell—nobody seems to be hurt.' In passing, he shook my hands gravely: 'Where've you been, Cecilia?'

'You going out there, Monroe?' Father asked.

'When all the news is in: One of the power lines is off, too—I've sent for Robinson.'

He made me sit down with him on the couch and tell about the quake again.

'You look tired,' I said, cute and motherly.

'Yes,' he agreed, 'I've got no place to go in the evenings, so I just work.'

'I'll arrange some evenings for you.'

'I used to play poker with a gang,' he said thoughtfully, 'before I was married. But they all drank themselves to death.'

Miss Doolan, his secretary, came in with fresh bad news.

'Robby'll take care of everything when he comes,' Stahr assured Father. He returned to me. 'Now there's a man—that Robinson. He was a trouble-shooter—fixed the telephone wires in Minnesota blizzards—nothing stumps him. He'll be here in a minute—you'll like Robby.'

He said it as if it had been his life-long intention to bring us together, and he had arranged the whole earthquake with just that in mind.

'Yes, you'll like Robby,' he repeated. 'When do you go back to college?'

'I've just come home.'

'You get the whole summer?'

'I'm sorry,' I said. 'I'll go back as soon as I can.'

I was in a mist. It hadn't failed to cross my mind that he might have some intention about me, but if it was so, it was in an exasperatingly early stage—I was merely 'a good property'. And the idea didn't seem so attractive at that moment—like marrying a doctor. He seldom left the studio before eleven.

'How long,' he asked my father, 'before she graduates from college. That's what I was trying to say.'

And I think I was about to sing out eagerly that I needn't go back at all, that I was quite educated already—when the totally admirable Robinson came in. He was a bowlegged young redhead, all ready to go.

'This is Robby, Cecilia,' said Stahr. 'Come on, Robby.'

So I met Robby. I can't say it seemed like fate—but it was. For it was Robby who later told me how Stahr found his love that night.

Under the moon the back lot was thirty acres of fairyland—not because the locations really looked like African jungles and French châteaux and schooners at anchor and Broadway at night, but because they looked like the torn picture books of childhood, like fragments of stories dancing in an open fire. I never lived in a house with an attic, but a back lot must be something like that, and at night of course in an enchanted distorted way, it all comes true.

When Stahr and Robby arrived, clusters of lights had already picked out the danger spots in the flood.

'We'll pump it out into the swamp on Thirty-Sixth Street,' said Robby after a moment. 'It's city property—but isn't this an act of God? Say—look there!'

On top of a huge head of the Goddess Siva, two women were floating down the current of an impromptu river. The idol had come unloosed from a set of Burma, and it meandered earnestly on its way, stopping sometimes to waddle and bump in the shallows with the other debris of the tide. The two refugees had found sanctuary along a scroll of curls on its bald forehead and seemed at first glance to be sightseers on an interesting bus-ride through the scene of the flood.

'Will you look at that, Monroe!' said Robby. 'Look at those dames!'

Dragging their legs through sudden bogs, they made their way to the bank of the stream. Now they could see the women, looking a little scared but brightening at the prospect of rescue.

'We ought to let 'em drift out to the waste pipe,' said Robby gallantly, 'but DeMille needs that head next week.'

He wouldn't have hurt a fly, though, and presently he was hip deep in the water, fishing for them with a pole and succeeding only in spinning it in a dizzy circle. Help arrived, and the impression quickly got around that one of them was very pretty, and then that they were people of importance. But they were just strays, and Robby waited disgustedly to give them hell while the thing was brought finally into control and beached.

'Put that head back!' he called up to them. 'You think it's a souvenir?'

One of the women came sliding smoothly down the cheek of the idol, and Robby caught her and set her on solid ground; the other one hesitated and then followed. Robby turned to Stahr for judgement.

'What'll we do with them, chief?'

Stahr did not answer. Smiling faintly at him from not four feet away was the face of his dead wife, identical even to the expression. Across the feet of moonlight, the eyes he knew looked back at him, a curl blew a little on a familiar forehead; the smile lingered, changed a little according to pattern; the lips parted—the same. An awful fear went over him, and he wanted to cry aloud. Back from the still sour room, the muffled glide of the limousine hearse, the falling concealing flowers, from out there in the dark—here now warm and glowing. The river passed him in a rush, the great spotlights swooped and blinked—and then he heard another voice speak that was not Minna's voice.

'We're sorry,' said the voice. 'We followed a truck in through a gate.'

A little crowd had gathered—electricians, grips, truckers, and Robby began to nip at them like a sheep dog.

'. . . get the big pumps on the tanks on Stage 4 . . . put a cable around this head . . . raft it up on a couple of two by fours . . . get the water out of the jungle first, for Christ's sake . . . that big "A" pipe, lay it down . . . all that stuff is plastic. . . .'

Stahr stood watching the two women as they threaded their way after a policeman towards an exit gate. Then he took a tentative step to see if the weakness had gone out of his knees. A loud tractor came bumping through the slush, and men began streaming by him—every second one glancing at him, smiling, speaking: 'Hello, Monroe . . . Hello, Mr. Stahr wet night, Mr. Stahr . . . Monroe . . . Monroe . . . Stahr . . . Stahr . . . Stahr.'

He spoke and waved back as the people streamed by in the darkness, looking, I suppose, a little like the Emperor and the Old Guard. There is no world so but it has its heroes, and Stahr was the hero. Most of these men had been here a long time—through the beginnings and the great upset, when sound came, and the three years of depression, he had seen that no harm came to them. The old loyalties were trembling now, there were clay feet everywhere; but still he was their man, the last of the princes. And their greeting was a sort of low cheer as they went by.

BETWEEN THE night I got back and the quake, I'd made many observations.

About Father, for example. I loved Father—in a sort of irregular graph with many low swoops—but I began to see that his strong will didn't fill him out as a passable man. Most of what he accomplished boiled down to shrewd. He had acquired with luck and shrewdness a quarter interest in a booming circus—together with young Stahr. That was his life's effort—all the rest was an instinct to hang on. Of course, he talked that double talk to Wall Street about how mysterious it was to make a picture, but Father didn't know the ABC's of dubbing or even cutting. Nor had he learned much about the feel of America as a bar boy in Ballyhegan, nor did he have any more than a drummer's sense of a story. On the other hand, he didn't have concealed paresis like——; he came to the studio before noon, and, with a suspiciousness developed like a muscle, it was hard to put anything over on him.

Stahr had been his luck—and Stahr was something else again. He was a marker in industry like Edison and Lumière and Griffith and Chaplin. He led pictures way up past the range and power of the theatre, reaching a sort of golden age, before the censorship.

Proof of his leadership was the spying that went on around him—not just for inside information or patented process secrets—but spying on his scent for a trend in taste, his guess as to how things were going to be. Too much of his vitality was taken by the mere parrying of these attempts. It made his work secret in part, often devious, slow—and hard to describe as the plans of a general, where the psychological factors become too tenuous and we end by merely adding up the successes and failures. But I have determined to give you a glimpse of him functioning, which is my excuse for what follows. It is drawn partly from a paper I wrote in college on *A Producer's Day* and partly from my imagination. More often I have blocked in the ordinary events myself, while the stranger ones are true.

In the early morning after the flood, a man walked up to the outside balcony of the Administration Building. He lingered there some time, according to an eyewitness, then mounted to the iron railing and dove head first to the pavement below. Breakage—one arm.

Miss Doolan, Stahr's secretary, told him about it when he buzzed for her at nine. He had slept in his office without hearing the small commotion.

'Pete Zavras!' Stahr exclaimed, '—the camera man?'

'They took him to a doctor's office. It won't be in the paper.'

'Hell of a thing,' he said. 'I knew he'd gone to pot—but I don't know why. He was all right when we used him two years ago—why should he come here? How did he get in?'

'He bluffed it with his old studio pass,' said Catherine Doolan. She was a dry hawk, the wife of an assistant director. 'Perhaps the quake had something to do with it.'

'He was the best camera man in town,' Stahr said. When he had heard of the hundreds dead at Long Beach, he was still haunted by the abortive suicide at dawn. He told Catherine Doolan to trace the matter down.

The first dictagraph messages blew in through the warm morning. While he shaved and had coffee, he talked and listened. Robby had left a message: 'If Mr. Stahr wants me tell him to hell with it I'm in bed.' An actor was sick or thought so; the Governor of California was bringing a party out; a supervisor had beaten up his wife for the prints and must be 'reduced to a writer'—these three affairs were Father's job—unless the actor was under personal contract to Stahr. There was early snow on a location in Canada with the company already there—Stahr raced over the possibilities of salvage, reviewing the story of the picture. Nothing. Stahr called Catherine Doolan.

'I want to speak to the cop who put two women off the back lot last night. I think his name's Malone.'

'Yes, Mr. Stahr. I've got Joe Wyman—about the trousers.'

'Hello, Joe,' said Stahr. 'Listen—two people at the sneak preview complained that Morgan's fly was open for half the picture . . . of course they're exaggerating, but even if it's only ten feet . . . no, we can't find the people, but I want that picture run over and over until you find that footage. Get a lot of people in the projection room—somebody'll spot it.'

> *'Tout passe.—L'art robuste*
> *Seul a l'éternité.'*

'And there's the Prince from Denmark,' said Catherine Doolan. 'He's very handsome.' She was impelled to add pointlessly, '—for a tall man.'

'Thanks,' Stahr said. 'Thank you, Catherine, I appreciate it that I am now the handsomest small man on the lot. Send the Prince out on the sets and tell him we'll lunch at one.'

'And Mr. George Boxley—looking very angry in a British way.'

'I'll see him for ten minutes.'

As she went out, he asked: 'Did Robby phone in?'

'No.'

'Call sound, and if he's been heard from, call him and ask him this. Ask him this—did he hear that woman's name last night? Either of those women. Or anything so they could be traced.'

'Anything else?'

'No, but tell him it's important while he still remembers. What were they? I mean what kind of people—ask him that, too. I mean were they——'

She waited, scratching his words on her pad without looking.

'—oh, were they—questionable? Were they theatrical? Never mind—skip that. Just ask if he knows how they can be traced.'

The policeman, Malone, had known nothing. Two dames, and he had hustled 'em, you betcha. One of them was sore. Which one? One of them. They had a car, a Chevvy—he thought of taking the licence. Was it—the good looker who was sore? It was one of them.

Not which one—he had noticed nothing. Even on the lot here Minna was forgotten. In three years. So much for that, then.

Stahr smiled at Mr. George Boxley. It was a kindly fatherly smile Stahr had developed inversely when he was a young man pushed into high places. Originally it had been a smile of respect towards his elders, then as his own decisions grew rapidly to displace theirs, a smile so that they should not feel it—finally emerging as what it was: a smile of kindness—sometimes a little hurried and tired, but always there—towards anyone who had not angered him within the hour. Or anyone he did not intend to insult, aggressive and outright.

Mr. Boxley did not smile back. He came in with the air of being violently dragged, though no one apparently had a hand on him. He stood in front of a chair, and again it was as if two invisible attendants seized his arms and set him down forcibly into it. He sat there morosely. Even when he lit a cigarette on Stahr's invitation, one felt that the match was held to it by exterior forces he disdained to control.

Stahr looked at him courteously.

'Something not going well, Mr. Boxley?'

The novelist looked back at him in thunderous silence.

'I read your letter,' said Stahr. The tone of the pleasant young headmaster was gone. He spoke as to an equal, with a faint two-edged deference.

'I can't get what I write on paper,' broke out Boxley. 'You've all been very decent, but it's a sort of conspiracy. Those two hacks you've teamed me with listen to what I say, but they spoil it—they seem to have a vocabulary of about a hundred words.'

'Why don't you write it yourself?' asked Stahr.

'I have. I sent you some.'

'But it was just talk, back and forth,' said Stahr mildly. 'Interesting talk but nothing more.'

Now it was all the two ghostly attendants could do to hold Boxley in the deep chair. He struggled to get up; he uttered a single quiet bark which had some relation to laughter but none to amusement, and said:

'I don't think you people read things. The men are duelling when the conversation takes place. At the end one of them falls into a well and has to be hauled up in a bucket.'

He barked again and subsided.

'Would you write that in a book of your own, Mr. Boxley?'

'What? Naturally not.'

'You'd consider it too cheap.'

'Movie standards are different,' said Boxley, hedging.

'Do you ever go to them?'

'No—almost never.'

'Isn't it because people are always duelling and falling down wells?'

'Yes—and wearing strained facial expressions and talking incredible and unnatural dialogue.'

'Skip the dialogue for a minute,' said Stahr. 'Granted your dialogue is more graceful than what these hacks can write—that's why we brought you out here. But let's imagine something that isn't either bad dialogue or jumping down a well. Has your office got a stove in it that lights with a match?'

'I think it has,' said Boxley stiffly, '—but I never use it.'

'Suppose you're in your office. You've been fighting duels or writing all day and you're too tired to fight or write any more. You're sitting there staring—dull, like we all get sometimes. A pretty stenographer that you've seen before comes into the room and you watch her—idly. She doesn't see you, though you're very close to her. She takes off her gloves, opens her purse and dumps it out on a table——'

Stahr stood up, tossing his key-ring on his desk.

'She has two dimes and a nickel—and a cardboard match box. She leaves the nickel on the desk, puts the two dimes back into her purse and takes her black gloves to the stove, opens it and puts them inside. There is one match in the match box and she starts to light it kneeling by the stove. You notice that there's a stiff wind blowing in the window—but just then your telephone rings. The girl picks it up, says hello—listens—and says deliberately into the phone, "I've never owned a pair of black gloves in my life." She hangs up, kneels by the stove again, and just as she lights the match, you glance around very suddenly and see that there's another man in the office, watching every move the girl makes ——'

Stahr paused. He picked up his keys and put them in his pocket.

'Go on,' said Boxley, smiling. 'What happens?'

'I don't know,' said Stahr. 'I was just making pictures.'

Boxley felt he was being put in the wrong.

'It's just melodrama,' he said.

'Not necessarily,' said Stahr. 'In any case, nobody has moved violently or talked cheap dialogue or had any facial expression at all. There was only one bad line, and a writer like you could improve it. But you were interested.'

'What was the nickel for?' asked Boxley evasively.

'I don't know,' said Stahr. Suddenly he laughed. 'Oh, yes—the nickel was for the movies.'

The two invisible attendants seemed to release Boxley. He relaxed, leaned back in his chair and laughed.

'What in hell do you pay me for?' he demanded. 'I don't understand the damn stuff.'

'You will,' said Stahr grinning, 'or you wouldn't have asked about the nickel.'

CHRISTOPHER ISHERWOOD

(b. 1904)

Christopher Isherwood's Prater Violet *(1946) was, in effect, a postscript to the 1930s—in particular the high summer of British film production when the rise of Fascism in Europe was driving some of its finest artists to Britain. It is a comedy which is resonant with horrors to come. Isherwood, of course, is also the author of* Mr. Norris Changes Trains *and* Goodbye to Berlin *upon which two successful films—*I am a Camera *and the Bob Fosse musical,* Cabaret*—were based. This extract is from Chapter 10 of* Prater Violet.

Prater Violet

IN THOSE days Imperial Bulldog was still down in Fulham. (They didn't move out to the suburbs until the summer of 1935.) It was quite a long taxi-ride. Bergmann's spirits rose, as we drove along.

'You have never been inside a film-studio before?'

'Only once. Years ago.'

'It will interest you, as a phenomenon. You see, the film-studio of today is really the palace of the sixteenth century. There one sees what Shakespeare saw: the absolute power of the tyrant, the courtiers, the flatterers, the jesters, the cunningly ambitious intriguers. There are fantastically beautiful women, there are incompetent favourites. There are great men who are suddenly disgraced. There is the most insane extravagance, and unexpected parsimony over a few pence. There is enormous splendour which is a sham; and also horrible squalor hidden behind the scenery. There are vast schemes, abandoned because of some caprice. There are secrets which everybody knows and no one speaks of. There are even two or three honest advisers. These are the court fools, who speak the deepest wisdom in puns, lest they should be taken seriously. They grimace, and tear their hair privately, and weep.'

'You make it sound great fun.'

'It is unspeakable,' said Bergmann with relish. 'But to us all this does not matter. We have honourably done our task. Now, like Socrates, we pay the penalty of those who tell the truth. We are thrown to the Bulldog to be devoured, and the Umbrella will weep a crocodile tear over our graves.'

The outside of the Studio was as uninteresting as any modern office-building: a big frontage of concrete and glass. Bergmann strode up the steps to the swinging door, with such impetus that I couldn't follow him until it had stopped whirling around. He scowled, breathing ferociously, while the doorman took our names, and a clerk telephoned to announce our arrival. I caught his eye and grinned, but he wouldn't smile back. He was obviously planning his final speech for the defence. I had no doubt that it would be a masterpiece.

Chatsworth confronted us, as we entered, across a big desk. The first things I saw were the soles of his shoes and the smoke of his cigar. The shoes stood upright on their heels, elegantly brown and shiny, like a pair of ornaments, next to two bronze horses, which were rubbing necks over an inkstand. Sitting apart from him, but still more or less behind the desk, were Ashmeade and a very fat man I didn't know. Our chairs were ready for us, facing them, isolated in the middle of the room. It really looked like a tribunal. I drew nearer to Bergmann, defensively.

'Hullo, you two!' Chatsworth greeted us, very genial. His head was tilted sideways, holding a telephone against his jaw, like a violin. 'Be with you in a moment.' He spoke into the phone: 'Sorry, Dave. Nothing doing. No. I've made up my mind. . . . Well, he may have told you that last week. I hadn't seen it then. It stinks. . . . My dear fellow, I can't help that. I didn't know they'd do such a rotten job. It's bloody awful. . . . Well, tell them anything you like. . . . I don't care if their feelings *are* hurt. They damn well ought to be hurt. . . . No. Good-bye.'

Ashmeade was smiling subtly. The fat man looked bored. Chatsworth took his feet off the desk. His big face came up into view.

'I've got some bad news for you,' he told us.

I glanced quickly across at Bergmann, but he was watching Chatsworth with the glare of a hypnotist.

'We've just changed our schedule. You'll have to start shooting in two weeks.'

'Impossible!' Bergmann discharged the word like a gun.

'Of course it's impossible,' said Chatsworth, grinning. 'We're impossible people, around here . . . I don't think you know Mr. Harris? He sat up all last night doing designs for your sets. I hope you'll dislike them as much as I do. . . . Oh, another thing: we can't get Rosemary Lee. She's sailing for New York tomorrow. So I talked to Anita Hayden,

46

and she's interested. She's a bitch, but she can sing. In a minute I want you to come and listen to Pfeffer's arrangement of the score. It's as noisy as hell. I don't mind it, though. . . . I've put Watts on to the lighting. He's our best man. He knows how to catch the mood.'

Bergmann grunted dubiously. I smiled. I liked Chatsworth that morning.

'What about the script?' I asked.

'Don't you worry about that, my lad. Never let a script stand in our way, do we, Sandy? Matter of fact, I can lick that ending of yours. Thought about it this morning, while I was shaving. I have a great idea.'

Chatsworth paused to re-light his cigar.

'I want you to stay with us,' he told me, 'right through the picture. Just keep your ears and eyes open. Watch the details. Listen for the intonations. You can help a lot. Bergmann isn't used to the language. Besides, there may be re-writes. From now on I'm giving you two an office here in the building, so I'll have my eye on you. If you want anything, just call me. You'll get all the co-operation you need. . . . Well, I think that takes care of everything. Come along, Doctor. Sandy, will you show Isherwood his new dungeon?'

Thus, as the result of ten minutes' conversation, the whole rhythm of our lives was abruptly changed. For Bergmann, of course, this was nothing new. But I felt dazed. It was as though two hermits had been transported from their cave in the mountains into the middle of a modern railway station. There was no privacy any more. The process of wasting time, which hitherto had been orientally calm and philosophical, now became guilty and apprehensive.

Our 'dungeon' was a tiny room on the third floor, forlornly bare, with nothing in it but a desk, three chairs and a telephone. The telephone had a very loud bell. When it rang we both jumped. The window commanded a view of sooty roofs and the grey winter sky. Outside, along the passage, people went back and forth, making what seemed a deliberately unnecessary amount of noise. Often their bodies bumped against the door; or it opened, and a head was thrust in. 'Where's Joe?' a stranger would ask, somewhat reproachfully. Or else he would say: 'Oh, sorry——' and vanish without explanation. These interruptions made Bergmann desperate. 'It is the third degree,' he would groan. 'They torture us, and we have nothing to confess.'

We were seldom together for long. The telephone, or a messenger, would summon Bergmann away, to confer with Chatsworth, or the casting-director, or Mr. Harris, and I would be left with an unfinished scene and his pessimistic advice 'to try and think of something'. Usually, I didn't even try. I stared out of the window, or gossiped with Dorothy. We had a tacit understanding that, if anybody looked in, we would immediately pretend to be working. Sometimes Dorothy herself left me. She had plenty of friends in the Studio, and would slip away for a chat when the coast seemed clear.

Nevertheless, under the pressure of this crisis, we advanced. Bergmann was reckless now. He was ready to pass even the weakest of my suggestions with little more than a sigh. Also, I myself was getting bolder. My conscience no longer bothered me. The dyer's hand was subdued. There were days when I could write page after page with magical facility. It was really quite easy. Toni joked. The Baron made a pun. Toni's father clowned. Some inner inhibition had been removed. This was simply a job. I was doing it as well as I could.

In the meanwhile, whenever I got a chance, I went exploring. Imperial Bulldog had what was probably the oldest studio-site in London. It dated back to early silent days, when directors yelled through megaphones to make themselves heard above the carpenters' hammering; and great flocks of dazed, deafened, limping, hungry extras were driven hither and thither by aggressive young assistant directors, who barked at them like sheepdogs. At the time of the panic, when Sound first came to England, and nobody's job was safe, Bulldog had carried through a hasty and rather hysterical reconstruction programme. The whole place was torn down and rebuilt at top speed, most of it as cheaply as possible. No one knew what was coming next: Taste, perhaps or Smell, or Stereoscopy, or some device that climbed right down out of the screen and ran around in the audience. Nothing seemed impossible. And, in the interim, it was unwise to spend much money on equipment which might be obsolete within a year.

The result of the rebuilding was a maze of crooked stairways, claustrophobic passages, abrupt dangerous ramps and Alice in Wonderland doors. Most of the smaller rooms were overcrowded, underventilated, separated only by plywood partitions and lit by naked bulbs hanging from wires. Everything was provisional, and liable to electrocute you, fall on your head, or come apart in your hand. 'Our motto,' said Lawrence Dwight, 'is: "If it breaks, it's Bulldog." '

Lawrence was the head cutter on our picture: a short, muscular, angry-looking young man of about my own age, whose face wore a frown of permanent disgust. We had made friends, chiefly because he had read a story of mine in a magazine, and growled crossly that he liked it. He limped so slightly that I might never have noticed; but after a few minutes' conversation he told me abruptly that he had an artificial leg. This he referred to as 'my stump'. The amputation had followed a motor accident, in which his wife had been killed a month after their marriage.

'We'd just had time to find out that we couldn't stand each other,' he told me, angrily watching my face to see if I would be shocked. 'I was driving. I suppose I really wanted to murder her.'

'I don't know what the hell you imagine you're doing here,' he said, a little later. 'Selling your soul, I suppose? All you writers have such a bloody romantic attitude. You think you're too good for the movies. Don't you believe it. The movies are too good for you. We don't need any romantic nineteenth-century whores. We need technicians. Thank God I'm a cutter. I know my job. As a matter of fact I'm damned good at it. I don't treat film as if it were a bit of my intestine. It's all Chatsworth's fault. He's a romantic, too. He *will* hire people like you. Thinks he's Lorenzo the Magnificent. . . . I bet you despise mathematics? Well, let me tell you something. The movies aren't drama, they aren't literature: they're pure mathematics. Of course, you'll never understand that as long as you live.'

Lawrence took great pleasure in pointing out to me the many inefficiencies of the Studio. For instance, there was no proper storage-room for scenery. Sets had to be broken up as soon as they had been used; the waste of materials was appalling. And then, Bulldog carried so many passengers. 'We could do a much better job with two-thirds of our present staff. All these assistant directors, fussing about and falling over each other. . . . They even have what they call dialogue-directors. Can you imagine? Some poor stooge who sits around on his fat behind and says yes whenever anybody looks at him.'

I laughed. 'That's what I'm going to do.'

But Lawrence wasn't in the least embarrassed. 'I might have known it,' he said disgustedly. 'You're just the right type. So bloody tactful.'

His deepest scorn was reserved for the Reading Department, officially known as Annexe G. The back lot of Imperial Bulldog sloped down to the river: Annexe G had originally been a warehouse. It reminded me of a lawyer's office in a Dickens novel. There were cobwebbed shelves, rows and rows of them, right up to the roof; and not a crack anywhere wide enough to insert your little finger. The lower rows were mostly scripts; scripts in duplicate and triplicate, treatments, rough drafts, every scrap of paper on which any Bulldog writer had ever scribbled. Lawrence told me that the rats had gnawed long tunnels through them, from end to end. 'They ought to be dumped in the Thames,' Lawrence added, 'but the river police would prosecute us for poisoning the water.'

And then there were books. These were the novels and plays which the Studio had bought to make into pictures. At any rate, that was what they were supposed to be. Had Bulldog ever considered filming Bradshaw's Railway Timetable for 1911? Well, perhaps that had come originally from the Research Department. 'But will you explain to me,' said Lawrence, 'why we have twenty-seven copies of *Half Hours with a Microscope*, one of them stolen from the Woking Public Library?'

Rather to my surprise, Lawrence approved of Bergmann and admired him. He had seen several of the pictures Bergmann had directed in Germany; and this, of course, delighted Bergmann, although he would never admit it. Instead, he praised Lawrence's character, calling him 'ein anstaendiger Junge'. Whenever they met, Bergmann addressed him as 'Master'. After a while, Lawrence started to reciprocate. Whereupon Bergmann, never to be outdone, began to call Lawrence 'Grand Master'. Lawrence took to calling me 'Herr Talk-Director'. I called him 'Herr Cut-Master'.

I was careful, however, not to inform Bergmann of Lawrence's political opinions. 'All this fascist-communist nonsense,' said Lawrence, 'is so bloody old-fashioned. People rave about the workers. It makes me sick. The workers are just sheep. Always have been. Always will be. They choose to be that way, and why shouldn't they? It's their life. And they dodge a lot of headaches. Take the men at this place. What do they know or care about anything, except getting their pay-cheques? If any problem arises outside their immediate job they expect someone else to decide it for them. Quite right too, from their point of view. A country has to be run by a minority of some sort. The only thing is, we've got to get rid of these damned sentimental politicians. All politicians are amateurs. It's as if we'd handed over the Studio to the Publicity Department. The only people who really matter are the technicians. They know what they want.'

'And what do they want?'

'They want efficiency.'

'What's that?'

'Efficiency is doing a job for the sake of doing a job.'

'But why should you do a job, anyway? What's the incentive?'

'The incentive is to fight anarchy. That's all Man lives for. Reclaiming life from its natural muddle. Making patterns.'

'Patterns for what?'

'For the sake of patterns. To create meaning. What else is there?'
'And what about the things that won't fit into your patterns?'
'Discard them.'
'You mean kill Jews?'
'Don't try to shock me with your bloody sentimental, false analogies. You know perfectly well what I mean. When people refuse to fit into patterns they discard themselves. That's not my fault. Hitler doesn't make patterns. He's just an opportunist. When you make patterns you don't persecute. Patterns aren't people.'
'Who's being old-fashioned now? That sounds like Art for Art's sake.'
'I don't care what it sounds like . . . technicians are the only real artists, anyway.'
'It's all very well for you to make patterns with your cutting. But what's the use, when you have to work on pictures like *Prater Violet*?'
'That's Chatsworth's worry, and Bergmann's, and yours. If you so-called artists would behave like technicians and get together, and stop playing at being democrats, you'd make the public take the kind of picture you wanted. This business about the box-office is just a senti-mental democratic fiction. If you stuck together and refused to make anything but, say, abstract films, the public would have to go and see them, and like them . . . still, it's no use talking. You'll never have the guts. You'd much rather whine about prostitution, and keep on making *Prater Violets*. And that's why the public despises you, in its heart. It knows damn well it's got you by the short hairs. Only, one thing: don't come to me with your artistic sorrows, because I'm not interested.'

We started shooting the picture in the final week of January. I give this approximate date because it is almost the last I shall be able to remember. What followed is so confused in my memory, so transposed and foreshortened, that I can only describe it synthetically. My recol-lection of it has no sequence. It is all of a piece.

Within the great barn-like sound-stage, with its high, bare, padded walls, big enough to enclose an airship, there is neither day nor night: only irregular alternations of activity and silence. Beneath a firmament of girders and catwalks, out of which the cowled lamps shine coldly down, like planets, stands the inconsequent, half-dismantled archi-tecture of the sets; archways, sections of houses, wood and canvas hills, huge photographic backdrops, the frontages of streets; a kind of Pompeii, but more desolate, more uncanny, because this is, literally, a half-world, a limbo of mirror images, a town which has lost its third dimension. Only the tangle of heavy power-cables are solid, and apt to trip you as you cross the floor. Your footsteps sound unnaturally loud: you find yourself walking on tiptoe.

In one corner, amidst these ruins, there is life. A single set is brilliantly illuminated. From the distance, it looks like a shrine, and the figures standing around it might be worshippers. But it is merely the living-room of Toni's home, complete with period furniture, gaily coloured curtains, a canary-cage and a cuckoo-clock. The men who are putting the finishing touches to this charming, life-size dolls' house go about their work with the same matter-of-fact, unsmiling efficiency which any carpenters and electricians might show in building a garage.

In the middle of the set, patient and anonymous as tailors' dummies, are the actor and actress who are standing in for Arthur Cromwell and Anita Hayden. Mr. Watts, a thin bald man with gold-rimmed spectacles, walks restlessly back and forth, regarding them from various angles. A blue glass monocle hangs from a ribbon around his neck. He raises it repeatedly to observe the general effect of the lighting; and the gesture is incongruously like that of a Regency fop. Beside him is Fred Murray, red-haired and wearing rubber shoes. Fred is what is called 'the Gaffer', in Studio slang. According to our etiquette, Mr. Watts cannot condescend to give orders directly. He murmurs them to Fred; and Fred, as if translating into a foreign language, shouts up to the men who work the lamps on the catwalk, high above.

'Put a silk on that rifle. Take a couple of turns on number four. Kill that baby.'

'I'm ready,' says Mr. Watts, at length.

'All right,' Fred Murray shouts to his assistants. 'Save them.' The arcs are switched off and the house-lights go on. The set loses its shrine-like glamour. The stand-ins leave their postions. There is an atmosphere of anti-climax; as though we were about to start all over again from the beginning.

'Now then, are we nearly ready?' This is Eliot, the assistant director. He has a long, pointed nose and a public school accent. He carries a copy of the script, like an emblem of office, in his hand. His manner is bossy, but self-conscious and unsure. I feel sorry for him. His job makes him unpopular. He has to fuss and keep things moving; and he doesn't know how to do it without being aggressive. He doesn't know how to talk to the older men, or the stagehands. He is conscious of his own high-pitched, cultured voice. His shirt-collar has too much starch in it.

'What's the hold-up?' Eliot plaintively addresses the world in general. 'What about you, Roger?'

Roger, the sound-recordist, curses under his breath. He hates being rushed. 'There's a baffle on this mike,' he explains, with acid patience. 'It's a bloody lively set. Shift your boom a bit more round to the left, Teddy. We'll have to use a flower-pot.'

The boom moves over, dangling the microphone, like a fishing-rod. Teddy, who works it, crosses the set and conceals a second microphone behind a china figure on the table.

Meanwhile, somewhere in the background, I hear Arthur Cromwell calling: 'Where's the invaluable Isherwood?' Arthur plays Toni's father. He is a big handsome man who used to be a matinée idol: a real fine old ham. He wants me to hear him his part. When he forgets a line, he snaps his fingers, without impatience.

'What's the matter, Toni? Isn't it time to go to the Prater?'

'Aren't you going to the Prater today?' I prompt.

'Aren't you going to the Prater today?' But Arthur has some mysterious actor's inhibition about this. 'Bit of a mouthful, isn't it? I can't hear myself saying that, somehow. How about: "Why aren't you at the Prater?"'

'All right.'

Bergmann calls: 'Isherwood!' (Since we have been working in the Studio, he always addresses me by my surname in public.) He marches away from the set with his hands behind his back, not even glancing around to see if I am following. We go through the double doors and out on to the fire-escape. Everybody retires to the fire-escape when they want to talk and smoke, because smoking isn't allowed inside the building. I nod to the doorman, who is reading the *Daily Herald* through his pince-nez. He is a great admirer of Soviet Russia.

Standing on the little iron platform we can see a glimpse of the chilly grey river, beyond the roof-tops. The air smells damp and fresh, after being indoors, and there is a breeze which ruffles Bergmann's bushy hair.

'How is the scene? Is it all right like this?'

'Yes, I think so.' I try to sound convincing. I feel lazy, this morning, and don't want any trouble. We both examine our copies of the script; or, at least, I pretend to. I have read it so often that the words have lost their meaning.

Bergmann frowns and grunts: 'I thought, maybe, if we could find something. It seems so bare, so poor. . . . Couldn't perhaps Toni say: "I cannot sell the violets of yesterday. They are unfresh"?'

' "I can't sell yesterday's violets. They wither so quickly." '

'Good. Good. . . . Write that down.'

I write it into the script. Eliot appears at the door. 'Ready to rehearse now, sir.'

'Let us go.' Bergmann leads the way back to the set, with Eliot and myself following: a general attended by his staff. Everybody watches us, wondering if anything important has been decided. There is a childish satisfaction in having kept so many people waiting.

Eliot goes over to the door of Anita Hayden's portable dressing-room. 'Miss Hayden,' he says, very self-conscious, 'would you come now, please? We're ready.'

Anita, looking like a rather petulant little girl in her short flowered dress, apron and frilly petticoats, emerges and walks on to the set. Like nearly all famous people, she seems a size smaller than her photographs.

I approach her, afraid that this is going to be unpleasant. I try to grin. 'Sorry! We've changed a line again.'

But Anita, for some reason, is in a good mood.

'Brute!' she exclaims, coquettishly. 'Well, come on, let's hear the worst.'

Eliot blows his whistle. 'Quiet there! Dead quiet! Full rehearsal! Green light!' This last order is for the doorman, who will switch on the sign over the sound-stage door. 'Rehearsal. Enter quietly.'

At last we are ready. The rehearsal begins.

Toni is standing alone, looking pensively out of the window. It is the day after her meeting with Rudolf. And now she has just received a letter of love and farewell, cryptically worded, because he cannot tell her the whole truth: that he is the Prince and that he has been summoned back to Borodania. So Toni is heartbroken and bewildered. Her eyes are full of tears. (This part of the scene is covered by a close-up.)

The door opens. Toni's father comes in.

Father: 'What's the matter, Toni? Why aren't you at the Prater?'

Toni (inventing an excuse): 'I—I haven't any flowers.'

Father: 'Did you sell all you had yesterday?'

Toni (with a far away look in her eyes, which shows that her answer is symbolic): 'I can't sell yesterday's violets. They wither so quickly.'

She begins to sob, and runs out of the room, banging the door. Her father stands looking after her, in blank surprise. Then he shrugs his shoulders and grimaces, as much as to say that woman's whims are beyond his understanding.

'Cut.' Bergmann rises quickly from his chair and goes over to Anita.

'Let me tell you something, madame. The way you throw open that door is great. It is altogether much too great. You give to the movement

54

a theatrical importance beside which the slaughter of Rasputin is just a quick breakfast.'

Anita smiles graciously. 'Sorry, Friedrich. I *felt* it wasn't right.' She *is* in a good mood.

'Let me show you, once.' Bergmann stands by the table. His lips tremble, his eyes glisten; he is a beautiful young girl on the verge of tears. 'I cannot sell violets of yesterday. They wither.' He runs, with face averted, from the room. There is a bump behind the scenes, and a muttered: 'Verflucht!' He must have tripped over one of the cables. An instant later Bergmann reappears, grinning, a little out of breath. 'You see how I mean? With a certain lightness. Do not hit it too hard.'

'Yes.' Anita nods seriously, playing up to him. 'I *think* I see.'

'All right, my darling,' Bergmann pats her arm. 'We shoot it once.'

'Where's Timmy?' Anita demands, in a bored, melodious voice. The make-up man hurries forward. 'Timmy, darling, is my face all right?'

She submits it to him, as impersonally as one extends a shoe to the bootblack; this anxiously pretty mask which is her job, her source of income, the tool of her trade. Timmy dabs at it expertly. She glances at herself coldly, without vanity, in his pocket-mirror. The camera-operator's assistant measures the distance from the lens to her nose, with a tape.

A boy named George asks the continuity-girl for the number of the scene. It has to be chalked on the board which he will hold in front of the camera, before the take.

Roger calls from the sound-booth: 'Come in for this one, Chris, I need an alibi.' He often says this, jokingly, but with a certain veiled resentment, which is directed chiefly against Eliot. Roger resents any criticism of the sound-recording. He is very conscientious about his job.

I go into the sound-booth, which is like a telephone box. Eliot begins to shout bossily: 'Right! Ready, sir? Ready, Mr. Watts? Bell, please. Doors! Red light!' Then, because some people are still moving about: 'Quiet! This is a take!'

Roger picks up the headphones and plugs in to the sound-camera room, which is in a gallery, overlooking the floor. 'Ready to go, Jack?' he asks. Two buzzes: the okay signal.

'Are we all set?' asks Eliot. Then, after a moment: 'Turn them over.'

'Running,' the boy at the switchboard tells him.

George steps forward and holds the board up before the camera.

Roger buzzes twice to the sound-camera. Two buzzes in reply. Roger buzzes twice to signal Bergmann that Sound is ready.

Clark, the boy who works the clappers, says in a loud voice: 'One hundred and four, Take One.' He claps the clappers.

Bergmann, sitting grim in his chair, hisses between shut teeth: 'Camera!'

I watch him, through the take. It isn't necessary to look at the set: the whole scene is reflected in his face. He never shifts his eyes from the actors for an instant. He seems to control every gesture, every intonation, by a sheer effort of hypnotic power. His lips move, his face relaxes and contracts, his body is thrust forward or drawn back in its seat, his hands rise and fall to mark the phases of the action. Now he is coaxing Toni from the window, now warning against too much haste, now encouraging her father, now calling for more expression, now afraid the pause will be missed, now delighted with the tempo, now anxious again, now really alarmed, now reassured, now touched, now pleased, now very pleased, now cautious, now disturbed, now amused. Bergmann's concentration is marvellous in its singleness of purpose. It is the act of creation.

When it is all over he sighs, as if awaking from sleep. Softly, lovingly, he breathes the word: 'Cut.'

He turns to the camera-operator: 'How was it?'

'All right, sir, but I'd like to go again.'

Roger gives two buzzes.

'Okay for sound, sir,' says Teddy.

Joyce, the continuity-girl, checks the footage with the operator. Roger put his head out of the booth. 'Teddy, will you favour round towards Miss Hayden a bit? I'm afraid of that bloody camera.'

This problem of camera-noise is perpetual. To guard against it, the camera is muffled in a quilt, which makes it look like a pet poodle wearing its winter jacket. Nevertheless, the noise persists. Bergmann never fails to react to it. Sometimes he curses, sometimes he sulks. This morning, however, he is in a clowning mood. He goes over to the camera and throws his arms around it.

'My dear old friend, we make you work so hard! It's too cruel! Mr. Chatsworth should give you a pension, and send you to the meadow to eat grass with the retired race-horses.'

Everybody laughs. Bergmann is quite popular on the floor. 'He's what I call a regular comedian,' the doorman tells me. 'This picture will be good, if it's half as funny as he is.'

Mr. Watts and the camera-operator are discussing how to avoid the mike-shadow. Bergmann calls it 'the Original Sin of the Talking Pictures'. On rare occasions, the microphone itself somehow manages to get into the shot, without anybody noticing it. There is something sinister about it, like Poe's Raven. It is always there, silently listening.

A long buzz from the sound-camera room. Roger puts on the head-phones and reports: 'Sound-camera reloading, sir.' Bergmann gives a grunt and goes off into a corner to dictate a poem to Dorothy. Amidst all this turmoil, he still finds time to compose one nearly every day. Fred Murray is shouting directions for the readjustment of various lamps on the spot-rail and gantry; the tweets, the snooks and the baby spots. Joyce is typing the continuity report, which contains the exact text of each scene, as acted, with details of footage, screen-time, hours of work and so forth.

'Come on,' shouts Eliot. 'Aren't we ready, yet?'

Roger calls up to the camera-room: 'Going again, Jack.'

Teddy notices that Eliot is inadvertently standing in front of Roger's window, blocking our view of the set. He grins maliciously, and says, in an obvious parody of Eliot's most officious tone: 'Clear the booth, please!' Eliot blushes and moves aside, murmuring: 'Sorry.' Roger winks at me. Teddy very pleased with himself, swings the microphone-boom over, whistling, and warning his crew: 'Mind your heads, my braves!'

Roger generally lets me ring the bell for silence and make the two-buzz signal. It is one of the few opportunities I get of earning my salary. But, this time, I am mooning. I watch Bergmann telling something funny to Fred Murray, and wonder what it is. Roger has to make the signals himself. 'I'm sorry to see a falling off in your wonted efficiency, Chris,' he tells me. And he adds, to Teddy: 'I was thinking of giving Chris his ticket, but now I shall have to reconsider it.'

Roger's nautical expressions date back to the time when he was a radio operator on a merchant ship. He still has something of the ship's officer about him, in his brisk movements, his conscientiousness, his alert, pink, open-air face. He studies yachting magazines in the booth, between takes.

'Quiet! Get settled down. Ready? Turn them over.'

'Running.'

'One hundred and four, Take Two.'

'Camera . . .'

'Cut.'

'Okay, sir.'

'Okay for sound, Mr. Bergmann.'

'All right. We print this one.'

'Are you going again, sir?'

'We shoot it once more, quickly.'

'Right. Come on, now. Let's get this in the can.'

But the third take is N.G. Anita fluffs a line. In the middle of the fourth take the camera jams. The fifth take is all right, and will be printed. My long, idle, tiring morning is over, and it is time for lunch.

S. J. PERELMAN

(b. 1904)

The comic genius of S. J. Perelman has been employed variously by Mike Todd (for whom he laboured on the screenplay of Around the World in Eighty Days*), the* New Yorker *and the Marx Brothers, to whose team of script-writers Perelman was once shackled. Earlier on he tried his hand as cartoonist for a magazine whose editors, he complains, were inexplicably unmoved by such masterpieces from his drawing board as one showing 'a distraught gentleman careening into a doctor's office clutching a friend by the wrist and whimpering "I've got Bright's disease and he has mine." ' As a biographical note he has released the comment of one who knew him well (or as well as he wanted to know him) : 'Just before they made S. J. Perelman, they broke the mould.'*

Strictly From Hunger

YES I was excited, and small wonder. What boy wouldn't be, boarding a huge, mysterious, puffing steam train for golden California? As Mamma adjusted my reefer and strapped on my leggings, I almost burst with impatience. Grinning redcaps lifted my luggage into the compartment and spat on it. Mamma began to weep into a small pillow-case she had brought along for the purpose.

'Oh, son, I wish you hadn't become a scenario writer!' she sniffled.

'Aw, now, Moms,' I comforted her, 'it's no worse than playing the piano in a call house.' She essayed a brave little smile, and, reaching into her reticule, produced a flat package which she pressed into my hands. For a moment I was puzzled, then I cried out with glee.

'Jelly sandwiches! Oh, Moms!'

'Eat them all, boy o' mine," she told me, 'they're good for boys with hollow little legs.' Tenderly she pinned to my lapel the green tag reading 'To Plushnick Productions. Hollywood, California'. The whistle shrilled and in a moment I was chugging out of Grand Central's dreaming spires followed only by the anguished cries of relatives who would now have to go to work. I had chugged only a few feet when I realised

59

that I had left without the train, so I had to run back and wait for it to start.

As we sped along the glorious fever spots of the Hudson I decided to make a tour of inspection. To my surprise I found that I was in the only passenger car of the train; the other cars were simply dummies snipped out of cardboard and painted to stimulate coaches. Even 'passengers' had been cunningly drawn in coloured crayons in the 'window', as well as ragged tramps clinging to the blinds below and drinking Jamaica ginger. With a rueful smile I returned to my seat and gorged myself on jelly sandwiches.

At Buffalo the two other passengers and I discovered to our horror that the conductor had been left behind. We finally decided to divide up his duties; I punched the tickets, the old lady opposite me wore a conductor's hat and locked the washroom as we came into stations, and the young man who looked as if his feet were not mates consulted a Hamilton watch frequently. But we missed the conductor's earthy conversation and it was not until we had exchanged several questionable stories that we began to forget our loss.

A flicker of interest served to shorten the trip. At Fort Snodgrass, Ohio, two young and extremely polite road-agents boarded the train and rifled us of our belongings. They explained that they were modern Robin Hoods and were stealing from the poor to give to the rich. They had intended to rape all the women and depart for Sherwood Forest, but when I told them that Sherwood Forest as well as the women were in England, their chagrin was comical in the extreme. They declined my invitation to stay and take a chance on the train's pool, declaring that the engineer had fixed the run and would fleece us, and got off at South Bend with every good wish.

The weather is always capricious in the Middle West, and although it was midsummer, the worst blizzard in Chicago's history greeted us on our arrival. The streets were crowded with thousands of newsreel cameramen trying to photograph one another bucking the storm on the Lake Front. It was a novel idea for the newsreels and I wished them well. With only two hours in Chicago I would be unable to see the city, and the thought drew me into a state of composure. I noted with pleasure that a fresh coat of grime had been given to the Dearbon Street station, though I was hardly vain enough to believe that it had anything to do with my visit. There was the usual ten-minute wait while the porters withdrew with my portable typewriter to a side room and flailed it with hammers, and at last I was aboard the 'Sachem', crack train of the B.B.D. & O. lines.

It was as if I had suddenly been transported into another world. 'General Crook', in whom I was to make my home for the next three days, and his two neighbours, 'Lake Tahoe' and 'Chief Malomai', were everything that the word 'Pullman' implies; they were Pullmans. Uncle Eben, in charge of 'General Crook', informed me that the experiment of air-cooling the cars had been so successful that the road intended trying to heat them next winter.

'Ah suttinly looks fo'd to dem roastin' ears Ah's gwine have next winter, he, he, he!' he chuckled, rubbing soot into my hat.

The conductor told me he had been riding on trains for so long that he had begun to smell like one, and sure enough, two brakemen waved their lanterns at him that night and tried to tempt him down a siding in Kansas City. We became good friends and it came as something of a blow when I heard the next morning that he had fallen off the train during the night. The fireman said that we had circled about for an hour trying to find him but that it had been impossible to lower a boat because we did not carry a boat.

The run was marked by only one incident out of the ordinary. I had ordered breaded veal cutlet the first evening, and my waiter, poking his head into the kitchen, had repeated the order. The cook, unfortunately, understood him to say '*dreaded* veal cutlet', and resenting the slur, sprang at the waiter with drawn razor. In a few seconds I was the only living remnant of the shambles, and at Topeka I was compelled to wait until a new shambles was hooked on and I proceeded with dinner.

It seemed only a scant week or ten days before we were pulling into Los Angeles. I had grown so attached to my porter that I made him give me a lock of his hair. I wonder if he still has the ten-cent piece I gave him? There was a gleam in his eye which could only have been insanity as he leaned over me. Ah, Uncle Eben, faithful old retainer, where are you now? Gone to what obscure ossuary? If this should chance to meet your kindly gaze, drop me a line care of *Variety*, won't you? They know what to do with it.

— II —

The violet hush of twilight was descending over Los Angeles as my hostess, Violet Hush, and I left its suburbs headed towards Hollywood. In the distance a glow of huge piles of burning motion-picture scripts lit up the sky. The crisp tang of frying writers and directors whetted my appetite. How good it was to be alive, I thought, inhaling deep lungfuls of carbon monoxide. Suddenly our powerful Gatti-Cazazza slid to a stop in the traffic.

'What is it, Jenkin?' Violet called anxiously through the speaking-tube to the chauffeur (played by Lyle Talbot).

A *suttee* was in progress by the roadside, he said—did we wish to see it? Quickly Violet and I elbowed our way through the crowd. An enormous funeral pyre composed of thousands of feet of film and scripts, drenched with Chanel Number 5, awaited the torch of Jack Holt, who was to act as master of ceremonies. In a few terse words Violet explained this unusual custom borrowed from the Hindus and never paid for. The worst disgrace that can befall a producer is an unkind notice from a New York reviewer. When this happens, the producer becomes a pariah in Hollywood. He is shunned by his friends, thrown into bankruptcy, and like a Japanese electing hara-kiri, he commits *suttee*. A great bonfire is made of the film, and the luckless producer, followed by directors, actors, technicians, and the producer's wives, immolate themselves. Only the scenario writers are exempt. These are tied between the tails of two spirited Caucasian ponies, which are then driven off in opposite directions. This custom is called 'a conference'.

Violet and I watched the scene breathlessly. Near us Harry Cohl, head of Moribund Studios, was being rubbed with truck towels preparatory to throwing himself into the flames. He was nonchalantly smoking a Rocky Ford five-center, and the man's courage drew a tear to the eye of even the most callous. Weeping relatives besought him to eschew his design, but he stood adamant. Adamant Eve, his plucky secretary, was being rubbed with crash towels preparatory to flinging herself into Cohl's embers. Assistant directors busily prepared spears, war bonnets and bags of pemmican which the Great Chief would need on his trip to the 'Happy Hunting Grounds'. Wampas and beads to placate the Great Spirit (played by Will Hays) were piled high about the stoical tribesman.

Suddenly Jack Holt (played by Edmund Lowe) raised his hand for silence. The moment had come. With bowed head Holt made a simple invocation couched in one-syllable words so that even the executives might understand. Throwing his five-center to a group of autograph hunters, the great man poised himself for the fatal leap. But from off-scene came the strident clatter of coconut shells, and James Mohl, Filmdom's fearless critic, wearing the uniform of a Confederate guerrilla and the whiskers of General Beauregard, galloped in on a foam-flecked pinto. It was he whose mocking review had sent Cohl into Coventry. It was a dramatic moment as the two stood pitted against each other—

Cohl against Mohl, the Blue against the Gray. But with true Southern gallantry Mohl was the first to extend the hand of friendship.

'Ah reckon it was an unworthy slur, suh,' he said in manly tones. 'Ah-all thought you-all's pictuah was lousy but it opened at the Rialto to sensational grosses, an' Ah-all 'pologies. Heah, have a yam.' And he drew a yam from his tunic. Not to be outdone in hospitality, Cohl drew a yam from his tunic, and soon they were exchanging yams and laughing over the old days.

When Violet and I finally stole away to our waiting motor, we felt that were were somehow nearer to each other. I snuggled luxuriously into the buffalo laprode Violet had provided against the treacherous night air and gazed out at the gleaming neon lights. Soon we would be in Beverly Hills, and already the quaint native women were swarming alongside in their punts urging us to buy their cunning beadwork and mangoes. Occasionally I threw a handful of coppers to the Negro boys, who dove for them joyfully. The innocent squeals of the policemen as the small blackamoors pinched them were irresistible. Unable to resist them, Violet and I were soon pinching each other till our skins glowed. Violet was good to the touch, with a firm fleshy texture like a winesap or pippin. It seemed but a moment before we were sliding under the porte-cochère of her home, a magnificent rambling structure of beaver-board patterned after an Italian ropewalk of the sixteenth century. It had recently been remodelled by a family of wrens who had introduced chewing gum into the left wing, and only three or four obscure Saxon words could do it justice.

I was barely warming my hands in front of the fire and watching Jimmy Fidler turn on a spit when my presence on the Pacific Slope made itself felt. The news of my arrival had thrown international financial centres into an uproar, and sheaves of wires, cables, phone messages, and even corn began piling up. An ugly rumour that I might reorganise the motion-picture industry was being bruited about in the world's commodity markets. My brokers, Whitelipped & Trembling, were beside themselves. The New York Stock Exchange was begging them for assurances of stability and Threadneedle Street awaited my next move with drumming pulses. Film shares ricocheted sharply, although wools and meats were sluggish, if not downright sullen. To the reporters who flocked around me I laughingly disclaimed that this was a business trip. I was simply a scenario writer to whom the idea of work was abhorrent. A few words murmured into the transatlantic telephone, the lift of an eyebrow here, the shrug of a shoulder there, and equilibrium was soon restored. I washed sparsely, curled my moustache with a heated hairpin, flicked a drop of Sheik Lure on my lapel, and rejoined my hostess.

After a copious dinner, melting-eyed beauties in lacy black underthings fought with each other to serve me kummel. A hurried apology, and I was curled up in bed with the Autumn 1927 issue of *The Yale Review*. Halfway through an exciting symposium on Sir Thomas Aquinas' indebtedness to Professors Whitehead and Spengler, I suddenly detected a stowaway blonde under the bed. Turning a deaf ear to her heartrending entreaties and burning glances, I sent her packing. Then I treated my face to a feast of skin food, buried my head in the pillow and went bye-bye.

— III —

Hollywood Boulevard! I rolled the rich syllables over on my tongue and thirstily drank in the beauty of the scene before me. On all sides nattily attired boulevardiers clad in rich stuffs strolled nonchalantly, inhaling cubebs and exchanging epigrams stolen from Martial and Wilde. Thousands of scantily draped but none the less appetizing extra girls milled past me, their mouths a scarlet wound and their eyes clearly defined in their faces. Their voluptuous curves set my blood on fire, and as I made my way down Mammary Lane, a strange thought began to invade my brain: I realised that I had not eaten breakfast yet. In a Chinese eatery cunningly built in the shape of an old shoe I managed to assuage the inner man with a chopped glove salad topped off with frosted cocoa. Charming platinum-haired hostesses in red pyjamas and peaked caps added a note of colour to the surroundings, whilst a gypsy orchestra played selections from Victor Herbert's operettas on musical saws. It was a bit of old Vienna come to life, and the sun was a red ball in the heavens before I realised with a start that I had promised to report at the Plushnick Studios.

Commandeering a taxicab, I arrived at the studio just in time to witness the impressive ceremony of changing the guard. In the central parade ground, on a snowy white charger, sat Max Plushnick, resplendent in a producer's uniform, his chest glittering with first mortgage liens, amortizations, and estoppels. His personal guard, composed of picked vice-presidents of the Chase National Bank, was drawn up stiffly about him in a hollow square.

But the occasion was not a happy one. A writer had been caught trying to create an adult picture. The drums rolled dismally, and the writer, his head sunk on his chest, was led out amid a ghastly silence. With the aid of a small stepladder Plushnick slid lightly from his steed. Sternly he ripped the epaulets and buttons from the traitor's tunic, broke his sword across his knee, and in a few harsh words demoted him to the mail department.

'And now,' began Plushnick, 'I further condemn you to eat . . .'

'No, no!' screamed the poor wretch, falling to his knees and embracing Plushnick's jackboots. 'Not that, not that!'

'Stand up, man,' ordered Plushnick, his lip curling; 'I condemn you to eat in the studio restaurant for ten days and may God have mercy on your soul.' The awful words rang out on the still evening air and even Plushnick's hardened old mercenaries shuddered. The heartrending cries of the unfortunate were drowned in the boom of the sunset gun.

In the wardrobe department I was photographed, fingerprinted, and measured for the smock and Windsor tie which were to be my uniform. A nameless fear clutched at my heart as two impassive turnkeys headed me down a corridor to my supervisor's office. For what seemed hours we waited in an anteroom. Then my serial number was called, the leg-irons were struck off, and I was shoved through a door into the presence of Diana ffrench-Mamoulian.

How to describe what followed? Diana ffrench-Mamoulian was accustomed to having her way with writers, and my long lashes and peachblow mouth seemed to whip her to insensate desire. In vain, time and again, I tried to bring her attention back to the story we were discussing, only to find her gem-incrusted fingers straying through my hair. When our interview was over, her cynical attempt to 'date me up' made every fibre of my being cry out in revolt.

'P-please,' I stammered, my face burning, 'I—I wish you wouldn't. . . . I'm engaged to a Tri Kappa at Goucher—'

'Just one kiss,' she pleaded, her breath hot against my neck. In desperation I granted her boon, knowing full well that my weak defences were crumbling before the onslaught of this love tigree. Finally she allowed me to leave, but only after I had promised to dine at her penthouse apartment and have an intimate chat about the script. The basket of slave bracelets and marzipan I found awaiting me on my return home made me realise to what lengths Diana would go.

I was radiant that night in blue velvet tails and a boutonnière of diamonds from Cartier's, my eyes starry and the merest hint of cologne at my ear-lobes. An inscrutable Oriental served the Lucullian repast and my vis-à-vis was as effervescent as the wine.

'Have a bit of the wing, darling?' queried Diana solicitously, indicating the roast Long Island airplane with apple sauce. I tried to turn our conversation from the personal note, but Diana would have none of it. Soon we were exchanging gay bantam over the mellow Vouvray, laughing as we dipped fastidious fingers into the Crisco parfait for which Diana was famous. Our meal finished, we sauntered into the rumpus room and Diana turned on the radio. With a savage snarl the radio turned on her and we slid over the waxed floor in the intricate maze of the jackdaw strut. Without quite knowing why, I found myself hesitating before the plate of liqueur candies Diana was pressing on me.

'I don't think I should—really, I'm a trifle faint—'

'Oh, come on,' she urged masterfully. 'After all, you're old enough to be your father—I mean I'm old enough to be my mother. . . .' She stuffed a brandy bonbon between my clenched teeth. Before long I was eating them thirstily, reeling about the room and shouting snatches of coarse drunken doggerel. My brain was on fire, I tell you. Through the haze I saw Diana ffrench-Mamoulian, her nostrils dilated, groping for me. My scream of terror only egged her on, overturning chairs and tables in her bestial pursuit. With superhuman talons she tore off my collar and suspenders. I sank to my knees, choked with sobs, hanging on to my last shirt-stud like a drowning man. Her Svengali eyes were slowly hypnotising me; I fought like a wounded bird—and then, blissful unconsciousness.

When I came to, the Oriental servant and Diana were battling in the centre of the floor. As I watched, Yen Shee Gow drove a well-aimed blow to her mid-section, following it with a right cross to the jaw. Diana staggered and rolled under a table. Before my astonished eyes John Chinaman stripped the mask from his face and revealed the features of Blanche Almonds, a little seamstress I had long wooed unsuccessfully in New York. Gently she bathed my temples with Florida water and explained how she had followed me, suspecting Diana ffrench-Mamoulian's intentions. I let her rain kisses over my face and lay back in her arms as beaming Ivan tucked us in and cracked his whip over the prancing bays. In a few seconds our sleigh was skimming over the hard crust towards Port Arthur and freedom, leaving Plushnick's discomfited officers gnashing one another's teeth. The wintry Siberian moon glowed over the tundras, drenching my hair with moonbeams for Blanche to kiss away. And so, across the silvery steppes amid the howling of wolves, we rode into a new destiny, purified in the crucible that men call Hollywood.

JEFFREY DELL

(b. 1904)

Jeffrey Dell's Nobody Ordered Wolves *(1939) hilariously harks back to a time when British film production was dominated by émigrés of occasional genius and unrelenting* chutzpah. *The ghost of Alexander Korda is never far distant from the happenings in this excerpt. Dell himself is a veteran screen-writer (most often for the Boulting Brothers) and the director of such comedies as the gentle and engaging* Don't Take It To Heart.

Nobody Ordered Wolves

CHAPTER 12

THE SITE for the new studios proved to be a delightfully secluded estate containing a great deal of timber and surrounded by a high stone wall. A wide stream bisected the Park; and, on the rising ground overlooking the stream, stood an immense eighteenth-century mansion with many of the windows broken or boarded up.

Uxbridge parked the car among half a dozen others on what had once been a lawn and was now a hay-field. They strolled towards the house and sat down on the balustrade of a terrace choked with dandelions and chickweed. It was a lovely morning, with scarcely a breeze, and the lichen-covered stones were warm to the touch. They lit cigarettes and smoked for some time without speaking.

Though it was no longer dawn, birds sang as Uxbridge had said they would and Phillip noticed a stream of bees going in and out of a hole in a first-floor window.

At length Uxbridge said reflectively: 'Well, I must say it's a nice spot for making pictures.'

'Yes, until they start making them,' amended Phillip. 'What will the house be used for?' He was looking up at the vast façade, somewhat reminiscent of Blenheim Palace, and wondering how many stages it would contain when adapted.

'Naps is going to live in it,' replied Uxbridge.

'My hat!' exclaimed Phillip. 'He'll need some servants.'

'Oh, I don't know. Naps is quite a simple chap when you get to know him. The trout stream is the principal attraction so far as he's concerned. You know, when they first decided to build it was a toss up between this place and about three others. But some of the blokes in the head office got old Naps enthused about fishing and the trout settled it.'

'Three million seems a hell of a price for trout,' said Phillip.

'Oh, it's been enormously exaggerated,' objected Uxbridge. 'They're not spending more than two and a half at the outside. Naps is like a kid with a new toy over that stream. He's crazy about it. Thinks he'll get the P.M. down for weekends.'

Uxbridge crossed the terrace and cut a buttonhole from among the tea-roses which straggled untidily along the wall. 'Come on!' he called. Let's go and see what's doing.'

They passed round the end of the house and through a huge columned archway into a yard like a barrack-square, surrounded by stables and coach-houses. No sooner had they set foot on the cobbles than a mournful howl shattered the midday peace. It was immediately taken up by other voices, whose agonised wailing echoed eerily among the deserted buildings. Phillip stopped dead.

'Good Lord! What's that?' he asked.

Uxbridge pointed. 'Look! Some old friends of yours,' he said.

Over the cracked and flaking surface of one of the stable doors had been nailed a freshly painted notice-board with the words: *DANGER. Beware of the Wolves.*

'Do you mean to say they've still got those wretched animals?' Phillip asked.

'Yes,' said Uxbridge. 'But I didn't know they were down here. There's been quite a bit of bother, you know, one way and another. I shouldn't be surprised if *you* hear about them before very long.'

'Me?' Phillip turned and looked keenly at Uxbridge. 'Do you know something?' he demanded suspiciously.

'Nothing very definite,' answered Uxbridge airily. 'Let's get out of here. I can't stand that row.'

He turned to leave the stable-yard by the way they had entered; but Phillip was not going to be put off like this.

'Come on! Let's have it! I suppose you mean I'm going to be assigned to another story especially written for them, is that it?'

'Well, I did hear a vague rumour about a loan to C.B.A.'

'What do you mean, a loan? Who's going to be loaned? Me?'

'You *and* the wolves, old boy. Now, don't fly off the handle. It may

68

not come off. But something's obviously got to be done with them soon. The Siberian gag is beginning to lose some of its youthful charm and freshness and the finance wallahs have started asking rather pointed questions again.'

'I don't wonder,' muttered Phillip bad-temperedly.

'You're as unreasonable as they are,' declared Uxbridge. 'It's your city mind. Anyone with a particle of imagination would say that if Naps erects the new studios he ought to be encouraged and given a breather, not distracted by a lot of irritating quibbles.'

They went in silence through the kitchen-gardens, which were a wilderness of thistles and burdocks; past long ranges of forcing-houses, where few of the panes remained intact; through a belt of sweet chestnuts; and so into a paddock, bordered on two sides by elm-trees and on the third, where the ground fell away to the stream, by a line of pollarded willows. Uxbridge paused and shaded his eyes.

'There's the unit over there,' he said. But they don't seem to be doing much.'

From a distance the group had the appearance of a picnic-party. They were prostrate in the shade near the stream. A little way off stood a camera, a sound truck, and one or two small piles of gear, about which a few sheep were grazing. It was a peaceful scene.

'We'll just go over and say "How-do",' said Uxbridge.

'Where did you get all this from?' asked Phillip, still busy with his own thoughts, as they started across the paddock.

'Get what from? What are you talking about?' demanded Uxbridge.

'Why, all this about C.B.A. and the wolves.'

'Oh, I dunno. It's just one of those things. You know how they fly around. For heaven's sake don't say *I* told you.'

'If they think they're going to hawk me around as a job lot with a parcel of wolves . . .' began Phillip, heatedly.

'Oh, forget it!' Uxbridge interrupted him. 'The mere fact that it's actually discussed is quite sufficient to prevent it ever happening. You've been in this racket long enough to know that . . . Hullo, old boy!'

The last words were addressed to Bud Roscoe, the cameraman. He was lying flat on his stomach surrounded by a group of giggling girls in bathing-costumes who were contending for the privilege of tickling the back of his neck with feathery grasses.

'Hullo! Hullo! Hullo!' he said, raising himself on to his elbow. 'What brings you boys out here?'

'Oh, just inspecting the estate,' explained Uxbridge. 'You know Hardcastle?'

'Sure!' Roscoe nodded to Phillip. He did not look very sure.

'What's the hold-up?' enquired Uxbridge.

'We're just waiting for Naps.'

'Hasn't he turned up?'

'He turned up right enough; but he's gone off again some place. Say, Mabel! Just cut out that stuff, willyer?'

Amid shrieks of laughter he brushed the tormenting grasses aside. But Mabel, it seemed, was not prepared to cut it out. Nor were the others prepared to let Mabel cut them out, and Mr. Roscoe disappeared beneath an agitated heap of vivid costumes and writhing limbs, to the accompaniment of much shrill laughter. It was difficult to carry on conversation with him under these conditions, and Uxbridge and Phillip wandered off along the bank of the stream.

'That's all those fellows ever think about,' sighed Uxbridge.

They followed the stream for perhaps half a mile through meadows and woods when suddenly, as they emerged into a clearing, Uxbridge seized Phillip's arm. There, a few yards away, sat Mr. Bott, fishing. Or rather, to be exact, he was fishing by proxy. That is to say he lay in a wicker chaise-longue, with his eyes closed and a large cigar in his mouth, while on a camp-stool by the water sat his chauffeur. The latter was holding a rod and gazing at a brightly coloured celluloid float the size of a duck's egg, which lay on the surface of the stream.

By Mr. Bott's side stood a garden table bearing a bottle of Vichy, a glass and a pile of morning papers. The *Financial Times* lay open on his lap.

At their approach, he raised his head with a jerk, and frowned in their direction.

'Ssh!' he commanded.

The chauffeur jumped.

'Beg pardon, sir?' he asked.

'Not you! Not you!' snapped Mr. Bott. 'You watch that . . . whatever-it-is and you don't take your eyes away for one second!'

'Yes, sir,' replied the chauffeur. He sounded scared.

Mr. Bott was plainly excited and as usual this was inclined to affect his English. He stared at the enormous float and whispered: 'Sit down! You see something in a minute, very likely.'

They sat on the grass beside a pile of lines, spinners and other gear, and watched the float.

For some time there was no sound except the buzz of insects and the faint drone of a distant threshing machine. Phillip began to feel drowsy. He would have liked to lie flat on the grass and close his eyes, but felt courtesy demanded that he should show an interest in the fishing. After a while Uxbridge got out a cigarette and closed his case with a snap.

'Ssh!' hissed Mr. Bott. 'Be careful!'

'Sorry!' said Uxbridge in a low voice. 'What are you fishing for, Naps?'

'Because I like to fish! It is nice to fish. Mr. Chamberlain does it.'

'I mean, what sort of fish are you trying to catch?'

'Trout. This is a trout stream.'

'But what about flies?'

'They're bloddy awful, ole boy! They've been biting me all the morning.'

Uxbridge gave it up and lay back with his hands under his head. After a few moments Phillip suddenly became aware that Mr. Bott was staring at him with every appearance of fury. As he had made no sound for several minutes he was at a loss to account for it. He endeavoured to show even more interest in the float, but could not help hearing Mr. Bott whisper fiercely to Uxbridge.

'What does this fellow want?'

'Nothing . . . he's on the scenario staff,' whispered Uxbridge, in reply.

'Yes, of course,' said Mr. Bott without conviction.

Phillip was again conscious of being closely scrutinised. Fortunately, at this moment a diversion was created by a loud splash some distance away.

Mr. Bott turned sharply and gazed along the water.

'That was a trout!' he announced anthoritatively, getting to his feet.

'Probably a moor-hen,' said Uxbridge without stirring.

'It was a trout, I tell you!' shouted Mr. Bott, now very excited. 'An enormous trout. Huggett! Go along there! By that post. If you are quick we have him.'

The chauffeur obediently wound in his line, revealing first a large silver spinner and subsequently two substantial lead weights. Uxbridge got up and took hold of the spinner.

'I say, Naps,' he protested. 'You can't catch trout with that thing.'

'Why not?' demanded Mr. Bott defensively.

'Well, for one thing he couldn't get it in his mouth. It's darn nearly as big as he is.'

Mr. Bott scowled at the spinner, then at the chauffeur. The man shuffled his feet uneasily.

'You hear that?' challenged Mr. Bott. 'Why do you buy this damn-fool thing?'

'I don't know nothin' about fishin', sir. I got what they said in the shop was right.'

The colour began to drain from Mr. Bott's cheeks.

'I tell you on the telephone to say to them that you want some things to go trout-fishing!'

'I thought you said to go out fishing,' replied the chauffeur sheepishly, and then made matters worse by adding: 'I expect that's why they give me the wrong things.'

A strangled sound came from Mr. Bott's throat. For a moment Phillip expected to see the chauffeur assaulted. The situation was saved, however, by Uxbridge, who had been sorting over the pile of gear and now produced a box.

'Look, Naps! Those spinners you're using are for pike,' he said, opening the box. 'These are the chaps you want.'

He exhibited two neat rows of flies. But Mr. Bott seemed to have lost his enthusiasm. After a cursory glance at the flies he remarked: 'We try some other time.'

He turned to the chauffeur.

'You waste all this bloddy time when I have to make pictures!' he complained peevishly. 'You go back to the shop and get them to show you how to fix these things.'

He started off along the bank of the stream; but after going a few yards he stopped and looked back.

'Come!' he said, and beckoned.

'Me?' enquired Phillip, at whom he appeared to be looking.

'Yes, yes! Come!'

As Phillip joined him, Mr. Bott put an arm through his and started to walk towards the location.

'I'm so awful tired,' he groaned.

Phillip could think of nothing to say and in a moment or two Mr. Bott continued: 'How do you like to make a picture for C.B.A.? An Alaskan picture?'

Phillip's heart sank. As if to confirm his fears a distant howl came from the direction of the stables.

'It is terrific!' Mr. Bott went on with enthusiasm. 'I have seen the script. It's colossal! As a matter of fact I sell them the story.'

'But . . . didn't you mean I was to write the script?' queried Phillip.

'Writing is a lousy business,' proclaimed Mr. Bott. 'You don't want to bother with that. No. You will be the dialogue director. You teach their bloddy actors to speak English. It is a nice job for you. I see you have a good credit.'

'Well, thank you,' said Phillip doubtfully. 'But I . . .'

'It is nothing, my dear fellow.' Mr. Bott brushed it aside with a wave of his hand. 'I like very much to do something for you.'

He was peculiarly foreign this morning, thought Phillip. The episode of the pike spinner had evidently upset him. But his charm was unfailing. He borrowed Phillip's matches and re-lit his cigar.

'It's a fine story!' he repeated, putting the matches into his pocket. 'My God! What a story!'

'Can you give me some idea what it's about?' prompted Phillip.

Mr. Bott was looking intently at a bright blue dragonfly which had just settled on the pink, waxen cup of a water-lily. He waited until it rose and soared over their heads. Then he resumed both the walk and the conversation.

'It's about some wolves,' he said, and went on quickly: 'They may want you to polish up their script a little. You know, just a line here and there. They haven't any good writers. We have all the good writers.'

He smiled benevolently at Phillip, who tried, not very successfully, to smile back.

They came out of the wood and started to cross a field.

'You know Cripps of C.B.A.?' Mr. Bott asked suddenly.

Phillip confessed that he did not.

'He is a nice fellow,' declared Mr. Bott. 'You will like working with him.'

Phillip had many times heard it stated that of the things which were wrong with the industry, Mr. Cripps of C.B.A. took pride of place; but Mr. Bott's voice carried such conviction that he was slightly reassured.

'How long shall I be . . . on loan?' he asked.

'Oooooh!' The cigar described an expressive arc of time. 'Two weeks? Three weeks? You like to do this, eh? You see, we have no picture good enough for you just now.'

It was on the tip of Phillip's tongue to point out that they had had no picture for him during the preceding two years, either good enough or otherwise. He was tempted to seize this opportunity to clear up many questions which had long tormented him—questions about the Malayan picture, the Siberian picture, and his engagement. But Mr. Bott's voice was now so full of wistful fatigue that he hadn't the heart to do so. Instead he enquired when his new work would begin.

'Right away, ole boy, if you like,' replied Mr. Bott, as if Phillip were pressing him for permission to start. 'I can fix that for you. I must do some work now.'

The spasm of fatigue had passed. Roscoe and his companions were now in sight and, with a smile and pat on the arm, Mr. Bott strode briskly across the paddock. As soon as they saw him coming, they started scrambling to their feet.

Phillip turned and strolled slowly back in search of Uxbridge.

The conversation had developed most unsatisfactorily. Somehow his conversations with Mr. Bott always did. He tried to persuade himself that he was glad to have a job at last. He found himself hard to convince.

He discovered Uxbridge instructing Huggett in the manipulation of a fly. At every cast, the chauffeur, looking grimly determined, was catching a Portugal laurel.

'You said something about having breakfast,' Phillip said, rather petulantly. 'I suppose you know it's half-past one?'

Uxbridge picked up his hat.

'Lunch'll be just as good,' he said cheerfully. 'There's nothing like fishing for giving you an appetite.'

They walked towards the car.

'Well?' he asked. 'What was all that about? Did you land yourself a nice job?'

'I did!' said Phillip bitterly. 'I'm to teach the wolves to speak English!'

BUDD SCHULBERG

(b. 1915)

Budd Schulberg is the son of Hollywood producer B. P. Schulberg. One of his first assignments as a young screen-writer was to accompany a sick and drunken Scott Fitzgerald to the Dartmouth Winter Carnival to absorb atmosphere for a Walter Wanger musical. The expedition ended disastrously (Malcom Cowley has called it Fitzgerald's 'biggest, saddest, most desperate spree') and Schulberg finished the film alone. He utilised the experience for his novel about Fitzgerald, The Disenchanted—*a documentary process he was to repeat with considerably less affection in* What Makes Sammy Run? *in which the heel-hero, who hustles his way to movie prominence over the beds and bodies of his contemporaries, is based on the late film producer, Jerry Wald (this extract is from Chapter 10). Schulberg has written many screenplays and in 1954 was awarded an Oscar for* On the Waterfront.

What Makes Sammy Run?

SAMMY WAS a crude dancer, but he wasn't like so many bad dancers who can't make up their minds. Because he wasn't self-conscious about it and forced her to follow all his mistakes, he got away with it. It wasn't exactly a thing of beauty, but you had to hand it to him, he had a sense of rhythm. Back in the New York office if anybody had told me that three years later I would be sitting in a Hollywood night club watching my copy boy dance the rhumba with one of those Vassar smarty-pants I would have called the Bellevue psychopathic ward to come down and take him away. But now that I was actually at a ringside table watching it happen, I couldn't make myself feel too surprised. He had about as much interest in dancing the rhumba as he had in writing. But I had begun to take for granted his ability to do everything just well enough so it wouldn't break his stride.

She was dancing under wraps but looked as though she really enjoyed it, even with Sammy. But not he. He looked desperate and

75

busy. He was working at it, he was working at having fun. Recreation never seemed to come naturally to him. In fact the only activity that did, seemed to be that damned running. I don't think he ever drank because he liked the taste of whisky or frequented the Black Lot through any craving for hot music. He just went through the motions of relaxing because he was quick to discover and imitate how gentlemen of his rank were supposed to spend their leisure. It wouldn't have surprised me if this even extended to sex. He seemed to be a lusty little animal, but I think if Zanuck offered to give up his job to Sammy on the condition that Sammy never touched a woman again our hero would have gone impotent before you could say general-manager-in-charge-of-production.

The waiter set our drinks up again. They went on dancing. I kept an eye on Billie doing a little drink promoting at the bar. They came back to the table because the floor was getting too crowded, and the waiter went for another round.

Kit fixed a cigarette to her long holder and eyed the dance crowd with frowning amusement.

'Kirstein says folk dancing is a swell barometer of a country's society,' she said. 'Just look at ours—no more group spirit—every man for himself, covered with sweat and trying to push all the other couples off the floor.'

Trying to follow her and watch Sammy at the same time was distracting. I noticed that Sammy hadn't been listening. He was preoccupied with somebody on the other side of the room.

She turned her head for an instant, caught on and gave him a patient smile. 'Go ahead,' she said, 'go over and see him, you're practically over there anyway.'

Her voice was that of a mother trying to practise child psychology on a delinquent child.

He rose, thrusting his cigar through his lips, and there was something pugnacious about the way he clenched it between his teeth in the corner of his mouth. It stuck out in front of him like a cannon levelled at the world.

'I'll try to get him over for a drink,' he said.

He didn't circle the dance floor to reach the other side. He walked straight across it, pushing his way through the dancers.

'Who's he sucking around now?' I said.

'A good-natured lush called Franklin Collier,' she said. 'He was married to one of the big silent stars, I forget-her-name. When she got tired of him she packed him off to Iceland to make a picture.

He surprised her and everybody else in town by not only coming back alive but bringing *Pengi* with him.'

Pengi was the epic that was so beautifully acted by a cast of penguins, one of the sensations of the twenties.

'Is Collier a good . . .'

She had the disturbing habit of beginning to answer your questions before you had finished asking them.

'He's always had a flair for outdoor pictures,' she said. 'He's sort of a one-man Last Frontier. But when it comes to stories, I don't think he knows his ass from a hole-in-the-script.'

She didn't use those words the way women usually do, conscious they're making you think they're talking like men, but having to get a running start for every word not considered fit for ladies or dictionaries.

Sammy returned with a tall man in his late forties, with a red face and baldspot, slimly built except for a pot belly which made me think of a thin neck with a large Adam's apple. He wasn't navigating too well under his own power and Sammy, almost a head shorter, guiding him to our table, looked like a busy little tug piloting a liner into port.

'Mr. Manheim,' Sammy said with his best Sunday manners, 'I want you to meet not only one of the greatest producers in town but one of my favourite people.'

I almost expected Mr. Collier to start making an after-dinner speech. I thought that was going a little too far, even for Sammy, but Mr. Collier took it very gracefully, or perhaps it was only drunkenly. He seemed to be bowing, but it turned out he was only aiming his bottom cautiously at the seat of the chair. The waiter brought his drink over from the other table and Collier stared into it with an expression that might have been either thoughtful or thirsty.

'Now what was I just saying, son?' Collier began.

'What Mr. Rappaport told you about my work,' Sammy prompted.

'Correct,' Collier said. The only effect his drinking seemed to have on his mind was to throw it into slow motion. 'Rappy tells me you did a hell of a job on *Girl Steals Boy*, Glick. Hell of a job.'

'We'll know better after the sneak,' Sammy said. 'And we'll know best when we see whether Mr. and Mrs. Public buy tickets.'

Later Kit told me Collier's favourite beef was that writers didn't care what made money and what didn't as long as their stuff went over with the Hollywood first-nighters. And Sammy didn't sound as if he were exactly stabbing in the dark.

Collier looked around at us in triumph. 'If only more of you writers talked that language!'

Then he turned back to Sammy as if he were going to kiss him. 'Well, you and I could talk pictures till all hours of the morning. But I'm in a spot, son, hell of a spot, and maybe a bright young kid like you can help me out. I've got Dorothy Lamour for a South Sea picture that's supposed to start in six weeks. It opens at the Music Hall Easter week. It's got a surefire title, *Monsoon*. All I need now is the story.'

Sammy jerked the cigar from his mouth as if it were a stopper checking his flow of words. 'South Sea story! You're looking for a South Sea story! Well, of all the goddam coincidences I ever heard of!'

Hold your hats, girls and boys, I thought, here we go again.

'Don't tell me you've got one!'

'Have I!' Sammy yelled. 'It this a break for both of us! I've only got the greatest South Sea story since *Rain*, that's all.'

It was so convincing it even made me wonder if he hadn't been holding out on us.

'I'll tell you something about me,' Collier said happily. 'I never made a mistake in my life when I played my own hunch. Something just told me you might come through on this.'

He took a little notebook from his pocket and wrote in a large, precise, drunk-under-control hand: Glick—*Monsoon*.

'You folks won't mind if Sammy tells us his yarn right here?' he asked us.

'Go right ahead,' Kit said, 'maybe we can even get the boys to play us a little South Sea music.'

I tried to figure out how she felt about him, but it wasn't simple. She was as eager as I to put him on the spot, but I don't think she was hoping to see him go on his trim little can the way I was. I think she was just pushing him off the high board because she enjoyed the spectacle of seeing him straighten out and get his balance before knifing into the water.

It made me panicky just to imagine myself out on that kind of limb, but Sammy didn't even look ruffled. As the boys in the band started working again, he said, in a voice buttered with boyish sincerity, 'Listen, Mr. Collier, I'd love to tell you the story now, but it wouldn't be fair to you. When you hear this story I want you to hear it right. Now what if I came out to your house next Sunday? . . .'

He had side-stepped his tackler beautifully and was off again.

Sammy not only had his lunch date Sunday but Collier was urging him to come early and try the pool.

Sammy hardly let Collier get out of earshot before he asked his question.

'Neither of you happen to know of a good South Sea story I could use? I'd split the sale with you.'

I stared at Sammy as if I were practising to be an X-ray machine. I just couldn't seem to take him easy. Kit was leaning back, relaxed, but with her eyes busy, as if she were enjoying a football game in which she wasn't rooting for either side.

'Sammy,' I started to say and then I stopped because I knew I couldn't think of anything equal to the occasion. So all I finally said was *'Sammy Glick'*, using it like a swear word.

'A little birdie tells me that lunch is going to cost him just about ten G's,' Sammy said.

'This time you've lost me,' Kit confessed. 'How can you sell anything while you're under contract? The studio owns everything you write.'

'Everything I write after I began working for them,' Sammy said coyly. 'It wouldn't be fair for the studio to own everything I wrote before I came to Hollywood would it? So who has to know when I wrote my South Sea story?'

All he had to do was say *South Sea story* once more and I'd begin to believe he had really written one. The only answer I could think of was, 'What South Sea story?'

'Don't worry,' Kit assured me, 'he'll have it. It would be different if he had to write the greatest South Sea story since *Rain* overnight. But he has three whole days.'

'That reminds me,' Sammy said, 'what's *Rain* about?'

'Holy Jesus,' I said with reverence.

'Sammy, now I *know* you're a great man,' she said. 'What other writer in the world could compare his story, which he hasn't written, with a classic he's never read?'

'I didn't have to read it,' Sammy explained. 'I saw the movie. But I was such a little kid that all I can remember is Gloria Swanson shaking her cute little can in a minister's face.'

'That's the plot all right,' she said. 'What more can I tell you about it?'

'Come on, Kit, stop the clowning, give out with *Rain*.'

Sammy was through playing for the evening. She began to tell Maugham's story. She told it well. You could feel the machinery in his mind breaking it down. I kept my eyes on his face. Sharp, well chiselled, full of the animal magnetism that passes for virility, his skin blue-complexioned from his close-shaved heavy beard adding five years to his appearance, he was almost handsome. If it wasn't for that ferret look. In moments like this when he was on the scent of something you could see the little animal in him poking its snout into a rabbit hole.

Just as she was reaching the climax, where the good Sadie starts giving way to the old Sadie again, Sammy suddenly leaned forward and cut in.

'Wait a minute I got an angle! I've got it!'

There was an old junk dealer in my youth who used to collect all our old newspapers to grind into fresh pulp again. That was the kind of story mind Sammy was developing. Without even warning us he launched into one of the most incredible performances of impromptu story telling I have ever heard—or ever want to.

'All you gotta do to that story is give it the switcheroo. Instead of the minister you got a young dame missionary, see. Dorothy Lamour. Her old man kicked off with tropical fever and she's carrying on the good work. You know, a Nice Girl. Then instead of Sadie Thompson you got a louse racketeer who comes to the Island to hide out. Dorothy Lamour and George Raft in *Monsoon*! Does that sound terrific? So Dotty goes out to save George's soul and he starts feeding her the old oil. Of course, all he's out for is a good lay, but before very long he finds himself watching the sunrise without even thinking of making a pass at her. The soul crap is beginning to get to him, see? He tells her she's the first dame he ever met he didn't think about that way. Now give me a second to dope this out . . .'

I told him I would be much more generous than that, I would gladly give him several decades, but he didn't stop long enough to hear me.

'Oh, yeah, how about this—just about the time George is ready to break down and sing in her choir every Sunday morning they get caught in a storm on one of the nearby islands. They have to spend the night in a cave huddled together. Well, you can see what's coming, she can't help herself and lets him slip it to her. When they realise what they've done they both go off their nut. He goes back to his booze, shooting his mouth off about all dames looking alike when you turn them upside down, and Dotty feels she's betrayed her old man, so she goes to the edge of the cliff and throws herself into the ocean. But good old George manages to get there in time and jumps in after her. Then you play a helluva scene in the ocean where you get over the idea that the water purifies 'em. Jesus, can't you see it, George coming up for the third time with Dotty in his arms hollering something like: 'Oh, God, if You get us outa this—I'll work like a bastard for You the rest of my life.' And you're into your final fade with Dorothy and George married and setting up shop together, in the market for new souls to save.'

Sammy looked at us the way a hoofer looks at his audience as he finishes his routine.

There was a moment of respectful silence.

'Of course,' Sammy explained, falling back on the official Hollywood alibi, 'I was just thinking out loud.'

'But where,' I said, 'does the monsoon come in?'

'Jesus,' he said, 'I'm glad you reminded me. What the hell is a monsoon?'

'A monsoon is a sequel to a typhoon,' Kit explained.

'Only bigger,' Sammy interpreted. 'So the monsoon'll have to be coming up all the time they're in the cave. It'll be a natural for inter-cutting. Symbolical. When she does her swan dive from that cliff she lands right in the middle of it. That will really give the rescue scene a wallop.'

'I'm glad you added the monsoon,' Kit said. 'I couldn't quite see how an ordinary ocean would purify them. But a monsoon makes it convincing.'

'What do you think of it, Al?' he said.

'I don't know much about art,' I said, 'I only know what I like. I think it stinks.'

He looked at her with a question mark. 'I think Collier will buy it,' she said seriously.

Sammy turned on me with a leer not quite hidden in a smile. 'That shows what you know about story values, Al.'

JOHN HOLLANDER

(b. 1929)

Movie-Going

Drive-ins are out, to start with. One must always be
Able to see the over-painted Moorish ceiling
Whose pinchbeck jazz gleams even in the darkness, calling
The straying eye to feast on it, and glut, then fall
Back to the sterling screen again. One needs to feel
That the two empty, huddled, dark stage-boxes keep
Empty for kings. And having frequently to cope
With the abominable goodies, overflow
Bulk and (finally) exploring hands of flushed
Close neighbours gazing beadily out across glum
Distances is, after all, to keep the gleam
Alive of something rather serious, to keep
Faith, perhaps, with the City. When as children our cup
Of joys ran over the special section, and we clutched
Our ticket stubs and followed the bouncing ball, no clash
Of cymbals at the start of the stage-show could abash
Our third untiring time around. When we came back,
Older, to cop an endless series of feels, we sat
Unashamed beneath the bare art-nouveau bodies, set
High on the golden, after-glowing proscenium when
The break had come. And still, now as always, once
The show is over and we creep into the dull
Blaze of mid-afternoon sunshine, the hollow dole
Of the real descends on everything and we can know
That we have been in some place wholly elsewhere, a night
At noonday, not without dreams, whose portals shine
(Not ivory, not horn in ever-changing shapes)

But made of some weird, clear substance not often used for gates.
Stay for the second feature on a double bill

Always: it will teach you how to love, how not to live,
And how to leave the theatre for that unlit, aloof
And empty world again. 'B'-pictures showed us: shooting
More real than singing or making love; the shifting
Ashtray upon the mantel, moved by some idiot
Between takes, helping us learn beyond a trace of doubt
How fragile are imagined scenes; the dimming-out
Of all the brightness of the clear and highly lit
Interior of the hero's cockpit, when the stock shot
Of ancient dive-bombers peeling off cuts in, reshapes
Our sense of what is, finally, plausible; the greys
Of living rooms, the blacks of cars whose window glass
At night allows the strips of fake Time Square to pass
Jerkily by on the last ride; even the patch
Of sudden white, and inverted letters dashing
Up during the projectionist's daydream, dying
Quickly—these are the colours of our inner life.

Never ignore the stars, of course. But above all,
Follow the asteroids as well: though dark, they're more
Intense for never glittering; anyone can admire
Sparklings against a night sky, but against a bright
Background of prominence, to feel the Presences burnt
Into no fiery fame should be a more common virtue.
For, just as Vesta has no atmosphere, no verdure
Burgeons on barren Ceres, bit-players never surge
Into the rhythms of expansion and collapse, such
As all the flaming bodies live and move among.
But there, more steadfast than stars are, loved for their being.
Not for their burning, move the great Characters: see
Thin Donald Meek, that shuffling essence ever so
Affronting to Eros and to Pride; the pair of bloated
Capitalists, Walter Connolly and Eugene Pallete, seated
High in their offices above New York; the evil,
Blackening eyes of Sheldon Leonard, and the awful
Stare of Eduardo Cianelli. Remember those who have gone—
(Where's bat-squeaking Butterfly McQueen? Will we see again

That ever-anonymous drunk, waxed-moustached, rubber-legged
Caught in revolving doors?) and think of the light-years logged
Up in those humbly noble orbits, where no hot

Spotlight of solar grace consumes some blazing hearts,
Bestowing the flimsy immortality of stars
For some great distant instant. Out of the darkness stares
Venus, who seems to be what once we were, the air
Form of emerging love, her nitrous atmosphere
Hiding her prizes. Into the black expanse peers
Mars, whom we in time will come to resemble: parched,
Xanthine desolations, dead Cimmerian seas, the far
Distant past preserved in the blood-coloured crusts; fire
And water both remembered only. Having shined
Means having died. But having been real only, and shunned
Stardom, the planetoids are what we now are, humming
With us, above us, ever into the future, seeming
Ever to take the shapes of the world we wake to from dreams.

Always go in the morning if you can; it will
Be something more than habit if you do. Keep well
Away from most French farces. Try to see a set
Of old blue movies ever so often, that the sight
Of animal doings out of the clothes of thirty-five
May remind you that even the natural act is phrased
In the terms and shapes of particular times and places.
Finally, remember always to honour the martyred dead.
The forces of darkness spread everywhere now, and the best
And brightest screens fade out, while many-antennaed beasts
Perch on the housetops, and along the grandest streets
Palaces crumble, one by one. The dimming starts
Slowly at first; the signs are few, as 'Movies are
Better than Ever', 'Get More out of Life. See a Movie' Or
Else there's no warning at all and, Whoosh! the theatre falls,
Alas, transmogrified: no double-feature fills
A gleaming marquee with promises, now only lit
With 'Pike and Whitefish Fresh Today' 'Drano' and 'Light
Or Dark Brown Sugar, Special', Try never to patronise
Such places (or pass them by one day a year). The noise
Of movie mansions changing form, caught in the toils
Of our lives' whithering, rumbles, resounds and tolls
The knell of neighbourhoods. Do not forget the old
Places, for everyone's home has been a battlefield.

I remember: the RKO COLONIAL; the cheap

84

ARDEN and ALDEN both; LOEW'S LINCOLN SQUARE'S bright shape;
The NEWSREEL; the mandarin BEACON, resplendently arrayed;
The tiny SEVENTY-SEVENTH STREET, whose demise I rued
So long ago; the eighty-first street, sunrise-hued,
RKO; and then LOEW'S: at eighty-third, which had
The colder pinks of sunset on it; and then, back
Across Broadway again, and up, you disembarked
At the YORKTOWN and then the STODDARD, with their dark
Marquees; the SYMPHONY had a decorative disk
With elongated 'twenties nudes whirling in it;
(Around the corner the THALIA, daughter of memory! owed
Her life to Foreign Hits, in days when you piled your coat
High on your lap and sat, sweating and cramped, to catch
'La Kermesse Heroique' every third week, and watched
Fritz Lang from among an audience of refugees, bewitched
By the sense of Crisis on and off that tiny bit
Of screen) Then north again: the RIVERSIDE, the bright
RIVIERA rubbing elbows with it; and right
Smack on a hundredth street, the MIDTOWN; and the rest
Of them: the CARLTON, EDISON, LOEW'S OLYMPIA, and best
Because, of course, the last of all, its final burst
Anonymous, the NEMO! These were once the pearls
Of two-and-a-half miles of Broadway! How many have paled
Into a supermarket's failure of the imagination?

Honour them all. Remember how once their splendour blazed
In sparkling necklaces across America's blasted
Distances and deserts: think how, at night, the fastest
Train might stop for water somewhere, waiting, faced
Westward, in deepening dusk, till ruby illuminations
Of something different from Everything Here, Now, shine
Out from the local Bijou, truest gem, the most bright
Because the most believed in, staving off the night
Perhaps, for a while longer with its flickering light.

These fade. All fade. Let us honour them with our own fading sight.

LARRY McMURTRY

(b. 1936)

Larry McMurtry comes from a family of ranchers and cowboys in north-west Texas, the setting and source of his two best-known novels (both of them filmed), Hud *and* The Last Picture Show *(1966). He writes about movies, not as an insider but a member of the audience for whom the images on screen have been companions rather than catalysts.*

The Last Picture Show

CHAPTER 2

LIKE SO many Saturdays, it was a long work day; when Sonny rattled back into Thalia after his last delivery it was almost 10 p.m. He found his boss, Frank Fartley, in the poolhall shooting his usual comical Saturday night eight-ball game. The reason it was comical was because Mr. Fartley's cigar was cocked at such an angle that there was always a small dense cloud of white smoke between his eye and the cue ball. He tried to compensate for not being able to see the cue ball by lunging madly with his cue at a spot where he thought it was, a style of play that made Sam the Lion terribly nervous because it was not only hard on the felt but also extremely dangerous to unwatchful kibitzers, one or two of whom had been rather seriously speared. When Sonny came in Frank stopped lunging long enough to give him his cheque, and Sonny immediately got Sam the Lion to cash it. Abilene was there, dressed in a dark brown pearl-buttoned shirt and grey slacks; he was shooting nine-ball at five dollars a game with Lester Marlow, his usual Saturday night opponent.

Lester was a wealthy boy from Wichita Falls who came to Thalia often. Ostensibly, his purpose in coming was to screw Jacy Farrow, but his suit was not progressing too well and the real reason he kept coming was because losing large sums of money to Abilene gave him a certain local prestige. It was very important to Lester that he do *something* big, and since losing was a lot easier than winning, he contented himself with losing big.

Sonny had watched the two shoot so many times that it held no interest for him, so he took his week's wages and walked across the dark courthouse to the picture show. Jacy's white Ford convertible was parked out front, where it always was on Saturday night. The movie that night was called *Storm Warning*, and the posterboards held pictures of Doris Day, Ronald Reagan, Steve Cochran, and Ginger Rogers. It was past 10 p.m. and Miss Mosey, who sold tickets, had already closed the window; Sonny found her in the lobby, cleaning out the popcorn machine. She was a thin little old lady with such bad eyesight and hearing that she sometimes had to walk halfway down the aisle to tell whether the comedy or the newsreel was on.

'My goodness, Frank oughtn't to work you so late on weekends,' she said. 'You done missed the comedy so you don't need to give me but thirty cents.'

Sonny thanked her and bought a package of Doublemint gum before he went into the show. Very few people ever came to the late feature; there were not more than twenty in the whole theatre. As soon as his eyes adjusted Sonny determined that Jacy and Duane were still out parking; Charlene Duggs was sitting about halfway down the aisle with her little sister Marlene. Sonny walked down the aisle and tapped her on the shoulder, and the two girls scooted over a seat.

'I decided you had a wreck,' Charlene said, not bothering to whisper. She smelled like powder and toilet water.

'You two want some chewin' gum?' Sonny offered, holding out the package. The girls each instantly took a stick and popped the gum into their mouths almost simultaneously. They never had any gum money themselves and were both great moochers. Their father, Royce Duggs, ran a dinky little one-man garage out on the highway; most of his work was done on pickups and tractors, and money was tight. The girls would not have been able to afford the toilet water either, but their mother, Beulah Duggs, had a secret passion for it and bought it with money that Royce Duggs thought was going for the girls' school lunches. The three of them could only get away with using it on Saturday night when Royce was customarily too drunk to be able to smell.

After the feature had been playing for a few minutes Sonny and Charlene got up and moved back into one of the corners. It made

Sonny nervous to sit with Charlene and Marlene both. Even though Charlene was a senior and Marlene just a sophomore, the two looked so much alike that he was afraid he might accidentally start holding hands with the wrong one. Back in the corner, he held Charlene's hand and they smooched a little, but not much. Sonny really wanted to see the movie, and it was easy for him to hold his passion down. Charlene had not got all the sweetness out of the stick of Doublemint and didn't want to take it out of her mouth just to kiss Sonny, but after a few minutes she changed her mind, took it out, and stuck it under the arm of her seat. It seemed to her that Sonny looked a little bit like Steve Cochran, and she began to kiss him energetically, squirming and pressing herself against his knee. Sonny returned the kiss, but with somewhat muted interest. He wanted to keep at least one eye on the screen, so if Ginger Rogers decided to take her clothes off he wouldn't miss it. The posters outside indicated she at least got down to her slip at one point. Besides, Charlene was always getting worked up in picture shows; at first Sonny had thought her fits of cinematic passion very encouraging, until he discovered it was practically impossible to get her worked up *except* in picture shows.

The movies were Charlene's life, as she was fond of saying. She spent most of her afternoons hanging around the little beauty shop where her mother worked, reading movie magazines, and she always referred to movie stars by their first names. Once when an aunt gave her a dollar for her birthday she went down to the variety store and bought two fifty-cent portraits to sit on her dresser: one was of June Allyson and the other Van Johnson. Marlene copied Charlene's passions as exactly as possible, but when the same aunt gave *her* a dollar the variety store's stock of portraits was low and she had to make do with Esther Williams and Mickey Rooney. Charlene kidded her mercilessly about the latter, and took to sleeping with Van Johnson under her pillow because she was afraid Marlene might mutilate him out of envy.

After a few minutes of squirming alternately against the seat arm and Sonny's knee, lost in visions of Steve Cochran, Charlene abruptly relaxed and sat back. She languidly returned the chewing gum to her mouth, and for a while they watched the movie in silence. Then she remembered a matter she had been intending to bring up.

'Guess what?' she said. 'We been going steady a year tonight. You should have got me something for an anniversary present.'

Sonny had been contentedly watching Ginger Rogers, waiting for the slip scene. Charlene's remark took him by surprise.

'Well, you can have another stick of gum,' he said. 'That's all I've got on me.'

'Okay, and I'll take a dollar, too,' Charlene said. 'It cost that much for me and Marlene to come to the show, and I don't want to pay my own way on my anniversary.'

Sonny handed her the package of chewing gum, but not the dollar. Normally he expected to pay Charlene's way to the show, but he saw no reason at all why he should spend fifty cents on Marlene. While he was thinking out the ethics of the matter the exit door opened down to the right of the screen and Duane and Jacy slipped in, their arms around one another. They came back and sat down by Sonny and Charlene.

'Hi you all, what are you doin' back here in the dark?' Jacy whispered gaily. Her pretty mouth was a little numb from two hours of virtually uninterrupted kissing. As soon as it seemed polite, she and Duane started kissing again and settled into an osculatory doze that lasted through the final reel of the movie. Charlene began nervously popping her finger joints, something she did whenever Jacy came around. Sonny tried to concentrate on the screen, but it was hard. Jacy and Duane kept right on kissing, even when the movie ended and the lights came on. They didn't break their clinch until Billy came down from the balcony with his broom and began to sweep.

'Sure was a short show,' Jacy said, turning to grin at Sonny. Her nose wrinkled delightfully when she grinned. She shook her head so that her straight blonde hair would hang more smoothly against her neck. Duane's hair was tousled, but when Jacy playfully tried to comb it he yawned and shook her off. She put on fresh lipstick and they all got up and went outside.

Miss Mosey had taken the *Storm Warning* posters down and was gallantly trying to tack up the posters for Sunday's show, which was *Francis Goes to the Army*. The wind whipped around the corners of the old building, making the posters flop. Miss Mosey's fingers were so cold she could barely hold the tacks, so the boys helped her finish while the girls shivered on the kerb. Marlene was shivering on the kerb too, waiting for Sonny to drop her off at the Duggses. Duane walked Jacy to her convertible and kissed her goodnight a time or two, then came gloomily to the pickup, depressed at the thought of how long it was until Saturday night came again.

When they had taken Marlene home and dropped Duane at the rooming house, Sonny and Charlene drove back to town so they could find out what time it was from the clock in the jewellery store window. As usual, it was almost time for Charlene to go home.

'Oh, let's go on to the lake,' she said. 'I guess I can be a few minutes late tonight, since it's my anniversary.

'I never saw anything like that Jacy and Duane,' she said. 'Kissing in the picture show after the lights go on. That's pretty bad if you ask me. One of these days Mrs. Farrow's gonna catch 'em an' that'll be the end of that romance.'

Sonny drove on to the city lake without saying anything, but the remark depressed him. So far as he was concerned Jacy and Duane knew true love and would surely manage to get married and be happy. What depressed him was that it had just become clear to him that Charlene really wanted to go with Duane, just as he himself really wanted to go with Jacy.

As soon as the pickup stopped Charlene moved over against him. 'Crack your window and leave the heater on,' she said. 'It's still too cold in here for me.'

Sonny tried to shrug off his depression by beginning the little routine they always went through when they parked: first he would kiss Charlene for about ten minutes; then she would let him take off her brassiere and play with her breasts; finally, when he tried to move on to other things she would quickly scoot back across the seat, put the bra back on, and make him take her home. Sometimes she indulged in an engulfing kiss or two on the doorstep, knowing that she could fling herself inside the house if a perilously high wave of passion threatened to sweep over her.

After the proper amount of kissing Sonny deftly unhooked her bra. This was the signal for Charlene to draw her arms from the sleeves of her sweater and slip out of the straps. Sonny hung the bra on the rear-view mirror. So long as the proprieties were observed, Charlene liked being felt; she obligingly slipped her sweater up around her neck.

'Eeh, your hands are like ice,' she said, sucking in her breath. Despite the heater the cab was cold enough to make her nipples crinkle. The wind had blown all the clouds away, but the moon was thin and dim and the choppy lake lay in darkness. When Sonny moved his hand the little dash-light threw patches of shadow over Charlene's stocky torso.

In a few minutes it became apparent that the cab was warming up faster than either Sonny or Charlene. He idly held one of her breasts in his hand, but it might have been an apple someone had given him just when he was least hungry.

'Hey,' Charlene said suddenly, noticing. 'What's the matter with you? You act half asleep.'

Sonny was disconcerted. He was not sure what was wrong. It did not occur to him that he was bored. After all, he had Charlene's breast in his hand, and in Thalia it was generally agreed that the one thing that was never boring was feeling a girl's breasts. Grasping for straws, Sonny tried moving his hand downward but it soon got entangled in Charlene's pudgy fingers.

'Quit, quit,' she said, leaning her head back in expectation of a passionate kiss.

'But this is our anniversary,' Sonny said. 'Let's do something different.'

Charlene grimly kept his hand at navel level, infuriated that he should think he really had licence to go lower. That was plainly unfair, because he hadn't even given her a present. She scooted back towards her side of the cab and snatched her brassiere off the mirror.

'What are you trying to do, Sonny, get me pregnant?' she asked indignantly.

Sonny was stunned by the thought. 'My lord,' he said. 'It was just my hand.'

'Yeah, and one thing leads to another,' she complained, struggling to catch the top hook of her bra. 'Momma told he how that old stuff works.'

Sonny reached over and hooked the hook for her, but he was more depressed than ever. It was obvious to him that it was a disgrace not to be going with someone prettier than Charlene, or if not prettier, at least someone more likeable. The problem was how to break up with her and get his football jacket back.

'Well, you needn't get mad,' he said finally. 'After so long a time I get tired of doing the same thing, and you do too. You wasn't no livelier than me.'

'That's because you ain't good lookin' enough,' she said coldly. 'You ain't even got a ducktail. Why should I let you fiddle around and get me pregnant. We'll have plenty of time for that old stuff when we decide to get engaged.'

Sonny twirled the knob on his steering wheel and looked out at the cold scudding water. He kept wanting to say something really nasty to Charlene, but he restrained himself. Charlene tucked her sweater back into her skirt and combed angrily at her brownish blonde hair. Her mother had given her a permanent the day before and her hair was as stiff as wire.

'Let's go home,' she said. 'I'm done late anyway. Some anniversary.'

Sonny backed the pickup around and started for the little cluster of yellow lights that was Thalia. The lake was only a couple of miles out.

'Charlene, if you feel that way I'd just as soon break up,' he said. 'I don't want to spoil no more anniversaries for you.'

Charlene was surprised, but she recovered quickly. 'That's the way nice girls get treated in this town,' she said, proud to be a martyr to virtue.

'I knew you wasn't dependable,' she added, taking the football jacket and laying it on the seat between them. 'Boys that act like you do never are. That jacket's got a hole in the pocket, but you needn't ask me to sew it up. And you can give me back my pictures. I don't want you showin' 'em to a lot of other boys and tellin' them how hot I am.'

Sonny stopped the pickup in front of her house and fished in his billfold for the three or four snapshots Charlene had given him. One of them, taken at a swimming pool in Wichita Falls, had been taken the summer before. Charlene was in a bathing suit. When she gave Sonny the picture she had taken a ballpoint pen and written on the back of the snapshot, 'Look What Legs!', hoping he would show it to Duane. The photograph showed clearly that her legs were short and fat, but in spite of it she managed to think of herself as possessing gazellelike slimness. Sonny laid the pictures on top of the football jacket, and Charlene scooped them up.

'Well, good-night,' Sonny said. 'I ain't got no hard feelings if you don't.'

Charlene got out, but then she bethought herself of something and held the pickup door open a moment. 'Don't you try to go with Marlene,' she said. 'Marlene's young, and she's a good Christian girl. If you try to go with her I'll tell my Daddy what a wolf you was with me and he'll stomp the you-know-what out of you.'

'You was pretty glad to let me do what little I did,' Sonny said, angered. 'You just mind your own business and let Marlene mind hers.'

Charlene gave him a last ill-tempered look. 'If you've given me one of those diseases you'll be sorry,' she said.

She could cheerfully have stabbed Sonny with an ice pick, but instead, to impress Marlene, she went in the house, woke her up, and cried for half the night about her blighted romance. She told Marlene Sonny had forced her to fondle him indecently.

'What in the world did it look like?' Marlene asked, bug-eyed with startled envy.

'Oh, the awfulest thing you ever saw,' Charlene assured her, smearing a thick coating of beauty cream on her face. 'Ouuee, he was nasty. I hope you don't ever get involved with a man like that, honey—they make you old before your time. I bet I've aged a year, just tonight.'

Later, when the lights were out, Marlene tried to figure on her fingers what month it would be when Charlene would be sent away in disgrace to Kizer, Arkansas to have her baby. They had an aunt who lived in Kizer. Marlene was not exactly clear in her mind about how one went about getting pregnant, but she assumed that with such goings on Charlene must have. It was conceivable that her mother would make Charlene leave the picture of Van Johnson behind when she was sent away, and that thought cheered Marlene very much. In any case, it would be nice to have the bedroom to herself.

JOHN COTTON

(b. 1925)

Old Movies

How I loved those old movies
they would show at the Roxys
and Regals amongst all that
gilt plaster, or in the Bijou
flea-pits smelling of Jeyes:
The men sleek-haired and suited,
with white cuffs and big trilbies,
their girls all pushovers,
wide-eyed with lashes
like venus fly traps and their
clouds of blonde candy floss
for hair. Oh those bosoms, hips
and those long long legs
I never saw in daylight!
And their apartments,
vast as temples,
full of undusted furniture,
the sideboards bending with booze,
and all those acres of bed!
She, in attendance, wearing
diaphanous, but never quite
diaphanous enough, nightwear.
And their lives!
Where the baddies only
if not always, stopped one,
and they loved and loved
and never ended up married.
Every time I get a whiff
of that disinfectant
I get nostalgic.

A. S. J. TESSIMOND

(1902–1962)

Chaplin

The sun, a heavy spider, spins in the thirsty sky.
The wind hides under cactus leaves, in empty doorways. Only the wry

small shadow accompanies Hamlet-Petrouchka Chaplin across the
    plain,
the wry small sniggering shadow preceding, then in train.

The cavalcade has passed towards impossible horizons again;
but still the mask—the quick-flick fanfare of the cane remains.

The diminuendo of footsteps even is done.
but there remain (Don Quixote) hat, cane, smile and sun.

Goliaths fall before the sling, but craftier ones than these
are ambushed—malice of sliding mats, revolving doors, strings in the
    dark and falling trees.

God kicks us in the pants and sets banana-skins on stairs;
and tall sombreroed centaurs win the tulip lips and aureoled hair,

while we, craned from the gallery, throw our cardboard flowers
and our feet jerk to tunes not played for ours.

TOM RAWORTH

(b. 1938)

Claudette Colbert by Billy Wilder

run, do not walk, to the nearest exit
spain, or is democracy doomed
we regret that due to circumstances beyond our control
we are unable to bring you the cambridge crew trials

if you're counting my eyebrows
i can tell you there are two
i took your letter out and read it to the rabbits

describe the sinking ship
describe the sea at night
he lived happily ever after in the café magenta

how to preserve peaches
they're counting on you for intimate
personal stuff about hitler and his gang
it's a chance i wouldn't miss for anything in the
wait in holland for
instance watching the windmills
that's more than flash gordon ever did

all those bugles blowing
in the ears of a confused liberal
so long
pretty woman
wake me up at the part where he claims milwaukee

ROBERT LOWELL

(b. 1917)

For Harpo Marx

Harpo Marx, your hand white-feathered the harp—
the only words, you ever spoke were sound.
The movie's not always the sick man of the arts,
yours touched the stars; Harpo, your changing picture
is an unchanging still life, not nature dead.
You dumbly memorised an unwritten script. . . .
I saw you first two years before you died,
near Fifth in Central Park, in fragile autumn:
old blond hair too blonde, old eyes too young.
Two movie trucks and five police lay spoke-wheel
like the covered wagon. The crowd as much or little.
I wish I had knelt; I age to your wincing smile—
Dante's movies, his groups of pain and motion;
the genus *happy* is one generic actor.

MAURICE DRUON

(b. 1918)

Maurice Druon is best known for his series of historical novels, The Iron Kings, *which were filmed for French television and subsequently screened by the B.B.C.* The Film of Memory *(1954) tells of the last dream-filled days of a great Italian courtesan and the aspirations of her maid, Carmela, whose own dreams are pinned on a career in movies.*

The Film of Memory

CHAPTER 10

SINCE MIDDAY Carmela had been standing in a shady corner, not daring to move from the spot where she had been told to wait. But time did not weigh upon her; there were so many things to see. Arab dancers, soldiers in strange uniforms, gentlemen in tails sweating profusely under their costumes and make-up, sank on to the benches and fanned themselves for a moment. Then, at the sound of a call, dragging their halberds or tucking up their skirts, they trooped back to one of the cement and corrugated-iron buildings.

Three films were in production at the same time. The studios, built behind the Palatine, backed on to the ruins of the old Roman wall of Belisarius, which dominates the courts of red mortar and crumbling brick, reflecting the heat like the tiles of an oven.

Carmela saw several famous actors and actresses, and each time she recognised one her heart beat faster. These grand people were perpetually surrounded by an agitated crowd of attendants. Fuming and worn out, they seemed to carry in their wigs all the responsibility of the universe. Carmela watched them through the window as they entered the canteen and sat down at a table. One day she might take her place among them.

She was not conscious of being hungry, but she was afraid she might have been forgotten. Merello had told her not to go to the hairdresser's and not to put on another frock; so she was dressed as usual. But she doubted whether Merello, in giving her that advice, had done her a good turn.

All of a sudden she saw the starlet from the hotel dragging herself along in gooseberry-coloured velvet, overwhelmed by the elegance of the Borgias. She hoped the French girl would not notice her. But in this she was disappointed.

'What are you doing here?' she asked acidly.

Instinctively Carmela lied.

'Dottore Merello promised to show me how films are made. I'm waiting for him.'

'So that's it. Well, we're starting again in a quarter of an hour. You'll see me, I expect,' said the starlet, as she moved away. Carmela went on waiting.

At last, when she had begun to give up hope, an assistant of Vicaria's came to fetch her, and she thought: 'This is it!' like a student going into the examination room, or a jockey mounting for his first race.

She was taken into a large shed and guided to a corner crowded with machines, where a dozen people were already assembled. She saw that neither Merello nor Vicaria was there, which did not help to reassure her. 'Obviously Dottore Merello doesn't love me, or he'd have come.'

She concentrated as much as she could on trying to understand what was wanted of her, and in doing it as well as possible. Some of the orders were contradictory. She was made up, then the make-up was removed. Enormous projectors flared up all round her. 'Is all this light for me?' she wondered in terror.

She couldn't really understand what was going on. The heat from the projectors, added to the weight of the atmosphere, was almost unbearable. Blinded by the lamps, Carmela could see nothing but shadows and could keep her bearings only by the sound of voices. Somebody came up to her with a tape-measure, stretched it out on the floor and disappeared behind a machine, shouting: '*Motore!*'

Carmela heard a whirring noise and thought that from that moment she was being filmed. But she wasn't sure.

A stage hand clicked a wooden object in front of her face, shouting: '*Provino uno!*'

'*Actione!*' cried another voice.

They told Carmela to walk, to move away, to come back, to sit down, to stand still, to turn in every direction, lift her head, wave her arm as if she were saying goodbye to someone at a station. *Motore* . . . click-clack . . . *Actione*. Her head whirled. She had never fainted in her life, but she thought she was going to now.

She heard them commenting out loud on her eyes, her figure, her legs.

'There's something unattractive in her chin when she smiles.'

'She moves well.'

'Yes, she's all right from the front, but not from the back.'

'Does she squint a bit?'

'No, it's a shadow.'

'Carlo, put a filter on the fifteen hundred to soften that shadow. *Motore!*'

'Anyhow she's not afraid of the camera.'

She was much too frightened of the people to be intimidated by a machine.

'Hasn't she got a scene to rehearse?' asked someone.

'No, no, God forbid. Absolutely not! Then she'd have tried to act, and it would have been hopeless. When you're lucky enough to find someone who knows nothing, you must make the most of it!'

Carmela recognised Vicaria's voice. Until then she had not been aware of his presence. Had he been there long or had he just arrived, after instructing his assistants to start work? She felt a renewal of emotion and confidence. Whatever else happened in her life, nothing would ever compare in importance with this moment. Everything was being decided here, on the spot. She felt it, she sensed it, in the blinding convergence of the projectors, between which she stood like an insect trapped by the light. If there was ever to be a miracle it was taking place now. If among the hundreds of thousands of girls it was she whose dreams were to come true, this was the moment of destiny. A lucky star was shining above her, a dazzling star, and she mustn't let it go out at any price.

Carmela was taken right up to the camera for a close-up.

'How do you feel, Carmela?' asked Vicaria.

'I'm hot, *dottore*.'

There was a general burst of laughter at the sincerity and ingenuity of her words. She thought she had covered herself with ridicule, whereas in fact she had won all their hearts.

'Stop! That one's fine,' cried the camera-man.

Vicaria left the group of shadows and came up to Carmela. She saw the light shine on his silvery hair.

'Stand right here,' he said to her, indicating a particular spot, 'and say to me: "So I shall never see you again?" and try to cry if you can. First do it just for me; the camera isn't working.'

She did what he told her and as she uttered the sentence, her eyes began to fill with tears.

'*Motore!*' cried Vicaria. 'Now do it again.'

The rattle clicked once more:

'*Provino sette.*'

'*Actione!*' said Vicaria.

Carmela looked despairingly at the handsome, striking face of the director, at his keen eyes and friendly smile.

'So I shall never see you again?' she said. And there were real tears running down her soft cheeks.

'Stop,' shouted Vicaria. 'That's good enough for me. Finished.'

And turning to his assistants, he said in a low voice: 'You see? She can certainly act. I don't know how it'll come out when it's developed, but if you can find me another girl to do as much in five minutes, without ever having been in front of a camera before—well, you'll have something good coming to you.'

Carmela had not heard these words. The projectors faded out, and suddenly the building, the machines, and the men looked grey and dusty. Even the sun, which she caught a glimpse of through the large doors, seemed leaden.

'It's all over,' said Vicaria. 'You can go.'

She thought that this was his verdict and that she had failed. She gave such a desperate 'Oh!' that he asked her what was the matter.

'So it was no good, *dottore!*'

'Nonsense, it went very well,' he replied, laughing. 'I'll tell you the result in a couple of days. Have we got your address? Yes, of course, the Hotel Imperatore. Merello will let you know.'

And as they were leaving the building, he added:

'How did you manage to cry at once when I asked you to?'

'I told myself that I must think of something very sad, something that would make me really unhappy. And I imagined that Countess Sanziani was dead.'

'I'm certain we'll make something of you,' said Vicaria.

In the street she was still trembling. It was four o'clock in the afternoon. She had nothing to do until the evening, so she went to the cinema.

JIM KIRKWOOD

(b. 1929)

Jim Kirkwood was born in Los Angeles of theatrical parents and began his own acting career when he was seventeen. He has performed on Broadway, in night-clubs, on radio and TV. There Must Be A Pony (1960) was his first novel. He dramatised it and a stage company toured America with Myrna Loy playing the narrator's actress mother. In 1976 Jim Kirkwood scored a great success as the author of the Broadway musical A Chorus Line.

There Must Be A Pony

CHAPTER 21

DURING THE period we were off the front pages my mother seemed to relax a little. Of course, friends and acquaintances were still rallying around like crazy. There wasn't an afternoon or evening that somebody or other didn't drop by. She's always had loads of friends, anyhow.

Lee and Sally were around almost every day. If one wasn't there the other was. Sally was getting items planted in all the columns about what a crime it was that Ben pulled this trick on my mother. Lee said things looked better for us every day the gangster thing dragged on. And it *was* dragging on, too. It started to die down after a few days, but then one of the local California gangsters was found stuffed in the trunk of his car on Mulholland Drive. I guess it was in retaliation for the bombing. Anyhow, that stirred up a hornet's nest again, and the papers were wild with stories about how California was going to be like Chicago in the twenties and thirties if the cops didn't take action pretty soon and stop all these massacres.

Jay came down one day and said the chances were great for the television series to be sold to a sponsor within a couple of weeks. He also got my mother the lead in one of those hour Westerns. Mainly, I think, because she'd got all the publicity about Ben. She worked five days on it, and it did her a lot of good. She stopped drinking and took up the early-to-bed early-to-rise routine.

Also we could use the money. We actually didn't have to worry, though, because Merwin was always wonderful about taking care of bills and things that we couldn't handle. But you didn't like to bleed him dry. He'd always take the curse off making you feel like a leech by bragging about whatever terrific salary he was making at the time. I think he over-quoted just to make us feel all right.

During that time *I* even got an offer to be in a movie. It was right after my mother had finished working on the Western. Jay came down one day, all excited, and handed me a script. 'Rita your son's got a picture offer!'

'What?' she said. 'Why, that's ridiculous! He's never acted in his life!'

'Recently he's been displaying definite tendencies,' Merwin cut in.

' "Never acted before in his life"!' Jay said. 'The kid's only fifteen. What do you want—a long list of credits? He's got to start somewhere.'

I was so excited I didn't know what to do. I had the script in my hand. *Hell Bent Teen-agers* was the title.

'How about it, Josh?' Jay asked me.

'I think it's great, Jay. How come they want me?'

'The producer, Sam Gutman, is a friend of mine. He saw your picture in the papers last week and thinks you're perfect for the part'.

'Now wait a minute! What's this all about?' My mother reached for the script, took one look at the title page, handed it back to Jay, and said, 'Oh, no! Not for a minute!'

'But, Mom, you haven't even read it,' I pleaded.

'I don't have to. I know Sam Gutman. It's one of those trashy teen-age quickies. I wouldn't want you to see it, let alone act in it. Besides, you know how I feel about that anyway!'

She's always been dead set against me being an actor. You see, in spite of all the crummy times we've been through, she's always tried to bring me up like the scion of some wealthy, old established, Boston Back Bay family. In theory, at least. It sure in hell hasn't worked out that way. But she's always had that conception in the back of her mind. That's why all the forays into military academies, boarding schools, and tutors.

Every time some woman would start drooling to my mother about what a lady killer I was going to grow up to be and how, if I decided to be an actor, I'd probably be a great hit in the movies—she'd throw cold water on it.

'I don't care if he turns out to be a cross between Apollo and Adonis' (once she said Apollo and Louis Jourdan—he's the other actor besides Cary Grant that really slays her), 'he's going to have no part of this rotten life. He's going to college and become a doctor or a lawyer or—'

'An Indian chief!' one woman cut in.

'Yes, by God, an Indian chief rather than an actor! At least that has a little dignity. An actor's life is for the birds, all other reports to the contrary.'

But Jay was a tenacious character. He kept pounding away at my mother. 'Just because the kid's got a small part in a picture—'

'Only a small part?' I asked.

'Listen to him!' Jay got a kick out of that. 'Well, it's not the star part but it's a good one. You play the kid brother of the leader of this teen-age gang. He worships you because you're the only decent thing in his life. You see, your parents are bums. Your mother's an alky, your father's a junkie. You get killed about half-way through the picture but—'

'I get killed—really! How?' That fascinated the hell out of me. From that moment I knew I'd put up a pitched battle to be in it.

Jay went on with the plot. 'Your brother takes you out drag strip-racing with his gang—against his better judgement. But you insist. You say, "Gee, I don't want to stay home. Mom's blind drunk again." Anyhow, you all pile into these hopped-up cars and drive out to the desert looking for kicks. There's a wreck. You get tossed out of your brother's car, but you're still alive. Then one of the cars behind him runs over you. By the time your brother gets out of the wreckage of his car and over to you—you die in his arms saying, "Try to keep Pop off the stuff!" '

'Jesus, that sounds terrific!' I was picturing my big death scene already.

'Josh, will you stop that swearing! You're getting worse every day!' In spite of the fact that practically every one of my mother's friends swore in front of me, she hated it when I talked that way. And, oddly enough, she hardly ever swore. Unless she absolutely lost complete control of her temper—then maybe she would, but not in everyday conversation. She looked at Jay as sarcastic as possible. 'Sounds like a perfectly delightful picture!'

'They use doubles and stunt men for the tricky stuff. There's no danger—'

'I'm not talking about that and you know it!' she said. 'I don't want Josh to be an actor, in the first place. In the second place, the reason Gutman's made the offer is to cash in on all the cheap publicity we've been getting.'

'Look, Rita—so the kid has a part in a picture. That doesn't mean he's going to grow up to be an actor, does it?'

'Don't try to wheedle me into it, Jay! And he's not "the kid". His name is Josh, if you don't mind.'

Boy, once she gets on her high horse about a major issue, she'll start picking on every tiny, insignificant, minor thing you say.

'*Josh*'—and he hit my name like a hammer—'Josh can earn five hundred per week, with a two-week guarantee!'

'Mom, please—I want to!'

'No.'

'But why not?'

'Sure. Why not?' Jay asked. 'You want the ki—Josh to go to college. Okay, you bank what he makes for him and use it towards—'

'Yeah,' I chimed in, 'that's a great idea. I can put myself through college. Then I'll be a lawyer or something.'

'I said no!'

Jay turned to Merwin. 'You talk to her. It's a great chance for the —It's a great chance for Josh!'

'I don't see the harm in it, Rita,' Merwin said. 'Might even be a good idea, after what's happened, just to keep him busy. Keep him from brooding—'

'Brooding!' she said. 'He's been having the time of his life from what I can see! Having his picture taken down by that hammock, giving out interviews . . .' She was really getting touchy.

'Oh, Rita, come now! I don't—'

'*Merwin!*' She has a way of saying your name when she gets in one of those moods that makes you feel if you utter one more sound the whole Swiss Alps will come sliding down on your head.

All of a sudden the discussion was over. Jay left shortly afterwards. As he got to the door he kind of threw over his shoulder, 'About Josh —I won't tell Sam it's off yet. Think it over for a day or two.' She didn't even answer him.

You get to a point with my mother where you know it's no use pursuing the subject any further. You might as well save your voice. You just have to lay low and bring it up at a later date. Or better yet, get a third party to bring it up for you. That point had definitely been reached, so I went upstairs to sulk for the rest of the day.

That's another thing: she hates it when I sulk. But I wanted to be in that picture so bad I could taste it, and I felt she was being unreasonable. I sat up in my room planning all kinds of tactics to get her to agree to let me do it. I'm the plotter of the world. I was rehearsing all kinds of speeches and rebuttals like—'You'd think, after getting me all involved in another one of your messy love affairs, and letting me find him with that hole in his head and all those goddam ants crawling over his face, you'd at least let me do something pleasant for a change!' Once I start cooking these things up in my mind I go way out. Like—'All right, Mom, if that's your attitude I'll be forced to tell the District Attorney that I heard you downstairs talking to Ben early that morning. That I peeked out of the window and saw you both walking down back of the house to the barbecue area. You were arguing. You sounded angry. Shortly after you disappeared down through the trees I heard you screaming at him. Then a shot rang out. You came back up to the house and went to bed!'

'Why, Josh, you know that's a lie!'

'Ah, yes! *I* know, Mother, and *you* know—but will *they* know? I think not! I believe you realise now how very important this movie job is to me. I refuse to let anything stand in the way of my career. Not even you, Mother!'

Anyhow, you can be damn sure I'd never go through with it. Not with *my* mother. Because when she turns on the cooling system she gets to be just like an iceberg. It destroys me.

After an hour or so I heard her walking down the hall towards my door. She stood there awhile, listening. Then she knocked.

'Josh?' she said. I didn't answer at first. 'Josh?'

I thought I'd make her wonder. She tried the door several times but I'd locked it.

'Josh, are you in there?'

'Yes.'

'What are you doing?'

'Nothing.'

'Then why is the door locked?'

'I don't know.' She always cows me into giving these vague answers when what I really wanted to say was, 'It's my room isn't it? Well, that's why the door's locked!'

'What do you mean—you don't know?'

'I just locked it, that's all.'

'I want to know *why* you locked it?'

106

'I'm resting.'

'Can't you rest with the door unlocked?'

'No.'

'Don't give me short answers, young man!' Boy, there's the danger signal—*young man*! That means there's trouble in the boiler-room, all right.

'What do you want me to say?' I asked.

'And don't get fresh!'

You can't win at a time like that. So I just didn't say anything.

'Josh, did you hear me!'

'Yes.'

'Well?'

'Well, what?'

'I'm telling you—don't get fresh!' She jiggled the door-knob again. 'All right, Josh, open the door! You and I are going to have a little talk!'

'I'll come downstairs later on. I don't feel like it now.' Boy, I was really getting nervy.

'Now listen—I'm just about fed up with you. And don't think you're fooling me. You're sulking—that's what you're doing in there. Sulking! Like a little girl!'

It was the last that did it. I loathe it when grown-ups get mean like that. I wasn't feeling at all like a sissy any more, but I guess my resentment to that kind of talk was still very strong.

'I know that's what you're doing!' Her voice was getting more shrill by the second. 'Well, isn't it?'

'Okay then, why do we have to go through the Spanish Inquisition —if you're so sure?'

'Josh, I'm telling you—I'm not enjoying standing out here one single bit. You'd better unlock that door and do it this minute.'

'Nobody's asking you to stand out there, you know!' I think I was being possessed by the devil at this point.

'You're going to get such a slap in the face it'll make your head spin!'

'That kind of talk isn't going to get me to open the door,' I said. Suddenly I felt this silly streak coming over me. Mainly, I guess, because we were both acting like kids, screaming at one another through the door. Also the nervous tension of having an argument with her made me kind of giggle.

'I'm not being funny,' she snapped. 'I meant what I just said!'

'If you keep telling me you're going to beat me up I'll never open the door.'

'Do you want me to call Merwin and have him hear the ridiculous way you're acting! I thought you were beginning to grow up, but apparently I was mistaken.'

I didn't want Merwin to get involved, so I didn't answer for a second while I was figuring out how to get out of this.

'All right, Josh, that's what I'm going to do.'

I heard her start to walk down the hall and something perverse as hell made me yell after her: 'While you're at it—why don't you get Ben? He could always handle me!'

Now what I said that for I'll never know. I suppose having this stupid fight was a way of letting off steam for both my mother and me. It was a pretty poor excuse; but you had to get rid of it somehow, so you picked the most trivial thing in the world and let go.

When I said it I heard her footsteps stop. She stood out in the hall for quite a while. Then I heard her walking away very softly.

I felt like a real monster.

About a half-hour later Merwin knocked on my door. 'Sweetie, may I come in?' I went to the door and opened it. 'Your mother's very upset,' he said.

'I know. I'm sorry about bringing up Ben,' I told him, 'but I'm upset, too. I don't understand why she won't let me take that part. It's only a couple of weeks, and we could use the money. What's so awful about it?'

'Sweetie, you've got to understand about your mother. God forbid, I don't want to sound like a Pollyanna, but she's only thinking of your own good. She doesn't want you to grow up and live the kind of life she's had.'

'Why would I do that? At least I wouldn't have all the rotten boy friends she's had. Or a lot of the cuckoo friends.'

'Don't you see, Josh—it's because of the instability of her professional life that she's got so mixed up in her personal life.'

I asked Merwin what had *really* happened with her career. I never quite understood why she hadn't stayed at the top. He tried to explain it to me.

'You've got to keep in mind that Rita came into the motion picture business when she was only a couple of years older than you are now. She'd had no experience, no training, no indoctrination of any sort. A beauty contest and, suddenly, by a fluke, the lead in a movie and a star at eighteen! She wasn't equipped for it. It was all too quick, too unprepared for. Oh, sure, five or six wonderful years, playing beautiful young things, requiring very little acting talent, but—'

'She's a good actress now,' I said.

'Of course, sweetie, but it took a long time and she learned the hard way. The first success came so easily I'm sure she felt everything else would follow just as naturally. But it takes serious work, hard work. Becoming a good actor or actress—a really good one—is no snap. Rita neglected her career those first few years. She got caught up in the glamour, the social life, the peripheral fluff of Hollywood— as was only natural for a beautiful, exciting, *and* excitable young girl.

'Then, eventually, she got thrown into a couple of roles that were beyond her. She began to slip. And, Josh, remember this: for every one person around to help boost your buns up the ladder, there's an even dozen ready to step on your shoulders on the way back down.

'Acting—probably the coldest, cruellest profession there is. Certainly the most unstable *and* the most personal, thus compounding the felony.'

I certainly couldn't argue with him about the dangers of it.

'I think I know how it went with your mother, Josh. You see, once she began getting rejected in her professional life, she started looking for acceptance doubly hard in her personal life. She began running around with the sophisticated set, the so-called sophisticates. Actually, on the inside, they're a fairly hollow bunch. They take what they can from a person: youth, beauty, fun. And the returns are meagre indeed: a pat on the back at first; then a kick in the ass when you're no longer a novelty.

'So your mother started looking for an exciting love-life. The minute you start that frantic search, you're in trouble. When it happens, it happens—but you can't do the Golden Fleece bit, baby. And when you can't find the one real person for you—and unfortunately, in your mother's case, whoever he is, he's managed to keep himself hidden—then you start settling for the attractive ones, the wealthy ones, the influential ones. Even worse—the fun ones! Pretty soon you're just looking for company, for someone to spend time with. That's what happened to Rita.

'If she weren't a good person, if she hadn't all the right instincts, this would be a condemnation. But your mother, Josh, has some remarkable qualities. She's loyal, she's kind, she's gentle. She has one failing: she falls in love with charming no-goods, thinking she can manage them, no doubt. She needs to be needed. Most of all, she's a thoroughly nice human being. But I think you know that.'

'Yes, I do,' I told him.

'Actually, if she ever finds the right man, she'll make a wonderful wife. God only knows, she gives herself completely, heart and soul.' He kind of chuckled. 'Why, Sugar-on-a-stick, I *am* sounding off. Old Granny Saltzman! Do I sound like an old poop?'

'No.' I laughed. 'It helps me straighten things out in my mind.'

'I'm not saying Rita's perfect, but then who is? The worst you can say about Rita is that she's soft and weak, and not the wisest of mortals. Oddly enough, those very qualities are redeeming in a way. If she were a little colder, harder, a shrewder woman, she might—on the outside at least—be more successful and therefore seem to be a happier woman. But she's a tried and true softie. Yet, conversely, she's got a marvellous strength. She's had to be strong to be able to keep her head above water after all she's been through. Thank God, she's an incurable optimist. Mainly, I think, because of you, Josh!'

'Because of me?' I asked.

'Yes. There's not a doubt in my mind that if it weren't for you she'd have given up long ago. She *wants* for you, baby! Do you understand what I mean?'

'Yes, I think so.'

'When I say *wants*, I mean not only things, but happiness, normalcy, a way of life. That's actually why she's against this movie thing.'

'Yes, but just because I'd be in a movie doesn't mean my career would turn out the same way hers did.'

'True, but she's indoctrinated by her own life and experiences. She wants to guard you against the same tough times, the struggles, and the heartbreaks.'

'I understand all that, but even so—'

'And remember, baby, this is a frightening period and we're not sure the worst is over—not by a long shot. So above all, make every effort to be kind and understanding to her.'

'I'm trying to,' I told him. I had been, and I felt like the lowest snake there is for the things I'd said when she was outside my door.

'At any rate, sweetie, she loves you dearly! Mind you, I still don't say there's anything wrong in your taking a flyer for two weeks to act in a movie.' He stood up from his chair. 'I'll still have a talk with her when she calms down and do my best to convince her.'

'You will? Honestly, Merwin?'

'But, of course! I can probably bore her into it. However, if she

doesn't come around, try to understand and let it go.' He put his
hands on my shoulders. 'You're so very young, Josh. You've got many
chances ahead of you. This is a drop in the bucket.'

'Okay. I promise I won't make a Federal Case out of it,' I told
him. 'I guess I'll go down and make up with her. Don't you think?'

'I'll cut you out of my will if you don't.' Merwin walked towards
the door. As he was going out into the hall, he stopped, turned around,
and said, 'You know, Josh, at times I almost wish I had a son like
you. But, of course, the whole idea is absurd. I'm really not built
for child-bearing. Too tiny around the pelvic region!' He slapped his
hands against his hips, looked up, and, as soon as he saw me smiling,
went to his room.

What a character! Merwin always knew how to say something wild
to snap you out of a mood when you had to do something you didn't
relish. And I wasn't looking forward too much to making up. I didn't
mind it once it was done. It was *how* to make up that always seemed
tricky. I hate to get involved in a lot of hashing-over talk. The best
way is to do it emotionally.

That's what I did that time. I took a deep breath, ran out of my
room, clomped down the stairs, and when I got to the bottom I yelled
out, 'Mom!'

'Yes?' She was in the kitchen.

I tore in. She was sitting at the breakfast table over a cup of coffee.
I ran right over to her and threw my arms around her. 'I'm sorry,
Mom. I was a jerk!'

She hugged me back. Then she said, 'You're not such a jerk. You're
pretty clever, Josh.' I guess she meant the way I just came in and
grabbed her to avoid any long, drawn-out scene.

It was Saturday and Cecelia was gone. The next thing you knew
we were talking about what to fix for dinner and everything was
relatively all right.

ALBERTO MORAVIA

(b. 1907)

*Alberto Moravia is the most celebrated of contemporary Italian writers.
He is a Jew and an anti-fascist who was forced into hiding during the
German occupation of Italy in the Second World War and his novels—
several of which, including* A Ghost At Noon, *have been made into films
—vividly reflect the concerns and crises of our own times. His journalism
includes a novella-length interview with Claudia Cardinale in which the
actress was invited to consider her own sexuality. 'The Film Test' comes
from* Roman Tales *(1956).*

The Film Test

SERAFINO AND I are friends although our work has taken us far
apart from one another; he is chauffeur to an industrialist and I am a
film cameraman and photographer. We are quite different in physical
appearance too: he has fair, curly hair and a pink, child-like face,
and his eyes, of a staring blue, are set flush with his face; whereas I
am swarthy, with the serious face of an adult man, and deep-set, dark
eyes. But the real difference lies in our characters: Serafino is a born
liar, wheras I am quite unable to tell lies. Well, one Sunday Serafino
let me know that he needed me: from his tone I suspected some sort
of embarrassment, for Serafino constantly gets into trouble through
his mania for cutting a dash. I went to keep the appointment at a café
in the Piazza Colonna; and a moment later, there he was, arriving
with Lie no. 1—the very expensive, 'special model' car belonging to
his employer, whom I knew to be away from Rome. He waved his
hand to me from some distance off, in a slightly conceited way, just
as though the car had been his own, and then went and parked it. I
looked at him as he came towards me: he was dressed in a foppish
kind of way, in short, narrow trousers of yellow corduroy, a jacket
with a slit at the back, and a coloured handkerchief round his
neck. A feeling of distaste came over me, for some reason, and, as

he sat down, I remarked somewhat acidly: 'You look like a millionaire.'

He answered emphatically: 'Today I *am* a millionaire'; and I did not at once understand what he meant. 'What about the car?' I persisted. 'Have you won a football pool?'

'It's the boss's new car,' he answered indifferently. For a moment he sat thinking, and then went on: 'Listen, Mario, two young ladies are coming here shortly . . . as you see, I thought of you too . . . one for each of us. . . . They're girls of good family, the daughters of a railway engineer. . . . You're a film producer—is that understood? Don't give me away.'

'And you—what are you?'

'I've already told you—a millionaire.'

I said nothing, but rose to my feet. 'What are you doing? Are you going away?' he said in alarm.

'Yes, I'm going,' I replied; 'you know I don't like lies. . . . Good-bye . . . enjoy yourself.'

'Wait, wait . . . You'll spoil my plan.'

'Don't worry, I won't spoil anything.'

'Wait a moment; these girls want to meet you.'

'But *I* don't want to meet *them*.'

In short, we argued for some time, he sitting down and I standing in front of him. In the end, since I am a good friend, I agreed to stay. However, I warned him: 'I don't guarantee to play this game of yours to the bitter end.' But he was paying no further attention to me. Beaming with pleasure, he said: 'Here they are.'

At first I could see nothing but hair. It looked as though they each of them had on their heads a large ball made of thick, frizzy, puffed-out hair. Then with some difficulty I caught sight, under these two vast masses, of their faces, peaked and thin, like two little birds peeping out of a nest. In figure, they were both of them supple and full of curves, all hips and bosom, with tiny wasp waists that could have gone through a napkin-ring. I thought they must be twins because they were dressed in the same way: tartan skirts, black jumpers, red shoes and bags. Serafino rose ceremoniously and performed the introductions: 'My friend Mario, the film producer; Signorina Iris, Signorina Mimosa.'

I could see them better, now that they were sitting down. From the careful attention he showed her, I realised that Serafino had reserved Iris for himself, leaving me Mimosa. They were not twins: Mimosa, who was clearly over thirty, had a more hungry-looking face, a longer nose, a bigger mouth and a more pronounced chin than Iris, and she was, in fact, almost ugly. Iris, on the other hand, must have been about twenty and was charming. I noticed, moreover, that they both had red, chapped hands—more like working women than young ladies. In the meantime Serafino, who with their arrival seemed to have become quite silly, was making conversation: what a pleasure it was to see them, how brown they were, where had they been for the summer? . . .

Mimosa began: 'At Ven——' But by that time Iris had answered: 'At Viareggio.' Then they looked at each other and started laughing. Serafino asked: 'What are you laughing at?'

'Don't take any notice,' said Mimosa; 'my sister is silly. . . . We were first at Venice, in an hotel, and then at Viareggio, in a little villa we have there.'

I knew she was lying because she lowered her eyes as she spoke. She was like me: I can't tell lies when I am looking someone in the face. Then she went on, coolly: 'Signor Mario, you're a film producer. . . . Serafino told us you would give us a film test.'

I was disconcerted; I looked at Serafino, but he turned away his head. 'Well, you know, Signorina,' I said, 'a film test is like a little film, it's not a thing that can be done at a moment's notice. . . . It needs a director, a cameraman, a studio. . . . Serafino doesn't quite understand. . . . But certainly, one of these days . . .'

'One of these days means never.'

'No, no, Signorina, I assure you . . .'

'Come on, be a good, kind man, do give us a test.' She was wriggling all over now, and had taken my arm and was pressing up against me. I realised that Serafino had turned her head with this story about a film test, and I tried again to explain to her that a film test was not a thing that could be done in a moment, there and then. Gradually she came, at length, to understand this; and she relaxed her hold on my arm. Then she said to her sister, who was chattering to Serafino: 'I told you it was just a story. . . . Well, what shall we do? Shall we go home?'

Iris, who was not expecting this, was ill at ease. She said, with some embarrassment: 'We might stay with them . . . until this evening.'

'Yes,' urged Serafino, 'let's all stay together. . . . Let's go out in the car.'

'You've got a car?' enquired Mimosa, almost reconciled.

'Yes, there it is.'

She followed the movement of his hand, saw the car and immediately changed her tone. 'Let's go, then. . . . Sitting in a café bores me.' We all four rose to our feet. Iris went in front with Serafino; and Mimosa walked beside me, saying: 'You're not offended, are you? But you know, we're sick and tired of promises. . . . Now, you *will* give me the test, won't you?'

So all my explanations had served no purpose at all: she still wanted the test. I made no answer, but got into the car and sat down beside her, at the back, while Serafino and Iris sat in front. 'Where shall we go?' asked Serafino.

Mimosa had now seized hold of my arm again, and had taken my hand in hers and was squeezing it. In a low voice, she tried to coax me: 'Come on, do be kind; tell him to go to the studio and we'll do the test.' For a moment, from sheer anger, I sat silent; and she took advantage of this to add, still in a low voice: 'Look, if you give me a test, I'll give you a kiss.'

I had a sudden inspiration, and suggested: 'Let's go to Serafino's house. . . . He has a lovely big house. . . . Then I'll be able to take a better look at you both, and I'll tell you if there's a chance of giving you this test.'

I noticed that Serafino threw me a look of reproach: he might pass off his employer's car as his own; but he had not yet had the courage to bring anyone into the house. He tried, in fact, to make objections: 'Wouldn't it be better to go for a nice drive?'; but the girls, Mimosa especially, insisted: they didn't want a drive, they wanted to discuss the question of the film test. So he resigned himself and we went off at full speed towards the Parioli district, where the house was. All the way there, Mimosa continued to press up against me, talking to me in a low, insinuating, caressing voice. I did not listen to her; but every now and then I caught that oft-repeated word, which she reiterated like a hammer striking a nail: 'The test . . . You'll give me a test? . . . If we do the test . . .'

We reached the Parioli district, with its empty streets between rows of expensive houses, all balcony and window. We reached the residence of Serafino's employer, with its black marble entrance-hall and its glass and mahogany lift. We went up to the third floor and, on entering, found ourselves in the dark, with a smell of naphthalene and stuffiness everywhere. 'I'm sorry, but I've been away,' Serafino informed us; 'the flat's all upside down.' We went into the sitting-room; Serafino threw open the windows; we sat down on a divan upholstered in grey cloth, in front of a piano covered in dust-sheets which were fastened with safety-pins. Then, putting my plan into action, I said: 'We two are going to take a look at you now; you must just walk up and down the room for a bit. . . . Then I shall be able to get an idea for the test.'

'Are we to show our legs?' asked Mimosa.

'No, no, not your legs . . . just walk about, that's enough.'

Obediently they started walking up and down in front of us, on the wax-polished wooden floor. No one could say they were not graceful, with those two big heads of hair, and their well-developed hips and busts and their thin waists. But I noticed that they had large, ugly feet as well as hands. And their legs were slightly crooked, stiff and clumsy in shape. They were, in fact, the sort of girls to whom film-producers do not give even a walking-on part. In the meantime they went on walking up and down, and each time they met in the middle of the room, they started laughing. All at once I called out: 'Halt! That's enough. Sit down!'

They went and sat down and looked at me with anxious faces. 'I'm sorry,' I said drily, 'but you won't do.'

'Why?'

'I'll tell you why, at once,' I explained seriously. 'For my films, I don't need refined, well-educated, distinguished, ladylike girls such as you. . . . What I need is working-class girls—girls who can even, if required, speak a few ugly words, girls who move in a provoking way, girls who are, in fact, awkward, ill-bred, unpolished. . . . You, on the other hand, are the daughters of an engineer, you come of a good family. . . . You're not what I'm looking for.'

I looked at Serafino: he had sunk back on the divan and appeared stupefied. 'But what d'you mean?' persisted Mimosa. 'We can surely pretend to be working-class girls, can't we?'

'No, you can't. There are some things that no one can do who isn't born to them.'

A short silence ensued. I had cast my hook and I was sure the fish would swallow it. And indeed, a moment later, Mimosa rose and went and whispered in her sister's ear. The latter did not appear pleased, but finally she made a gesture of consent. Then Mimosa placed her hands on her hips and swayed across to me; she gave me a punch in the chest and said: 'Come on, old sport, who d'you think you're talking to?'

If I were to say that she was transformed, it would be saying too much. In actual fact, it was herself, her own natural self. I replied, laughing: 'To the daughters of a railway engineer.'

'On the contrary, we're exactly what you want—two ordinary working-class girls. . . . Iris is in service, and I'm a nurse. . . .'

'And how about the villa at Viareggio?'

'There isn't one. We got our little bit of sunburn at Ostia.'

'But why did you tell so many lies?'

Iris said naïvely: 'I didn't want to . . . but Mimosa says you have to throw dust in people's eyes.'

'Anyhow, if we hadn't told lies,' Mimosa remarked flatly, 'Signor Serafino wouldn't have introduced us to you . . . so it served its purpose. . . . Well, now, what about that film test?'

'We've done it already,' I replied, laughing, 'and it served to show that you're a couple of nice working-class girls. . . . Besides, lie for lie: I'm not a film producer but an ordinary cameraman and photographer . . . and Serafino here, he's not the grand gentleman he pretends to be: he's a chauffeur.'

I must admit that Mimosa took the blow magnificently. 'Well, well, I was half expecting this,' she said sadly; 'we're unlucky . . . and if we meet a man with a car, of course he turns out to be a chauffeur. . . . Come on, Iris.'

At last Serafino roused himself. 'Wait a moment,' he said. 'Where are you going?'

'We're going away, Mr. Liar.'

All of a sudden I felt sorry for them, especially for Iris, who was so pretty and who seemed mortified and had tears in her eyes. I made a suggestion. 'Listen to me,' I said. 'We've all four of us told lies . . . but I propose that we let bygones be bygones and all go to the pictures together. . . . What about it?'

A discussion followed. Iris wanted to accept; Mimosa, who was still offended, did not; Serafino, crestfallen, hadn't the courage to speak. But I persuaded Mimosa by saying, finally: 'I'm a cameraman, not a producer . . . but I can introduce Iris to an assistant director that I know. . . . It won't be a great recommendation, but it's better than nothing. It's no good for you, I'm afraid, but possibly something might be done about Iris.'

So off we went to the pictures; but in a bus, not in the car. And Iris, in the cinema, pressed close up against Serafino, whom she liked in spite of his being both a liar and a chauffeur. Mimosa, on the other hand, kept to herself. And during an interval she said to me: 'I'm more or less of a mother to Iris. . . . She *is* a pretty girl, isn't she? Now remember you made a promise and you must keep it . . . there'll be the devil to pay if you don't.'

'It's only cowards who make promises and keep them,' I said jokingly.

'You made a promise and you're going to keep it,' said she; 'Iris is to have her film test, and have it she shall.'

GORE VIDAL

(b. 1925)

Gore Vidal's chosen role is that of the dandy and gadfly of current American letters. He has written some of the best novels (Burr), the best plays (Visit to a Small Planet) and the best film-scripts (The Best Man) of the past three decades between jousting in public print with politicians and fellow authors whose wit is less potent than their reputations. He is a polemicist whose target is America and in Myra Breckinridge *(1968), he created a trans-sexual hero/heroine who, deeply versed in movie-lore, challenged vital aspects of the American dream.*

Myra Breckinridge

CHAPTER 9

I CAN hardly bear it another moment! I am reborn or in the process of rebirth like Robert Montgomery in *Here Comes Mr. Jordan*.

I am seated in front of a French café in a Montmartre street on the back lot at Metro. Last year's fire destroyed many of the studio's permanent outdoor sets—those streets and castles I knew so much better than ever I knew the Chelsea area of Manhattan where Myron and I used to exist. I deeply regret the fire, mourn all that was lost, particularly the famous New York City street of brownstones and the charming village in Normandy. But, thank Heaven, this café still stands. Over a metal framework, cheap wood has been so arranged and painted as to suggest with astonishing accuracy a Paris bistro, complete with signs for BYRRH, while a striped awning shades metal tables and chairs set out on the 'sidewalk'. Any minute now, I expect to see Parisians. I would certainly like to see a waiter and order a Pernod.

I can hardly believe that I am sitting at the same table where Audrey Hepburn once awaited Gene Kelly so many years ago, and I can almost re-create for myself the lights, the camera, the sound boom, the technicians, all converged upon this one table where, in a blaze of artificial sunlight, Audrey—much too thin but a lovely face with eyes like mine—sits and waits for her screen lover while a man from make-up delicately dusts those famous features with powder.

From the angle where I sit I can see part of the street in Carvel where Andy Hardy lived. The street is beautifully kept up as the shrine it is, a last memorial to all that was touching and—yes—good in the American past, an era whose end was marked by two mushroom shapes set like terminal punctuation marks against the Asian sky.

A few minutes ago I saw Judge Hardy's house with its neatly tended green lawn and windows covered with muslin behind which there is nothing at all. It is quite eerie the way in which the houses look entirely real from every angle on the slightly curving street with its tall green trees and flowering bushes. Yet when one walks around to the back of the houses, one sees the rusted metal framework, the unpainted wood which has begun to rot, the dirty glass of the windows and the muslin curtains soiled and torn. Time withers all things human; although yesterday evening when I saw Ann Rutherford, stopped in her car at a red light, I recognised immediately the great black eyes and the mobile face. She at least endures gallantly, and I could not have been more thrilled! Must find where Lewis Stone is buried.

This is the happiest moment of my life, sitting here alone on the back lot with no one in sight, for I was able to escape the studio guide by telling him that I wanted to lie down in an empty office of the Thalberg Building; then of course I flew straight here to the back lot which is separated from the main studio by a public road.

If only Myron could have seen this! Of course he would have been saddened by the signs of decay. The spirit of what used to be has fled. Most dreadful of all, NO FILM is currently being made on the lot; and that means that the twenty-seven huge sound stages which saw the creation of so many miracles: Gable, Garbo, Hepburn (Katharine), Powell, Loy, Garland, Tracy and James Craig are now empty except for a few crews making television commercials.

Yet I must write the absolute truth for I am not Myron Breckinridge but myself and despite the intensely symbiotic relationship my husband and I enjoyed during his brief life and despite the fact that I do entirely support his thesis that the films of 1935 to 1945 inclusive were the high point of Western culture, completing what began that day in the theatre of Dionysos when Aeschylus first spoke to the Athenians,. I must confess that I part company with Myron on the subject of TV. Even before Marshall McLuhan, I was drawn to the grey shadows of the cathode tube. In fact, I was sufficiently *avant-garde* in 1959 to recognise the fact that it was no longer the movies but the television commercial that engaged the passionate attention of the world's best artists and technicians. And now the result of their extraordinary artistry is the new world, like it or not, we are living in: post-Gutenberg and pre-Apocalypse. For almost twenty years the minds of our children have been filled with dreams that will stay with them forever, the way those maddening jingles do (as I write, I have begun softly to whistle 'Rinso White', a theme far more meaningful culturally than all of Stravinsky or even John Cage). I submitted a piece on this subject to the *Partisan Review* in the summer of 1960. I believe, without false modesty, that I proved conclusively that the relationship between consumer and advertiser is the last demonstration of *necessary* love in the West, and its principal form of expression is the television commercial. I never heard from *PR* but I kept a carbon of the piece and will incorporate it into the book on Parker Tyler, perhaps as an appendix.

For almost an hour I watched a television commercial being made on the same stage where Bette Davis acted in *The Catered Affair*—that predictably unhappy result of the movies attempting to take over the television drama when what they should have taken over was the *spirit* of the commercials. Then I was given lunch in the commissary which is much changed since the great days when people in extraordinary costumes wandered about, creating the impression that one was inside a time machine gone berserk. Now television executives and technicians occupy all the tables and order what used to be Louis B. Mayer Chicken Soup only the name of Mayer has been, my guide told me, stricken from the menu. So much for greatness! Even more poignant as reminders of human transiency are the empty offices on the second floor of the Thalberg Building. I was particularly upset to see that the adjoining suites of Pandro S. Berman and the late Sam Zimbalist were both vacant. Zimbalist (immortal because of *Boom Town*) died in Rome while producing *Ben Hur* which saved the studio's bacon, and Pandro S. Berman (*Dragon Seed*, *The Picture of Dorian Gray*, *The Seventh Cross*) has gone into what the local trade papers refer to as 'indie production'. How tragic! M.G.M. without Pandro S. Berman is like the American flag without its stars.

No doubt about it, an era has indeed ended and I am its chronicler. Farewell the classic films, hail the television commercial! Yet nothing human that is great can entirely end. It is merely transmuted—in the way that the wharf where Jeanette MacDonald arrived in New

Orleans (*Naughty Marietta,* 1935) has been used over and over again for a hundred other films even though it will always remain, to those who have a sense of history, Jeanette's wharf. Speaking of history, there was something curiously godlike about Nelson Eddy's recent death before a nightclub audience at Miami. In the middle of a song, he suddenly forgot the words. And so, in that plangent baritone which long ago earned him a permanent place in the pantheon of superstars, he turned to his accompanist and said, 'Play "Dardanella," and maybe I'll remember the words.' Then he collapsed and died.

Play 'Dardanella'! Play on! In any case, one must be thankful for those strips of celluloid which still endure to remind us that once there were gods and goddesses in our midst and Metro-Goldwyn-Mayer (where I now sit) preserved their shadows for all time! Could the actual Christ have possessed a fraction of the radiance and the mystery of H. B. Warner in the first *King of Kings* or revealed, even on the cross, so much as a shadow of the moonstruck Nemi-agony of Jeffrey Hunter in the second *King of Kings,* that astonishing creation of Nicholas Ray?

HARRY BROWN

(b. 1917)

This is Merely Part of the Studio Tour

ON STAGE Seven we are shooting an historical epic,
And today we are taking angle shots of the Four Horsemen,
Who are somewhere in the background of every scene,
Four fine old actors hired through Central Casting,
Only one has grown fat, the others are very lean.

The stars of the picture are scattered about the set:
That one with the pout is the villain, this one dies in Reel Four,
That girl is fine in portrayals of outraged honour.
No one is ever sure whom she plays, and yet at her appearance
The audience cheers, and critics heap praise upon her.

The Assistant Directors have finished their shouts of 'Quiet!'
The stand-ins have ended their work beneath the Kliegs,
Now all is ready, and this is the actual take.
Microphones hang from their booms in the best positions
To pick up the thunderous noises the horsemen make.

They are riding a treadmill through manufactured smoke.
It will, on the screen, be a terrifying prospect,
Not recommended for children. Their mothers will protest,
Saying it makes them sweat or scream from their pillows,
Or somehow disturbs their innocent, silly rest.

O, watch those four old character actors, hired
Through Central Casting, one of them fat, three lean.
They perform as though they all were quite inspired,
And yet they all have moved across the screen
For longer than I can remember. They must be very tired.

KARL SHAPIRO

(b. 1913)

Movie Actress

I sit a queen, and am no widow, and shall see no sorrow

She is young and lies curved on the velvety floor of her fame
Like a prize-winning cat on a mirror of fire and oak,
And her dreams are as black as the Jew who uncovered her name;

She is folded in magic and hushed in the pride of her cloak
Which is woven of worship like silk for the hollows of eyes
That are raised in the dark to her image that shimmered and spoke;

And she speaks in her darkness alone and her emptiness cries
Till her voice is as shuddering tin in the wings of a stage,
And her beauty seems wrong as the wig of a perfect disguise;

She is sick with the shadow of shadow, diseased with the rage
Of the whiteness of light and the heat of interior sun,
And she faints like a pauper to carry the weight of her wage;

She is coarse with the honours of power, the duties of fun
And amazed at the regions of pleasure where skill is begun.

CHRISTOPHER LOGUE

(b. 1926)

During her first three months at Norten Art School she has been singing
with the local group.
Her song: **Don't Let Me Go.**
Before she left two third-year students fucked her.

She has been interviewed
'I have been singing all my life.'
The hotel bedroom looks onto the sea.

Her first big song: **True Love.**
The man who wrote it had her on the bed.
'Make sure your manager is queer' he said.
He liked the dog-and-bitch position best.
The flip side was called **Sleep.**

'Her image must be linked with joy and hope and youthful aspiration.'
She has signed.
Her sister liked him better than the rest.
'I have to urge her all the time.
Sometimes I let her know that I am pleased.'

Her first LP: **Love Is My World.**
Her photograph: Returning from a holiday in Greece.
Her clothes: silvered trapeze, chrome twill, grey foulard smock.
Her weight:
Her car:
Her age:

'FOR GOD'S SAKE MARRY ME!'

Two films: Drum City, Everything In Time.
Drum City Girl is her first gold.

Sometimes I let her know that I am pleased.
She buys her parents a dream bungalow.
He liked the dog-and-bitch position best.

Her nickname has become a household word.
The hotel bedroom looks onto the sea.
After the show he often sees her nude.
Her weight. Her car. Her photograph. Her age.

Fucked up the arse while touring America
polaroid snapshots of her being licked
are circulated in chic discotheques.

Then

Mountains seen through rain and cloud;
the wall is high; the house
a perspex smudge between the leaves.
Sometimes the tourists who call their dogs
back to them on the valley's northern slope,
notice, before a rubber hand pulls down a blind,
metallic glints among the foliage;
needles are hovering in the upper room
where she has come to rest.

She has a dog, dark glasses, and a book.
Now and again a plane flies overhead.
Thirty-five miles to the west
her money blossoms in a numbered vault.

When she returns she will be asked:
'What are your views about religion?'
And she will say:
'If God is love, then I believe in God.'

JAMES THURBER

(1894–1961)

*James Thurber's experiences with movie-making were fairly disastrous.
To his lasting and often-expressed regret he permitted Sam Goldwyn to
turn his short story 'The Secret Life of Walter Mitty' into a star vehicle
for Danny Kaye. And of his subsequent forays into the film business only
a British version of his story 'The Catbird Seat' (which was re-titled*
The Battle of the Sexes*) and a U.P.A. cartoon version of his fable
'The Unicorn in the Garden' convey the charm and the misanthropy of
the originals. 'The Man Who Hated Moonbaum' is taken from* Vintage
Thurber *(1963).*

The Man Who Hated Moonbaum

AFTER THEY had passed through the high, grilled gate they walked
for almost a quarter of a mile, or so it seemed to Tallman. It was
very dark; the air smelled sweet; now and then leaves brushed against
his cheek or forehead. The little, stout man he was following had
stopped talking, but Tallman could hear him breathing. They walked
on for another minute. 'How we doing?' Tallman asked, finally. 'Don't
ask me questions!' snapped the other man. 'Nobody asks me questions!
You'll learn.' The hell I will, thought Tallman, pushing through
the darkness and the fragrance and the mysterious leaves; the hell I
will, baby; this is the last time you'll ever see me. The knowledge
that he was leaving Hollywood within twenty-four hours gave him a
sense of comfort.

There was no longer turf or gravel under his feet; there was something that rang flatly: tile, or flagstones. The little man began to walk
more slowly and Tallman almost bumped into him. 'Can't we have
a light?' said Tallman. 'There you go!' shouted his guide. 'Don't
get me screaming! What are you trying to do to me?' 'I'm not trying
to do anything to you,' said Tallman. 'I'm trying to find out where
we're going.'

127

The other man had come to a stop and seemed to be groping around. 'First it's wrong uniforms,' he said, 'then it's red fire—red fire in Scotland, red fire three hundred years ago! I don't know why I ain't crazy!' Tallman could make out the other man dimly, a black, gesturing blob. 'You're doing all right,' said Tallman. Why did I ever leave the Brown Derby with this guy? he asked himself. Why did I ever let him bring me to his house—if he has a house? Who the hell does he think he is?

Tallman looked at his wristwatch; the dial glowed wanly in the immense darkness. He was a little drunk, but he could see that it was half past three in the morning. 'Not trying to do anything to me, he says!' screamed the little man. 'Wasn't his fault! It's never anybody's fault! They give me ten thousand dollars' worth of Sam Browne belts for Scotch Highlanders and it's nobody's fault!' Tallman was beginning to get his hangover headache. 'I want a light!' he said. 'I want a drink! I want to know where the hell I am!' 'That's it! Speak out!' said the other. 'Say what you think! I like a man who knows where he is. We'll get along.' 'Contact!' said Tallman. 'Camera! Lights! Get out that hundred-year-old brandy you were talking about.'

The response to this was a soft flood of rose-coloured radiance; the little man had somehow found a light switch in the dark. God knows where, thought Tallman; probably on a tree. They were in a courtyard paved with enormous flagstones which fitted together with mosaic perfection. The light revealed the dark stones of a building which looked like the Place de la Concorde side of the Crillon. 'Come on, you people!' said the little man. Tallman looked behind him, half expecting to see the shadowy forms of Scottish Highlanders, but there was nothing but the shadows of trees and of oddly shaped plants closing in on the courtyard. With a key as small as a dime, the little man opened a door that was fifteen feet high and made of wood six inches thick.

Marble stairs tumbled down like Niagara into a grand canyon of a living room. The steps of the two men sounded sharp and clear on the stairs, died in the soft depths of an immensity of carpet in the living room. The ceiling towered above them. There were highlights on dark wood medallions, on burnished shields, on silver curves and edges. On one wall a forty-foot tapestry hung from the ceiling to within a few feet of the floor. Tallman was looking at this when his companion grasped his arm. 'The second rose!' he said. 'The second rose from the right!' Tallman pulled away. 'One of us has got to snap out of this baby,' he said. 'How about that brandy?' 'Don't interrupt me!' shouted his host. 'That's what Whozis whispers to What's-His-Name—greatest love story in the world, if I do say so myself—king's wife mixed up in it—knights riding around with spears—Whozis writes her a message made out of twigs bent together to make words: "I love you"—sends it floating down a stream past her window—they got her locked in—goddamnedest thing in the history of pictures. Where was I? Oh—"Second rose from the right," she says. Why? Because she seen it twitch, she seen it move. What's-His-Name is bending over her, kissing her maybe. He whirls around and shoots an arrow at the rose—second from the right, way up high there—down comes the whole tapestry, weighs eleven hundred pounds, and out rolls this spy, shot through the heart. What's-His-Name sent him to watch the lovers.' The little man began to pace up and down the deep carpet. Tallman lighted a fresh cigarette from his glowing stub and sat down in an enormous chair. His host came to a stop in front of the chair and shook his finger at its occupant.

'Look,' said the little man. 'I don't know who you are and I'm telling you this. You could ruin me, but I got to tell you. I get Moonbaum here—I get Moonbaum himself here—you can ask Manny or Sol—I get the best arrow shot in the world here to fire that arrow for What's-His-Name—'

'Tristram,' said Tallman. 'Don't prompt me!' bellowed the little man. 'For Tristram. What happens? Do I know he's got arrows you shoot bears with? Do I know he ain't got caps on 'em? If I got to know that, why do I have Mitnik? Moonbaum is sitting right there—the tapestry comes down and out rolls this guy, shot through the heart—only the arrow is in his stomach. So what happens? So Moonbaum laughs! That makes Moonbaum laugh! The greatest love story in the history of pictures, and Moonbaum laughs!' The little man raced over to a large chest, opened it, took out a cigar, stuck it in his mouth, and resumed his pacing. 'How do you like it?' he shouted. 'I love it,' said Tallman. 'I love every part of it. I always have.' The little man raised his hands above his head. 'He loves it! He hears one—maybe two—scenes, and he loves every part of it! Even Moonbaum don't know how it comes out, and you love every part of it!' The little man was standing before Tallman's chair again, shaking his cigar at him. 'The story got around,' said Tallman. 'These things leak out. Maybe you talk when you're drinking. What about that brandy?'

The little man walked over and took hold of a bell rope on the wall, next to the tapestry. 'Moonbaum laughs like he's dying,' he said.

'Moonbaum laughs like he's seen Chaplin.' He dropped the bell rope. 'I hope you really got that hundred-year-old brandy,' said Tallman. 'Don't keep telling me what you hope!' howled the little man. 'Keep listening to what I hope!' He pulled the bell rope savagely. 'Now we're getting somewhere,' said Tallman. For the first time the little man went to a chair and sat down; he chewed on his unlighted cigar. 'Do you know what Moonbaum wants her called?' he demanded, lowering his heavy lids. 'I can guess,' said Tallman. 'Isolde.' 'Birds of a feather!' shouted his host. 'Horses of the same colour! Isolde! Name of God, man, you can't call a woman Isolde! What do I want her called?' 'You have me there,' said Tallman. 'I want her called Dawn,' said the little man, getting up out of his chair. 'It's short, ain't it? It's sweet, ain't it? You can say it, can't you?' 'To get back to that brandy,' said Tallman, 'who is supposed to answer that bell?' 'Nobody is supposed to answer it,' said the little man. 'That don't ring, that's a fake bell rope; it don't ring anywhere. I got it to remind me of an idea Moonbaum ruined. Listen: Louisiana mansion—guy with seven daughters—old-Southern-colonel stuff—Lionel Barrymore could play it—we open on a room that looks like a million dollars —Barrymore crosses and pulls the bell rope. What happens?' 'Nothing,' said Tallman. 'You're crazy!' bellowed the little man. 'Part of the wall falls in! Out flies a crow—in walks a goat, maybe—the place has gone to seed, see? It's just a hulk of its former self, it's a shallows!' He turned and walked out of the room. It took him quite a while.

When he came back he was carrying a bottle of brandy and two huge brandy glasses. He poured a great deal of brandy into each glass and handed one to Tallman. 'You and Mitnik!' he said, scornfully. 'Pulling walls out of Southern mansions. Crows you give me, goats you give me! What the hell kind of effect is that?' 'I could have a bad idea,' said Tallman, raising his glass. 'Here's to Moonbaum. May he maul things over in his mind all night and never get any spontaneity into 'em.' 'I drink nothing to Moonbaum,' said the little man. 'I hate Moonbaum. You know where they catch that crook— that guy has a little finger off one hand and wears a glove to cover it up? What does Moonbaum want? Moonbaum wants the little finger to *flap*! What do I want? I want it stuffed. What do I want it stuffed with? Sand. Why?' 'I know,' said Tallman. 'So that when he closes his hand over the head of his cane, the little finger sticks out stiffly, giving him away.' The little man seemed to leap into the air; his brandy splashed out of his glass. 'Suitcase!' he screamed.

'Not cane! Suitcase! He grabs hold of a suitcase!' Tallman didn't say anything; he closed his eyes and sipped his brandy; it was wonderful brandy. He looked up presently to find his host staring at him with a resigned expression in his eyes. 'All right, then, suitcase,' the little man said. 'Have it suitcase. We won't fight about details, I'm trying to tell you my story. I don't tell my stories to everybody.' 'Richard Harding Davis stole that finger gag—used it in "Gallegher",' said Tallman. 'You could sue him.' The little man walked over to his chair and flopped into it. 'He's beneath me,' he said. 'He's beneath me like the dirt. I ignore him.'

Tallman finished his brandy slowly. His host's chin sank upon his chest; his heavy eyelids began to close. Tallman waited several minutes and then tiptoed over to the marble stairs. He took off his shoes and walked up the stairs, carefully. He had the heavy door open when the little man shouted at him. 'Birds of a feather, all of you!' he shouted. 'You can tell Moonbaum I said so! Shooting guys out of tapestries!' 'I'll tell him,' said Tallman. 'Good night. The brandy was wonderful.' The little man was not listening. He was pacing the floor again, gesturing with an empty brandy glass in one hand and the unlighted cigar in the other. Tallman stepped out into the cool air of the courtyard and put on one shoe and laced it. The heavy door swung shut behind him with a terrific crash. He picked up the other shoe and ran wildly towards the trees and the oddly shaped plants. It was daylight now. He could see where he was going.

ALISON LURIE

(b. 1926)

Alison Lurie is one of the most skilled reporters of domestic in-fighting in contemporary fiction. Her novels—from Love and Friendship *to* The War Between the Tates—*are funny and mordant studies of the American marriage bound for the rocks.* The Nowhere City *(1965) seems to me a perfect—though chilling—description of Los Angeles, the setting here for further marital and professional disasters. Glory Green, the main character in this excerpt, is a starlet with ambitions.*

The Nowhere City

Part IV: Hollywood

CHAPTER 17

How to make more money!—How To Be A Success! Write Today For Free Information. Dept. M., Research Center of Success.

Los Angeles Times

Photographers! Shapely Model Available. Have all equipment.

Forest lawn has created the most beautiful and most enduring places of interment in the world for those who desire to honor their loved ones with the best. But, beauty costs money . . .

Simple girl wants not-too-bright man with Cad.

Los Angeles Mirror News

The empty sound stage was like the inside of an immense dark cardboard box; a vast cube of obscure space. Against the distant walls hung painted drop cloths representing in meticulous detail the landscape and architecture of the imaginary planet Nemo, setting of Glory's current picture, a science-fiction musical comedy. Assemblages of platforms and steps rose here and there in the darkness like hillocks on a plain, among herds of folding chairs. On the dusty ground, black electrical cables and wires of all sizes were coiled and crossed, in some

132

places resembling a nest of enormous snakes. Steel and aluminium skeletons supported the spotlights and floods, and the immense cameras on their travelling booms. More hanging lights, microphones, ropes, flats, and cables disappeared into the shadows far above.

All these lights were dark now; the only illumination came from the long strip of hot sunshine slanting in from the open doorway, fading as it fanned across the cement; and from the electric bulbs around the make-up mirror in Glory's trailer dressing-room.

It was hot everywhere today; densely hot and smoggy outdoors; only a little less so where Glory and her agent Maxie Weiss were sitting in front of her trailer on two wooden chairs. Glory's make-up was caked with sweat, for she had been working for three hours, rehearsing dance numbers; or standing about waiting in the excruciating boredom of film-making while other members of the cast rehearsed, or while the choreographer conferred endlessly with the director, the assistant director, the musical director, the dance coach, the man in charge of the extras, and his and their assistants. The tower of pink-blonde hair, though skewered to her head with innumerable pins, had begun to fray at the edges; her rehearsal clothes (black tights and loose sleeveless white top) were wrinkled and damp.

She sat in the naturally graceful pose of a dancer, one leg tucked under her, the other pointed out along the floor, drinking from a Thermos bottle a health-food drink called Frozen Tiger's Milk. Maxie was eating two pastrami sandwiches which had been wrapped in waxed paper; he looked hot, fat, and worried. He would have been lunching at Scandia, an air-conditioned restaurant near his air-conditioned office on Sunset Strip, and Glory would have been at the studio lunchroom, if they had not had to confer about a crisis.

The trouble had all started yesterday. It had been a bad day for Glory, an unlucky day. While she was eating breakfast, her girl friend, a starlet named Ramona Moon, had called up to warn her that Pluto was square with Neptune in her fourth house and she ought not to engage in any new or important professional ventures. Also she should avoid all occasions that might lead to serious emotional conflict; in fact about the best thing she could do would be to get right back into bed and stay there. Glory was not, like Mona, a follower of astrology; all the same, it would have been better if she had listened to her.

The first thing that happened was that she broke off one of her finger-nails starting the T-Bird. The traffic on the way to the studio was hell, and when she got there Roger, the best make-up man, was out sick. Then, while they were waiting around between takes, Petey Thorsley, a little dancer who was playing one of the other natives of Nemo, came over. He leaned on the back of a chair, in his green rubber costume with pink polka-dots and webbed hands like a duck, and remarked to Glory that Dr. Einsam had been seen eating cheesecake in Zucky's out in Santa Monica with a brunette, and what was the story? 'You tell me, don't ask me,' Glory said, thinking that Mona had been right. 'Gee, that's all I know,' Petey said, his wire antennae quivering. 'Listen, don't let it get you down. My friend said she was nothing anyhow, kind of an intellectual type. . . . Aw hell, Glory, I'm sorry.'

'That's okay, Petey, it doesn't bother me,' she had replied, manufacturing her smile.

Her real mistake had been to think that the stars were through with her after that one. She grew careless when nothing more went wrong on set the rest of the day; when she even got off early and beat some of the traffic driving home. She forgot about astrology; she had a big evening ahead.

There was a première that night of a picture call *Dancing Cowboy*, starring Rory Gunn. Rory was also the star of the musical that Glory was making now, and in which she had for the first time what might be called a second female lead, even if she did have to play it with antennae and green hands. As it was, naturally, top priority that Rory Gunn should be well disposed towards Glory, ever since the picture started Maxie had been putting out stories about how much she thought of him as an actor, and what a tremendous thrill it was for her to have the chance to play with him. For that evening he had arranged that after the showing, when Rory was on his way out of the theatre, Glory would rush up to him and kiss him in a spontaneous demonstration of her admiration; kind of kooky, but loveable, and really *sincere*. He had cleared this with the studio and with Rory's agent, and alerted the local papers and also two wire services. Glory had a new dress for the occasion, short white bouffant satin printed with pink roses, and she had borrowed a white mink stole from the studio. So it was all set.

Rory Gunn came out of the theatre first, right on schedule, taking it slow and giving the crowd behind the ropes a good look at his profile. Glory was close behind him, but at the door of the lobby she held back a couple of seconds, waiting for a good clear space to open up between her and the photographers. Then she stepped out, saw Rory, did a big take—excitement, adoration—and began to run.

She had waited a moment too long. As she approached Rory, a girl in the crowd, one of his fans, broke through the police line and also started racing towards him. They got to the star about the same time, and Glory stepped in front of the kid, but before she could open her mouth to speak this juvenile delinquent put her hand in Glory's face and gave her a violent push. Glory staggered back on her three-inch pink satin heels; tripped, screamed, and fell on her ass on the sidewalk, with a noise of ripping cloth. From this position she saw the girl fling her arms around Rory Gunn and kiss him passionately, while he just stood there looking dumb. Without stopping to think, boiling with fury, Glory scrambled up in the ruins of her dress, one shoe off, limped forward, and slammed the kid in the jaw. Even as the blow went home she knew she had made a terrible mistake; she heard a louder howl rise from the crowd and the flash bulbs popping, like all Mona's unlucky stars machine-gunning her down together.

Maxie had done what he could to mop up the mess. First he got the girl back into the lobby and started talking to her; come on, after all, he told her, Glory is a fan of Rory Gunn's same as you are; you ought to appreciate what she felt like when you shoved yourself in like that; beside you ruined her new two-hundred-dollar dress for her. It went over pretty well: at least the kid stopped crying, and Maxie got a taxi around to the stage door and sent her home before newspaper guys could get to her again. In the morning he ordered two lots of flowers delivered to the kid's house: some daffodils and a whole lot of other spring stuff from Glory, and three dozen red roses from Rory Gunn. Of course Maxie couldn't kill the story—but he spoke to the guys, giving them pretty much the same line: that Glory was so stuck on Rory Gunn and his marvellous performance in *Dancing Cowboy* that she just saw red when anybody got in her way. This story had appeared in the morning papers which lay about on the floor at Maxie's and Glory's feet. As he said now, it could have been a lot worse, even the photos.

'Uh-uh,' Glory uttered. 'Listen, thanks for everything, Maxie,' she added in a dull, throaty voice, and drank some Tiger's Milk. 'You're a doll.'

'That's okay. At least you appreciate.' Maxie wiped his face and began stripping the crusts off half a sandwhich. 'I wonder should I check up on that kid again this afternoon, how she's feeling, is she okay?'

'No,' Glory said. 'Let's drop it.'

'Maybe you're right. I sent flowers already; we don't want to start a correspondence.'

'Yeah. Besides, she hit me first,' Glory pointed out, not for the first time.

'She's a fan,' Maxie said. 'It doesn't make any difference what she did. You can't sock a fan. Also she's only fourteen years old. A kid.'

'Yeah, well, shit: how was I supposed to know that? You tell her next time she wants to push somebody in the face bring her birth certificate.'

Maxie winced. It always bothered him when Glory's language became too vulgar; he was trying to put her across as basically a sweet kid. He shifted around and sat sideways in his chair, facing her. 'Something else I got in my mind,' he said. 'I want to suggest a new image. We got to black out this picture you don't like fans. I thought of a gimmick this morning we could use, maybe. I want to put out a release—how does this sound?—Glory Green, now working in Superb's big new musical, etcetera, has a very *personal* relationship to her growing number of fans all over the world. Glory reads every day all the letters she receives, and she says she picks up lots of acting tips and good advice about her career from the girls and boys who follow her pictures: how does that sound?'

'Okay,' Glory said listlessly.

'Swell. Also I thought I'd call up Camilla at *Screen Scoops*, offer we could give her an exclusive. Maybe she can send somebody over this weekend and get some pictures. Like an example, I see you sitting at your antique writing-desk, nice outfit, serious expression, big piles of mail, dictating to your secretary. I like that.'

'Okay,' Glory repeated. 'My secretary? You think I should have a secretary? Don't you think that looks kind of too snooty?'

'Oh, nah. Everybody has a secretary. Liz Taylor has a secretary. Look at it this way: it shows how you're real serious about your responsibilities; it's like your business, these fan letters. I want to build up a nice picture. Anyhow, you got to get a secretary to answer the mail.'

Glory put the Thermos down and, turning her head slowly, looked at her agent through her fog of depression. 'Aw, Maxie,' she said. 'Do we really have to play this scene? I don't think I can make it.'

'Don't aggravate yourself. It'll be no trouble.' Maxie registered Glory's expression, and sought its probable cause. 'Hey, you had a conversation with Iz this morning?' he asked. 'Maybe he called you.'

Glory shook her head. 'Why should he call me? He's got nothing to talk to me about,' she said in a strained voice. 'He doesn't give a shit what happens to me.'

'Aw, Glory, baby. He's calling you all the time already. This last month he's phoned you eight, ten times.'

'Theven times,' she corrected him. 'Exactly theven times.'

'That's what I mean. He's obviously carrying the torch. And look at you: six months, and you're still very involved emotionally. I don't understand. Next time he phones, why don't you be a little nice to him?'

'That's how you thee it,' Glory said. She opened her mouth to relate Iz's latest betrayal, but could not bring herself to do so, and remained silent, staring into the dark spaces of the sound stage.

'Incidentally,' Maxie said, following his own train of thought. 'I spoke to Bo Habenicht this a.m.' Bo was Rory Gunn's agent. Maxie waited for Glory to ask 'Yeah?' As she did not, he continued. 'Rory's happy as a kid about the statement you gave. You know it's all gravy for him, that scene. Also he really appreciates your compliments. He wants to take you out some time this week, maybe tonight if you can make it.'

'You mean you and Bo want Gunn to take me out,' Glory said as flatly as was possible for her. This 'commercial socializing', as he called it, was one of the things Iz picked on most about her profession. 'What's the matter with him, doesn't he know I'm married yet?'

'Aw, come on now.' Maxie laid his sandwich down on its waxed paper. What with the trouble last night and his nervous stomach (he had something inside there that was probably planning to be an ulcer) he had got practically no sleep. But this was his job; he gathered his forces. 'What's the difference to you? All I'm asking is you should sit a table with Rory an hour or so in a couple of night spots. I'm not suggesting to spend a weekend with him.'

'With that fag? You better not. That guy's so minty he gives me the creeps.'

'Baby, you got to think of the publicity angle. If you show around town with Rory a couple times, all this trouble could blow over; it even could be to your advantage. Also, the studio would like it. How do you think it's going to look to them, you turn down a date with Rory Gunn? You should be flattered.'

Glory paid no attention to this hard sell, but continued with her own thoughts. 'I'll bet that's the first time in the fruit's life he ever had two women really fighting over him. No wonder he was stunned.' She gave a short laugh.

With a grating noise, the sliding door to the building slid open behind them. The strip of smog and sunlight widened across the floor, and a party of five or six new starlets entered the sound stage, accompanied by a minor studio executive named Baby Peterson, who was showing them over the lot.

'Glory, baby!' he called out. 'Hey, c'mon over here, girls! I want you to meet a kid who's really making it.'

Squeaking and tripping over the electric cables, the starlets crossed the floor towards Glory. They were all very young, more or less beautiful, and immensely got up, with laquered hair, nylon eyelashes, and layers of petticoats—exquisite dolls, dressed for a party by some little girl too old to play with dolls. One by one they held out their pink, sharp, manicured hands to Glory while Baby told her their brand-new studio names.

Glory responded politely. Four years ago she had been a kid like these; she had been through all it had taken to get them here and all they were about to be put through. They were the usual assortment —a couple of brunettes, one sultry and the other the ladylike type; a redhead who moved like a dancer; and some blondes of varying shades, at whom Glory looked hardest because there was a remote chance that one of them might be competition some day.

'And this is Maxie Weiss, one of the best agents in the business, or should I say the best, baby?' Peterson gave Glory a quite meaningless wink. It was unknown whether he was called 'Baby' because of his predilection for this epithet, or whether it was a nickname retained from his childhood, an era now some distance away. Detractors claimed that Baby was really over sixty; he admitted variously to fifty and forty-five, but dressed and deported himself like an extremely young man or boy. He had a deep tan and very white teeth, and wore a seersucker suit, perforated shoes, and some well-made artificial hair.

'And how're you, Glory; how're you doing today?' he asked noisily, meanwhile putting his arm round one of the blondes and pinching her haunch in a friendly way. 'Is the sun smiling on you?' It had sometimes been suggested that Baby had his dialogue written for him cheap by hack writers that had been dropped by the studio.

'Just fine, Baby.' Of course it was impossible that Baby had not seen the papers this morning. He would not speak about the brawl in front of these kids, but the look he gave her was greedily searching under the smile and the tan. Glory certainly pulled a boo-boo last night, it said. Is she cracking up, maybe? Is she already on the way out? 'How're you feeling yourself?' she counter-attacked, turning a sexy smile on and then fading it off, like an electronic door opening and closing in a supermarket.

'Ah, I'm in great condition. I was working out in the gym two hours this morning.' To demonstrate his vigour, Baby grabbed another one of the starlets, this time the redhead, with his spare arm, and squeezed her with some difficulty to his chest. 'I'm ready for anything!' This time he winked at Maxie.

'Isn't he a great guy, huh!' the blonde said, rubbing against Baby. He pinched her again, in gratitude.

'Well, got to get back to work,' he added in a heavily kidding voice. 'It was really fine to see you, baby. All right, girls.'

Squeaking, they trooped out.

'That guy makes me sick,' Glory said as they disappeared. 'He's a creep, that's what he is.'

'Aw, he's not so bad.' Maxie had returned to his sandwich. 'He's got good intentions.'

'He has my ass. Do you know he was blowing off to Petey Thorsley last week how he's screwed with two hundred and thirteen girls, or some number like that.'

'Yeah? Whew.' Maxie sighed, as when one hears of an exhausting athletic feat.

'The little blonde in pink wasn't bad-looking,' Glory went on, testing for reassurance.

'I liked the redhead better. She had a good walk.'

It was not exactly the right answer; what Maxie should have said was that none of the bunch would ever rate a look if she was around, or to that effect.

'Yeah, but did you get a look at her expression when Baby grabbed her like that. She really didn't like it.'

'Oh, she'll learn to play along.'

'Maybe,' Glory said, drinking from the Thermos.

'If she can't, there's plenty others where she came from.' Maxie's tone was quite neutral; still, it implied that the clients of a successful press agent, too, were not irreplaceable. He had the tact not to point his moral, but allowed a minute of silence for it.

'How about half a pastrami sandwich?' he asked then. 'I eat any more on a day like this, I'll get acid indigestion.'

'Uh-uh. . . . You want some Tiger's Milk? It's good for your stomach.'

'Uh, no thanks.' Maxie could not control a tone of distaste for this drink, which he knew to be made of orange juice, powered skim milk, brewer's yeast, vitamins, minerals, and raw egg. He shifted around and sat sideways on his chair again, facing Glory directly, but not looking at her.

'What I don't like to picture,' he said, beginning to fold the waxed paper around what was left of his sandwich. 'It's how Rory is going to feel when he hears you turned him down. Naturally, he's going to be hurt.' He finished wrapping the sandwich and put it into the paper bag. 'Aw yeah, he's going to think, all these nice statements she put out, she won't even have supper with me. She can't stand to talk to me for a couple hours with food. Actually she must hate me, probably.'

'Ah, Maxie, you know it's not like that,' Glory protested throatily. 'I mean, considering he's a complete lunk-head and a screaming queer, Gunn's a pretty straight guy. And he's a real dancer. He's got a style that won't quit.'

With the shrewdness born of hard experience, Maxie did not speak; he only looked at his client with a sad expression, waiting.

'You really figure he'll be all broken up if I don't go out with him?' Glory asked, in a tone half ironic, half serious.

Maxie shrugged. 'A guy like that, naturally he's sensitive. Already he's got the idea he can't make it with girls, not even as a friend. . . . An incident like this comes along and proves it, there's still less chance he's ever going to be able to relate normally.'

'Gee, you sound like my husband,' Glory said. She frowned, gazing up into the darkness above them. Maxie said nothing.

RONA JAFFE

(b. 1932)

Rona Jaffe's first novel The Best of Everything, *a glossy study of American career girls, was transferred—with equal gloss—to the screen. She writes, with deceptive simplicity, of a generation desperately playing what she has called* The Fame Game *(the title of her second novel) and this glimpse of two teeny-bopper stars joylessly at play is a trim example of her style and preoccupations. It is taken from a collection of short stories,* Mr. Right Is Dead *(1968).*

Guess Who This Is

RICHARD VIKING and Carlen Adams, brilliant inventions of the new Hollywood—you can see them on the screen whether you want to or not. If you are invited, you can see them at Hollywood parties— conspicuously young and uncomfortable among the middle-aged producers, directors and vanishing core of middle-aged stars. The young couple do not look out of place in their dinner clothes; they look as if they were on their way to the college prom. It is possible to look both superior and shy at the same time. They do. They talk to no one. Several people speak to them; the producers and directors make a point of stopping to say a few polite words to them and then move on.

Carlen and Dick know the names of most of these old people in the room, but not the names of their pictures. They have heard of Garbo (they once saw her in an art movie) and they put Gable in the same class with Hemingway: both are dead.

They are not child stars, as Mickey Rooney and Judy Garland were; they are adult stars. They do as they please. They make £200,000 apiece for one picture. They receive 10,000 fan letters a week. Before his recent marriage, a teenage magazine ran a nation-wide essay contest: WHY I WOULD LIKE TO HAVE A DATE WITH RICHARD VIKING. It drew 175,000 entries in indifferent penmanship, some enclosing snapshots.

In the reviews of their motion pictures no one has ever mentioned their acting, either to criticise or to praise it.

They live in a mansion built by a star they think they once heard of. But the guided bus tours that show visitors a distant vista of stars' homes still say 'This was once the home of Marlene Dietrich,' not 'This is the home of Carlen Adams and Richard Viking.' After all, very few teenagers have the patience for guided tours.

This October night the mansion at the top of Benedict Canyon looked like the *Queen Mary* at sea: hundreds of windows, all lighted, and everything around it black and still. It was a view never offered by the daytime tours. In the driveway, faintly illuminated from the picture window, were two small white sports cars with silver initials set into the doors: one marked HIS, the other marked ITS.

Richard Viking, the man of this house, wandered into the kitchen and searched around for the light switch. He was twenty-four years old, a little under six feet tall, with a handsome innocuous face. He was wearing long-sleeved flannel pyjamas striped black and white to simulate a prison uniform, and he was barefoot. Around his neck under the pyjamas he wore a thin gold chain bearing his wedding ring.

He found an opened box of chocolate-flavoured breakfast cereal and poured some into a soup bowl, tapping his cigarette ash on to the floor. He poured milk over the cereal, but from the first whiff he could tell the milk was sour, so he left the bowl with its contents on the draining-board and looked through the refrigerator again until he found a can of butterscotch-flavoured Metrecal which he poured into a beer stein and took with him into the den.

The den was a long mahogany-panelled room with no furniture. There was a bar built along one wall and curving around the corner of the room, perhaps fifteen feet long in all, and he set the beer stein of Metrecal on this while he searched for cigarettes. The only decorations in the den were half a dozen eight-by-ten studio head shots of Richard Viking, in silver frames, and half a dozen similar photographs of Carlen Adams. The pictures of Richard were inscribed 'To Carlen, with all my love', and the pictures of Carlen were inscribed 'To Dick, with love forever'. They were enlargements of the same photographs which Dick and Carlen sent to their fan clubs all over the country.

With two packets of cigarettes in one hand and the stein in the other, Dick left the den and walked through the living room on his way to the bedroom, which was at the opposite end of the house. The living room was enormous and empty. It was carpeted from wall to wall with thick pale-gold broadloom, spotlessly clean. The only furniture in the room was a large, pale-gold crescent-shaped couch, and against the opposite wall a colour television-stereophonic hi-fi console, which had been given to him as a present from the producer of his last picture. Above the console was a framed oil painting of Carlen standing on a hill with her hair blowing in the wind, wearing an evening gown and holding her poodle.

Carlen was lying on the bed. She was wearing black-and-white striped prison pyjamas to match her husband's, and without makeup she looked fourteen years old. She was actually twenty. She was a tiny girl with a pale, freckled, snub-nosed, frightened little face.

'How do you feel, honey?' he asked.

'Lousy. What have you got there?'

'There's nothing to eat in this house,' he said. 'For Crissakes, the milk is sour, there's nothing.' He propped up his pillows and lay on the bed beside her.

'I'm sorry, honey, I forgot to go to the store.'

'You're not supposed to *go* to the store, you're supposed to *call* the store,' he said.

'I forgot.' She started to giggle and then he laughed and hit her with the pillow.

'Stop it. I'm sick.'

'I forgot,' he said.

She hit him with the pillow for that, and he began to tickle her until she screamed and then he stopped.

'I'm bored,' she said. 'Let's call Gretchen.'

'You call her.'

She reached out lazily and dialled a number on the telephone that was on a cluttered table next to the bed. The entire bedroom was cluttered; in fact, it was the only room of the house that appeared to be lived in. It was furnished in seventeenth-century Spanish modern, and every available surface was covered with toys, dolls, teddy bears, framed photographs of Carlen and Dick, filled ashtrays, magazines, perfume bottles, ornaments, cosmetics and souvenirs. The bathroom, seen through the open door, looked like a department store make-up department. The closed toilet seat was covered with a ruffled black lace cover which their best friend, Gretchen, referred to as their 'Mr. John hat'.

Gretchen's voice, amplified and lifelike, came through a loudspeaker set into the wall above the bed. 'Hello?'

'This is the Forest Lawn Cemetery,' Dick said in sepulchral tones. 'Is this Miss Gretchen Tennieson?'

'Yes . . .?'

'I understand you have a pickup for us.'

'You must have the wrong number.'

'Is this Gretchen Tennieson?'

'Yes . . .'

'Well, you just go out in the garage and take a look. That's where it's supposed to be.'

'Carlen!' Gretchen's voice shrieked. 'Is that Dick?'

'Yes, it's us,' Carlen said.

'Who's dubbing your pictures lately, Richard?'

'Ha ha,' Dick said. 'I had you fooled.'

'Sure you did. What are you kids doing?'

'Carlen's sick.'

'Are you sick, Carlen?'

'I'm all right, I just have a headache.'

'Why don't you come over?' Dick said.

'I can't. I have a date.'

'Is he there now?'

'Yeah.'

'You both come over,' Carlen said.

'You're sick,' said Gretchen.

'I'm not that sick.'

'We have to go out and eat,' Gretchen said.

'Well, get some hamburgers or something and come over here,' Dick said.

'He wants to go out.'

'Oh, come on,' said Carlen. 'Don't be a pig. Come on over.'

'I can't. I'll talk to you tomorrow.'

'Oooh-oooh.' Dick began grunting, moaning and making obscene noises. 'Gretchen wants to be alone. Who is he, Gretch?'

'You go to hell,' Gretchen said. 'Get well soon, Carlen.' She hung up.

Dick and Carlen looked at each other and shrugged.

'What do you want to do?' Dick asked.

Carlen sighed. She tore open the packet and lit a cigarette. 'You want to play with the phone?'

'You want to?'

She brightened. 'Yah.'

He reached to the table on his side of the bed and took the phone book. He lit a cigarette, put an ashtray between them, and lay back, the opened telephone book on his stomach. 'Me first?'

'Yah.'

Dick closed his eyes and inscribed a circle in the air with his index finger. 'Mmm . . . round and round it goes, and where it stops *no-o-o*body knows. . . . Krowkalski, H. G.'

'What's the number?'

She dialled the number he gave her and they both listened, tensed and wide-eyed, as the loudspeaker on the wall sent forth the sound of the telephone ringing at the residence of Krowkalski, H. G.

'Yeah, hello.' The man's voice was tired and slightly accented.

'Is this Mr. Krowkalski?' Dick said.

'Yeah. Who's this?'

'Tell me, Mr. Krowkalski, do you go to the movies?'

'Yeah, sure. What's this, a poll?' Krowkalski sounded bored. Carlen put her hands over her mouth to suppress a giggle.

'Not exactly. Who is your favourite young actor, Mr. Krowkalski?'

'Huh?'

'Your favourite young actor. Your favourite star. For example . . . do you like Richard Viking?'

'Yeah, he's all right.'

'Have you seen his last two pictures?'

'Listen,' Krowkalski said, the voice sounding more tired, 'I got things to do. What's this about?'

'How would you like . . .' Dick said dramatically, 'how would you like to actually *talk* to Richard Viking on the telephone?'

'What for?'

'Hang up,' Dick said to Carlen. She did.

'I bet he's a plumber,' Carlen said. She lit another cigarette. 'He's watching TV. Krowkalski the plumber. Let me try one now.'

'No, I want to do another.'

'It's my turn. Come on . . . I'll do it for you, O.K.?'

'Oh, all right.' Dick flipped over a handful of pages. He closed his eyes and his pointed finger circled, hovered swooped down. 'Waterford, Mae.'

'Whee . . . that sounds like a good one.' Carlen dialled, her eyes round and bright. The loudspeaker emitted the sound of four rings.

'The television set is far away from the telephone,' Dick said. 'Hurry up, Mae; "Queen for a Day" is calling.'

'Shhh!'

'Hello.' The woman's voice was soprano and bright.

'Good evening, Mrs. Waterford,' Carlen said sweetly.

"*Miss* Waterford. Yes?'

'Miss Waterford, do you go to the movies?'

'In this town? What a question.'

'Oh, then you must have see all the latest pictures.'

'Who is this?'

'I'd just like to ask you a few question, if I may,' Carlen said.

'I'm used to questions,' Miss Waterford said gaily.

'Well . . . do you like Richard Viking?'

'Richard Viking. . . . He's one of those young kids, isn't he?'

'He's the biggest new young male star.'

'Star!' Mae Waterford said with contempt. 'All those no-face kids are alike to me; I can't tell one from the other. Oh, yeah, he's the one married to that Carolyn what's-her-name, I remember. *Star!* I'll tell you a *star*. John Garfield, that was a star. He had a face, at least; you knew who he was. I may have been only a character woman, but a lot of people knew *my* face if they didn't know my name, and I worked with some *real* stars, and I can tell you—'

Carlen hung up.

'Boy!' Dick said. 'Whew!' He turned up the collar of his pyjamas and shuddered:

'Did you ever hear of her?' Carlen asked. 'I didn't.'

'Old bitch. John Garfield . . .' he mimicked in a falsetto voice. 'I'll tell you a *star*. That Carolyn what's-her-name . . . let's try another number, *Carolyn*.'

Carlen hit him on the side of the head with her clenched fist.

'Hey! You'll ruin the profile.'

'You haven't got one,' she said.

'Yeah, I forgot. No face. Shall we find another peasant to give a thrill?'

'Your turn.'

'We'll try a nice, solid American family. Mmm . . . MacBrosnan, Robert L.'

Carlen dialled the number and the two of them straightened up against their pillows. After a moment a young-girl voice answered.

'Mrs. MacBrosnan?' Dick said.

'No, it's Janie. Who's this?'

'Miss Janie MacBrosnan?'

'Yes . . .'

Dick winked at Carlen. 'Tell me, Janie . . . do you like to go to the movies?'

'Sure.'

'And do you have a favourite male star?'

'Uh huh.'

'Who is it?'

'Well . . . Paul Newman. Um . . . do you want two?'

'Go right ahead.'

'Well . . .' There was an exhaling of breath. 'I just love Richard Viking.'

The cigarette she was holding burned Carlen's fingers and she dropped it on the sheet with a shower of sparks. She was still slapping them out when Dick went on.

'Janie, how would you like to actually *speak* to Richard Viking? On the telephone.'

The girl giggled. 'Huh?'

'I mean it,' he said.

'I'd love to,' she said shyly.

'Well, Janie . . .' Dick said, 'suppose this was Richard Viking talking to you right now . . .!'

'Huh?'

'Isn't my voice familiar?'

'I—don't know.'

'You said you just love Richard Viking. Well, this *is* Richard Viking.'

There was a silence. 'Oh, sure,' she said finally.

'It *is*.'

'Really? The real Richard Viking?'

'Of course.'

'Well . . . how come?' the girl asked, and giggled again.

'I can see you still don't believe me. All right, do you know who Richard Viking's wife is?'

'Sure. Carlen Adams.'

'Is Carlen Adams also one of your favourite movie stars?'

'Sure.'

Dick prodded Carlen on the leg with his bare toe. He nodded at her and pointed to the phone.

'Hello, Janie,' Carlen said softly.

'Hello . . .?' The voice from the loudspeaker was hushed, awed.

'Janie'—Carlen said, and now her voice was sure, louder, warm with generosity—'*Guess who this is!*'

147

JULIAN MACLAREN-ROSS

(1912–1964)

Julian Maclaren-Ross was a Soho celebrity (invariably sporting a clove carnation, gold-topped cane and dark glasses) whose cultivated air of indolence concealed a high capacity and appetite for writing of all sorts. He produced novels, short stories and journalism (including film criticism for Penguin New Writing*). For a time he wrote film scripts alongside Dylan Thomas and his tales of life on the raffish side of British film production—these stories come from* The Funny Bone *(1956)—have a wry authenticity. Maclaren-Ross died in 1964, with his final book,* Memoirs of the Forties, *uncompleted.*

Adventures In Film

(1) Getting into Pictures

ONE DAY a year or two ago I happened to be glancing idly through a ciné weekly in a barber's shop when I was confronted by a photograph of a well-known producer sitting at his desk in an attitude of dejection, his hair suitably dishevelled, the floor all around piled high with plays in typescript, novels in their dust-jackets, and rejected scenarios in a tattered condition.

'THE STORY'S THE THING' was the caption running in large type above the picture of the despondent executive: for the past six months, according to the article printed below, he had been trying without success to find a suitable screen-subject; everything else was fixed: studio-space, distribution-guarantee, stars under contract, finance ready for release: the whole bag of tricks in fact. But—no story; so he couldn't proceed.

I turned the page; the next article dealt with an identical theme: this time it was actually written by a producer *and* director, whose name was a Household Word. He too was at his wits' end for material: 'serious' writers, he deplored, took no interest in the medium; the standard of MSS. submitted fell far below that of the average published novel or play performed upon the stage; above all, they were not written 'visually', with cinematic requirements in mind.

My heart went out to these unhappy men in their plight: by the time my turn in the chair came and the fibrous towel was tucked in round my neck I had determined to help them. One of my earliest ambitions had been to write for the films; during the war I had been employed for that purpose by a documentary company; in a drawer at home lay a full-length feature-script, written primarily for the screen and overflowing with visual content. The plots of books marked down long ago as ideal for cinema adaptation; fragmentary scenes; snatches of dialogue: actual camera-angles surged up from my subconscious and swirled dizzily in montage through my head—at the moment being held down by the barber's ruthless Cypriot hand. Obviously I was the answer to the problems of these distressed impresarios; nor was my philanthropic desire to come to their aid unmixed with recollections of the fabulous sums which producers were reputed to pay for film rights; for, as usual, I was not overburdened with ready cash.

So, on leaving the hairdresser's, damp, shorn, and smelling of aromatic lotion, I at once entered a telephone-box and rang up the first producer, since his need seemed the most urgent.

'Sorry, Mr. Samuelson is down at the studio today,' an apathetic feminine voice informed me.

'Couldn't I contact him there?' I asked.

'If you have an appointment.'

'No, I meant by telephone.'

'Mr. Samuelson is allergic to the telephone, and he never sees anyone except by appointment.'

'It's about a story,' I said, playing what I believed to be my trump-card. I was evidently mistaken. Before, the voice had sounded merely bored; now, a perceptible note of contempt insinuated itself. 'Oh, I thought you wanted Mr. Samuelson himself. Just a moment, I'll put you through to the Scenario Department.'

A series of rapid clicks, one of which almost burst my ear-drum; then another voice, also female, but brusque to the point of incivility: 'Script editor speaking.'

'I have a story that might interest Mr. Samuelson. I believe he's looking for one.'

'The department's always looking for stories. Just send in a preliminary outline, typed, on a postcard. That will be sufficient for us to judge. If it shows promise we'll get in touch with you in due course. Good-bye.'

'Wait a second,' I said; 'this is a full shooting-script.'

'Haven't time to read 'em, I'm afraid, unless you're somebody frightfully well known. What d'you say your name . . .? Maclaren-Ross? Oh. Well, outline, synopsis, skeleton-treatment, full story-treatment, master-scene, that's the procedure. Shooting-script prepared by the director himself, if and when appointed. Not an orginal, is it?'

'Yes.'

'Originals considered only when submitted through a recognized and reputable agency. Inflexible company rule. Sorry.'

'But I've just read an article saying Mr. Samuelson's desperate for stuff.'

'Publicity Department's pigeon, that: not mine. Good-bye.'

The receiver clicked down decisively. I waited a minute for my annoyance to abate before dialling my second string: the Household Word. In the article signed by him his ready accessibility had been strongly emphasized: in frequent interviews that I'd read, this quality had also been stressed, together with insistent references to the lack of formality characteristic of him. I was certain that, in his own interests, he would listen to reason. Recalling my experience with editors, I foresaw already the invitation to lunch, the post-prandial rounds of cognac, the story retailed in synopsis over the coffee: 'Yes, that sounds the stuff, old boy. Just push it along and we'll get it done. As for the fee . . .'

'I don't,' I said, 'want to speak to his secretary, nor to the script-department, but to HIM in person. Is that clear?'

'Half a tick, sir. I'll connect you right away . . .'

'HIS personal secretary speaking.' (Female, undoubtedly, but dulcet and soothing this time. Dressed for a cert in something clinging and soft.) 'Can I help you at all?'

'By putting me on to HIM,' I said implacably.

'HE's out just at present, and I'm not sure HE'll be back this afternoon. But I can give you HIS private number at home; if you ring about seven you're sure to get HIM . . .'

On the stroke of seven I was again spinning the dial. A deep contralto answered: 'HIS personal secretary speaking.'

'Surely not the one I talked to this afternoon?'

'Oh no. That would be Miss Sims at the office. I'm HIS *home* secretary, so to speak.' (A low, gurgling laugh.) 'Unfortunately HE's left for the week-end. If you could give me a message . . . oh, a *story*!

But that's wonderful, the poor lamb doesn't know which way to turn for one. Best thing you can do is to write HIM a letter, and I'm sure HE'll ring you back Tuesday morning . . . yes, I'll see HE gets it directly HE comes in.'

But on Tuesday my telephone did not ring at all. Nor on Wednesday or Thursday. On Friday I rang the dulcet voice at the office. 'I'm afraid HE is week-ending in Paris . . . No reply to your letter? But that's most extraordinary . . . very unlike HIM *indeed*. Perhaps it never got there at all: lost in the post . . . most unreliable, the mails, nowadays. If you care to write again, though, and bring it down by hand, I can guarantee HE'll have it first thing on Wednesday when HE returns . . . Oh, you *will*? That's *very* kind: I do apologise for the trouble you've been put to . . .'

So once again I shoved it all down on paper: the names of the books I'd written, my documentary experience, agreement with the views expressed in HIS article, request for a brief interview; and enclosed the letter with a copy of my script, for which I obtained a receipt from the commissionaire: HIS secretary being out to lunch at the time of delivery.

No immediate reply came to that either. Meanwhile, in the columns of the ciné weekly, Mr. Samuelson continued to tear his hair for lack of stories; I wrote to the staff-reporter relating my own experience, but received no acknowledgement: then to the editor of the paper, with similar result. Instead, another article by HIM appeared, expressing HIS grief that the appeal HE made to writers had met with so singular a lack of response; I telephoned the office and was told by an entirely new secretary—who denied all knowledge of my letter and typescript—that her employer was away on a pleasure-cruise and not expected to return for several weeks.

Three months later a bulky package was delivered to me, wrongly addressed and re-forwarded at least twice through the dead-letter office. Inside was my script, removed from its spring-binder, roughly tied together with tape, and stained abundantly with tea and lipstick, accompanied by a typewritten note as follows:

DEAR MR. McCALLUM ROSE,—We are returning herewith your script which, addressed erroneously to HIM, eventually found its way to this Department. We regret that HE is too busy personally to read scenarios submitted by unknown authors, even in the rare event of these being recommended by a recognised literary agent; and though, in our opinion, your script shows ability above the average, we are not only provided with material sufficient for some time to come, but HIS personal preference is for works whose popular appeal has already been demonstrated by their circulation in volume form, rather than for plays written specially for the screen, whose chances of success would necessarily be of a problematical nature.

Yours very truly
ISOLA VAN DEN BOSSCHE
(President, Scenario Selection Board)

(2) The Shoestring Budget

THE LIFT was out of order: Pyrotechnic Pictures on the very topmost floor, behind a ground-glass panel blackly engraved with the Company's name and partly obscured by the shadow of many mackintoshes hanging from within. The anteroom beyond was crowded with persons of both sexes; a typewriter stopped clattering long enough for a sleek young woman with black hair centre-parted to frown up at me and say: 'Casting Director's down the studio, and anyway we're full up for now. Sorry.'

I said: 'Mr. Deepcar's expecting me, if you'll tell him I'm here.'

The aspirants to stardom glared round with expressions of indignation and dislike: the secretary made a tentative display of teeth, still uncertain that I wasn't an actor trying to get past by a trick. She said: 'Wing Commander Deepcar?'

'If that's his rank.'

'Well there's two of them—cousins, you see. Dennis is Pilot-Officer Deepcar. I think the Wing Co's what you want—he produces!'

As if to symbolize an English summer, a ray of sunshine split the rain-clouds, spotlighting the thickset Raff-moustached young man who rose, in shirt sleeves, from a swivel chair in the inner office, offering a pew and a fag with two waves of his freckled hairy hand.

'Neville's the name, o' boy,' said the Wing Co., heartily disclaiming any more formal mode of address; 'Out of the Service now, mercy beaucoup all the same.' His eyes, by no means devoid of native shrewdness, narrowed slightly as the removal of my raincoat revealed a corduroy jacket: *Bohemian, artistic, impractical,* he was clearly thinking; it would shortly be my duty to disabuse him of this latter notion.

The Wing Co. went into his spiel without further ado: he and his cousin Dennis had both read stuff of mine, and they wondered if I'd any original stories suitable for filming. Not scripts: just a few lines on paper. Synopsis form. Give the general outline, see? Then, providing the Distributors approved, I'd be asked to do a short treatment: scenes, sample dialogue, that sort of thing. 'And then' he said, 'a Full Treatment, a Master Scene Script, and a Shooting-Script—always providing the Distributors approve, naturally. In fact, they really decide what's what, and not you at all.'

'Well,' the sun was quite strong now, and the Wing Co. shifted uncomfortably, 'no producer's independent these days, o' boy. You can't make a movie without a distribution contract, now be reasonable, can you?'

'*I* can't make movies at all, unfortunately. No capital. And talking of money, how much would you pay? Supposing my synopsis went over big in Wardour Street, I mean?'

Deepcar gulped. He'd plainly not expected this. The persuasive smile he hurriedly assumed looked, in consequence, more like a cunning leer, or the involuntary grimace caused by a sudden twinge of toothache. Well, actually, o' boy, they expected writers to take a gamble with them in that respect. With this shoestring budget they were operating on, it just wasn't possible to lash out big sums simply for stories. Oh, admitted—no story no picture; only, let's face it, a story by itself had no star-value: 'less it was by Shakespeare or Greene or Balchin, or some wizard bloke like that', and they'd never raise the ante for any of those. 'You could always ask them to gamble with you,' I said.

'I can see you've a sense of humour, ha ha,' Neville Deepcar said. 'Seriously though, what else can we do, case like yours? If you'd written some plays now, it'd be a different cup. Got a great respect for the Drama, these Wardour-Street blokes. Take that play of Dennis's—they fairly ate it up.'

'Your cousin, Pilot-Officer Deepcar, is a dramatist?'

'No no, it's a script he heard on radio, had a copy somewhere, now what the heck's it called?' The door opened and a breezy blond chap grinned round it pointing a pipe like a pistol: obviously back from his midday pint. 'Lawfully deceased,' he said.

'*Lawfully Deceased* of course, what a man, what a memory! Shut the door, Dennis, join the fold; I was just thinking—suppose we briefed Julian here to do the script? Might even manage spot cash for once—how'd that suit, Julian o' boy?'

'How much spot cash?' I asked.

'Depends on what we've to pay for the rights,' the Wing Co. said.

'Well, let me know when you've got them.' With this I started to rise, but Dennis Deepcar intercepted me. 'Just wait while I give you the gen, really hot effort, happened to listen-in one evening, there's this wizard item coming over. Type's been dead seven years, see? Brown job, bought it in the war, only he's not actually dead at all, War Office made a bullock, he'd just lost his memory for a bit. Then, *bingo*! suddenly it all comes back to him, hops a crate, England, home and beauty—what's he find? Missus married another bloke meantime, real Gremlin type the new hubby, just after the dough that's all. But what's this poor perisher to do: been declared dead, R.I.P. past seven years, legally he's gone for a Burton. Now, hold it! here comes the cleverest part . . .'

'Murder,' I said resignedly. 'He plans to kill wife and husband, and the law can't do a thing because he's legally dead. Right?'

'Oh, you heard it, did you? Then you'll admit it's tops, bang on, right up your street too, eh?'

I couldn't have agreed less. Nor did I really expect to hear from the Deepcars again after the interview I've just described. But there I was wrong. During the following weeks Dennis called up several times, his excitement mounting progressively at each separate stage: negotiations were afoot; author being tricky; agent bluffing; distributors ready to sign: then—crescendo—they'd got the rights at last, when could I start on the script? The fee? Ah, not Dennis's pigeon, that: the Wing Co'd take it from there. 'Neville speaking, can't go higher than a century I'm afraid, well one-fifty perhaps, but that'd be the absolute ceiling. Half in advance? Why have a heart, o' boy, you must be Scotch. Bit down on delivery, yes, but half . . . Oh well, we'll go into a huddle, see what can be done, hang on till you hear from us.'

Again I expected to hear no more, and for three months I was right. Then my phone rang and a faintly Cockney voice said: 'Julian Rose? . . . What d'you mean—not exactly? . . . Oh, Ross is it, must have got the name muddled somehow. Well, Ross, this is Mister Boscobel. Pyrotechnic, you know. I'm to direct *Lawfully Deceased—You Can't Hang Me,* it's called now—and there's some work needs doing on the script . . . What's that? Money in advance? Well the Deepcars aren't here right now, have to talk to 'em later . . . Oh, and catch a cab over, will you—this is urgent!'

Mister Boscobel was younger than the Deepcars and not a R.A.F. type: more like a Company Office Corporal who'd been an insurance clerk in civvy street. Blue suit, suéde shoes, polished black hair and evasive eyes. He pushed a bundle of roneoed typescript across his desk with the stem of an unlit pipe and said: 'Now here's the provisional job. Pretty sound, only the dialogue's bit slow in patches. That's what we want you to tighten up, little job anyone can do really, take it on myself If I'd the time, only we go on the floor in a fortnight's time and I'm too pushed.'

'Who,' I asked him, 'is Gaylord Lennox?' That was the name on the screen-play. 'Gaylord?' said Mister Boscobel. 'Oh, he wrote a play couple of years ago, Sunday performance, surprised you've not heard of him, as Dennis says you write yourself . . . They were thinking of having you do the whole script at one point, but I felt we ought to get somebody a bit more experienced—with dialogue, I mean. Gaylord's a great pal of mine, actually.'

'Yet it's his dialogue that's weak, you say, and from the lines I'm reading here you seem to be 100 per cent right. Why doesn't he revise this himself?'

'Well matter of fact he reckons it's perfect as it stands—refused to alter anything. You know how these artists are: temperamental-like.' At this, there was a tramp of feet next door and both the Deepcars entered. 'Ah, Julian, glad you and Bill have got together, we figured you were just the job to help us out. Only needs a line changed here and there, piece of cake, do it in a couple of days easy, and we're prepared to pay out all we can . . .' 'Such as?' I said. Neville's eyes narrowed: 'Tenner do you?' 'Deepcar,' I said gently, 'if, as I suspect, this dialogue has to be rewritten entirely, what's the most you'll run to?' Neville rubbed his chin. 'Bad as that, eh?' 'If not worse,' I said. 'Now I'll take this stuff away and read it over lunch; we'll meet back here by three. Meantime you'd better have a ways-and-means palaver, if you expect to start shooting in a fortnight.' Neville turned to look at Boscobel whose glance became more evasive than ever under his producer's direct stare. 'Bill,' the Wing Co. said slowly, 'I believe your chum Gaylord's made a bellows of this script.'

He had. On the dot of three, with them all assembled in the office, I said: 'Bad news, I'm afraid, blokes. The whole thing needs re-doing. Not only dialogue—though that's some of the worst I've ever read —but the complete script: scenes, situations, everything. You're welcome to get another opinion if you like, but that's mine and I'm sticking to it.' Neville looked again at Boscobel: 'Bill,' he said, '*I'll talk to you later* . . . You too, Dennis,' and turning to me: 'How about twenty-five, o' boy— or do I hear a deathly hush.' 'You do,' I said. 'Double it.' 'Couldn't we knock it off Gaylord's fee?' said Dennis. 'N.B.G.,' said his cousin. 'We're bound by contract. My godfathers, another fifty quid!' 'And a proper dialogue credit,' I said. Boscobel looked up. 'Gaylord'll never stand for that,' 'Won't he?' said Neville. 'Why he won't even be *sitting* when I've done with him. . . . Script in four days, Julian: fifty in cash?' 'On the desk,' I said; 'Friday three o'clock.' 'Boy, you've saved our lives,' Neville told me, turning grimly towards Boscobel as I went out.

But on Friday at three, the office was empty except for the black-haired secretary, who smiled up at me as I stood before her, with the completely rewritten script in hand. 'Oh yes, just leave it on the desk, will you? Sorry they couldn't be here today, but actually something rather urgent cropped up and they'd to rush off in a flap. Neville said you were to drop the script and when he'd read it, he'd get in touch . . . were you looking for something?' 'Yes, a cheque. Or, rather, cash. Didn't he give it to you?' 'No, I'm afraid not . . . expect he means to send it on if the stuff's suitable and Mister Boscobel's passed the script, you know.' 'Unfortunately,' I said, 'he won't have that opportunity until I've been passed the money.' 'But, Mr. Maclaren, this is outrageous! The Wing Commander's instructions were . . .' I closed the office door carefully and continued on down the stairs with the script under my arm. The lift was still out of order and there were seven flights of stairs all told.

That night the Wing Co. rang up. 'Look here, m'lad, you don't do yourself any good behaving like this . . .' 'Deepcar,' I said, 'if you bring the dough round tonight, I'll still let you have the script for fifty. Tomorrow it'll have gone up ten.' 'Be reasonable, o' boy—where d'you think I'd get fifty this time of night?' 'Bargain's a bargain,' I told him. 'But,' he wailed, 'how do I know the script's okay?' 'It couldn't be worse than the one you had, or the play it's adapted from, and anyway that's your funeral. Take it or leave it, chum: I'll call in the morning and the sixty had better be there—no cheques.' 'This, I suppose,' the Wing Co. said bitterly, 'must be what they call the turn of the screw.'

I got my sixty quid right enough; and presumably Mister Boscobel passed the script, for the film was released a year later as a 'B' feature *(written by GAYLORD LENNOX, after a radio play by DUNSTAN GOUGH:* and—in small letters underneath—*Additional dialogue by Ross McLaren.)* The new title was *I'll Get Away with Murder!*—one which seemed particularly appropriate to me after a conversation I had with another script writer in a bar: 'Know a chappie called Gaylord Lennox?' he asked. 'Hadn't heard of him meself, but seems he scripted some little "B" picture that's going the rounds; one of the big shots happened to like it and signed him up straight away, three-year contract, eighty quid a week and expenses. Well, good luck to him, I suppose. Some people seem to have it all.'

JOHN O'HARA

(1905–1970)

John O'Hara was one of the most practised and prolific of American novelists and short-story writers. He achieved instant fame with his first novel, Appointment in Samarra, *in 1934 and maintained an amazing flow of fiction, essays and plays (which, despite their lack of success, he regarded as his best work) until his death in 1970. He wrote many screen-plays, including an acrid piece about jazz musicians for the omnibus film* On Our Merry Way, *described by Henry Fonda, who played one of the musicians opposite James Stewart, as his favourite screen part. O'Hara worked in Hollywood for many years but never came to love it. 'Can You Carry Me?' comes from his collection of stories,* Pipe Night *(1946).*

Can You Carry Me?

IT WAS one of those Beverly Hills afternoons when a fire in the fireplace is a good idea. The beautiful blonde saw that right away, the moment she entered the room. 'Jesus!' she said, and hugged her bosom. She was wearing white gabardine slacks and a white gabardine blouse. Over the left bosom, stitched on the pocket, were her initials, not less than six inches high, but adding no warmth. The blouse had only half sleeves and it was unbuttoned almost to the belt of her slacks. 'Alice!' There was no answer. 'That dumb dinge,' she said.

She opened her mouth to yell again, but changed her mind. Instead she lifted a glass-and-chromium lamp that was on an end table, and set it on top of a portable push button.

Alice appeared.

'Light the fire, will you?'

'Yes, Ma'am,' said Alice. 'It did get colder, din it, Miss B?' She bent down and lighted the gas, with which all Beverly Hills fires are started. Alice stood there until the logs had caught, and Miss B pushed her out of the way so that she could toast herself. She would warm her hands and then pass them over exposed portions of her body, and she was doing this when the doorbell rang. Alice went to answer the door, and Miss B jumped to the davenport.

Alice reappeared. 'It's Mr. Confelt. He said he——'

'But of course, don't keep him waiting, Alice.' She began to get off the sofa to greet Mr. Confelt, but reconsidered and slumped back, with her knees drawn up in front of her. When he came in she stuck out her left hand, which he took, pressed, and released. 'You're punctilious,' she said.

'Well, I try to be,' he said.

'Cigarettes there, in the white pigskin box. Drinks, whatever you prefer. I'm going to have a dry sherry, but don't let that influence you.'

Mr. Confelt cackled. 'It has to be whisky or brandy to influence me.'

She smiled, and indicated the cut-glass decanters.

'Well, Miss B,' said Mr. Confelt.

'*Miss*-ter C,' she said.

'You're a-lookin' might fine, mighty fine.'

'Thenk yaw, Mr. C. I guess it must be because I—I know how to take it. I guess I have a tough hide.'

'Not from where I sit I wouldn't say so. Oh, you mean that piece Duval wrote.'

'The same,' said Miss B. 'The very, very same. I was under the impression I had a great in at your magazine, but not after I saw Miss Duval's little autobiography.'

'Well, I wouldn't exactly call it an autobiography——'

'Well, you know what I mean. The article she wrote about me. You know what I have reference to.' She reached for her sherry, raised it to her eyes, and drank it. 'Bottoms up.'

'Bottoms up, if I can make it,' said Mr. Confelt. He didn't quite, but he finished quickly. 'I think we owe you an explanation on that piece.'

The explanation took a good half-hour, and when it was concluded Mr. Confelt went from the explanation to two or three other cases of actors and actresses who had been distressed by Miss Duval's writings. This addendum continued until the last of the Scotch and the last of the sherry.

'Uh-huh,' said Miss B. 'Push that button over there, will you?'

'What button?'

'The one on that table, it has a wire—oh, wouldn't you know. That damn Ethiopian, she—I bet she turned it off in the kitchen.'

'Oh, you mean this one, under the lamp.'

'*Alice!*'

Alice appeared. 'Yes, Ma'am. More Scotch and sherry. Ice. You want more soda, Mr. Confelt?'

'Sure he does,' said Miss B. 'Well—uh—oh, yes. Well, what I was gonna do, I was gonna go the Hays office and say look here, this Confelt's writers have got to be barred from the lot. All lots. All Confelt's writers. You remember a couple years ago, how these magazines, they got in plenty of trouble, Confelt, and you know it. And you hadda show us what you were going to print beforehand. You know that.'

'Yes, that's true.'

'Well, I was gonna do that, but then I talked to Rawson and he advised me against it. Rawson said he advised me against it. He said he wouldn't do it if he was me. I. So I took his advice. I didn't go the Hays office.' She stopped and smiled to herself. 'Hello, Confelt.'

'Hello, Miss B.'

'How're you feeling?'

'Top of the world. Never better.'

'Have a nice big drink,' said Miss B.

'Don't mind if I do,' he said. 'How about you?'

'No—all right. Sure. 'Cause I'm feeling good, too. I feel top of the *world.*'

He poured her sherry and mixed a highball. She was still smiling at him. 'So, I din go the Hays office.'

He smiled.

'*But!*' she said. 'You know what I *did* do, Connie my pigeon. *I* went to my *law*yer.'

'I——'

'And I said, "Joe, let's sue those sons of bitches for a million dollars." So Joe said all right, and so that's what we're doing, Connie. We're suing you for one million smackeroos. And I'm not the only one. At least three other friends of mine are going to sue you for a million smackeroos.' She smiled and raised her glass to him.

'Now listen, Miss B. I know all that.'

'So you knew it? Well, you had a hell of a nerve then, sticking that pan of yours in this house. My house. What are you gonna do, try and con me out of it? Well, guess again, pickle face. The stuff you printed about me.'

'I wasn't here. Duval was running the magazine. I was in the hospital. You know I'd never——'

'Sure. Sure. You'd never. Oh, no. Not much. Not much. You'd never print those things about me. Only you did, see? And you're gonna pay right through that pickle nose of yours.'

'You don't have to make personal remarks,' said Mr. Confelt.

'Oh? So I don't have to make personal remarks. Now the shoe fits you you don't like it so much. You can call me a drunken bum, practically, and all that stuff about the grips and the juicers and everybody and what a laugh they get from me when I get mad at something. Well, listen, you heel. My mother reads your goddam magazine. How do you think she felt when she read that stuff? What about the sisters?'

'What sisters? I didn't know you had a sister.'

'I haven't got a sister. I mean in school. The sisters that taught me. What if they saw your goddam——'

'Oh, nuns. Well, I don't think many nuns, uh——'

'Sure I mean nuns.' Miss B had a tear or two in her eye. 'I was almost one myself, and now what would they think? I wanted to be one. I coulda been if I didn't have to go to work when I was fifteen. Fif-teen.'

The tears were now more numerous, and Miss B was sniffling. Mr. Confelt gave her a handkerchief, which she applied. He watched her, and there was only a slight involuntary motion of his fingers when she took the handkerchief down from her face and tucked it in the pocket of her blouse.

He clapped his hands. 'I've got it. Marvellous!' he said.

'What have you got?'

'See what you think of this. Now, don't get me wrong. I'll print a retraction if you want me to, but there's no story in a retraction, Miss B. *You've* given me the idea, marvellous. Listen and see what you think of this. I'll write a piece. I'll write it myself. About your childhood. How you went to this school and you were the favourite of all the nuns. Led all your classes. The most religious one in the whole school, without any question. High hopes. Then your father dies——'

'He was put in jail.'

'No. He died. He died, and some talent scout saw you in a school play and just at the right moment, because right after your father's funeral, or right before he died, this mug comes along and offers you a contract——'

'You mean Earl Carroll?'

'I *don't* mean Earl Carroll. I mean Max Reinhardt, or Gilbert

Miller. I don't give a damn who it was right now. You get this offer when you're fifteen, and the only reason you take it is because your father's investments turned out——'

'My father didn't have any investments. Listen, Connie, I'm sure I don't know what the hell you're talking about. But I do know I'm sleepy. Can you carry me?'

'Why, sure, dear,' said Mr. Confelt.

GAVIN LAMBERT

(b. 1924)

Gavin Lambert was the co-founder with Lindsay Anderson of the influential magazine Sequence *which helped to set the tone of film criticism in Britain throughout the 1940s and 1950s. He turned script-writer—most notably for director Nicholas Ray—and now lives in California whose slipping coast-line provides the title,* The Slide Area *(1959), for the collection of stories from which 'The Closed Set' is taken.*

The Closed Set

ON A hot winter's day an open truck containing a papiermâché woman about fourteen feet high drove up Hollywood Boulevard and stopped outside one of the largest movie theatres. The woman had orange hair and wore a taut black evening dress with its skirt slashed between the thighs. One leg thrust contemptuously forward in a spangled stocking. I watched four workmen carry her out of the truck and fix her to the façade of the theatre, hoisting her into position on pulleys. Later, one of them climbed a ladder to paste a long sticker below her high-heeled shoes. It said, I HATE YOU HANNAH KINGDOM.

Slogans had been going up elsewhere for a week. All over the city you drove past black billboards with I HATE YOU HANNAH KINGDOM blocked out in massive gold type. In one of the newspapers, a lady columnist wrote:

Last night I saw Julie Forbe's new picture, *The Crime of Hannah Kingdom.* You'll be seeing it soon if you know what's good for you. It's a lulu. Julie should land another Oscar for this one. I told her so at the party after the showing, and she said: 'Yes, I feel I've done justice to a great character.' Coming from Julie that means a lot, because she's a perfectionist . . .

I looked forward to seeing the film, I always enjoy watching Julie Forbes on the screen. Who can forget those emotional boxing matches in which the characters give, take and parry great bruising blows of love and rage and hate? I refer of course to the later, more heavyweight works. Julie Forbes belongs to that group of star actresses in their late forties who retain a hold on the public by dramatically changing their style every five or ten years. Just when it seems impossible for them to continue any longer, when fashion threatens to leave them hopelessly behind, they undergo some mysterious process of renewal and come back more powerful than ever. It is like the secret rejuvenation course run by a specialist in Beverly Hills. For two thousand dollars you may spend ten days in her secluded mansion. You are blindfolded most of the time, and it is said that people who emerge are not always recognized by their closest friends.

The Julie Forbes of 1927 who made her first appearance in *Look Out, Sister!* was a chorus girl with a jaunty grin and busily tapping feet. In 1933 she surprised everyone as the simple country heroine of *Life Is Like That,* shy and innocent and wronged. A few years later she wore extravagant clothes with a kind of melancholy sophistication, and smoked cigarettes through a long holder, in comedies about the idle rich. Then came an uncertain period, beginning soon after the outbreak of the Second World War. She played a famous woman doctor who went blind, and a member of the Norwegian resistance. There were rumours that she was finished. She married a businessman from San Francisco and announced her retirement. They had a son, a divorce, and suddenly a 'new' Julie Forbes appeared once more. Mature but unravaged, she presented a ruthless schemer in *For Pity's Sake,* a woman who didn't care how many lives she destroyed in her quest for . . . what? She stole other women's husbands, became rich and feared and famous, drove her enemies to drunkenness or suicide, yet she never seemed happy. It led to even greater triumphs. For *The Big Angel* she won an Oscar.

Less than a month after the ceremonies, the same story appeared under enormous front page headlines in all the newspapers. Into Julie Forbe's swimming pool, drained of water because it was being cleaned, a man had fallen; cracked his skull; died immediately. It was three o'clock in the morning. When the police arrived they found the actress, her eleven-year-old son Timmy, her private secretary Mrs. Lynch and her agent Canning Wallace, all waiting stiff and tallow-faced in the living-room. Two questions were asked at once: who was the man, and how did he fall into the pool? Miss Forbes became hysterical and couldn't answer either of them. The agent and the private secretary spoke up. The stranger was a friend of Miss Forbes, they'd had dinner together that night, he'd driven her home. He was very drunk, and when Miss Forbes asked him to leave, he refused. He wanted to go for a swim in the pool. Miss Forbes pointed out this was impossible, because the pool was empty. The stranger became very angry and insisted that Miss Forbes make arrangements to have it filled immediately. There was a quarrel by the edge. The stranger lost his balance and fell in.

The only person who could corroborate or deny this story was Timmy. The boy had been asleep and didn't wake up until he heard his mother cry out, after the man fell in the pool. The police asked him what Miss Forbes did after that. He said that she calmed down and drank a glass of brandy. This made Timmy feel thirsty, and he went to the refrigerator for some milk. When he came back, his mother was telephoning Mrs. Lynch. Mrs. Lynch said she was going to telephone Mr. Wallace. A few minutes later, both came over to the house. Why didn't Miss Forbes call the police sooner? She was too upset, mightn't you be? said Mrs. Lynch. Her shock and grief were almost uncontrollable, said Canning Wallace.

It turned out that the stranger had once been a barman at a club in Beverly Hills. Timmy said he first came to the house about a year ago. He didn't think his mother saw him very often. He drank too much, and even hit her once. The actress had given him money to start his own bar, but it didn't catch on. At the inquest, the stranger's mother appeared. She was a dressmaker in Pasadena. While Julie Forbes repeated her story, she made a disturbance and was hustled out of court. Later she told reporters that her son never drank, but the police discovered she hadn't seen him for nearly two years.

The verdict was accidental death. No harm was done to Julie Forbes's career, and *The Big Angel* drew larger crowds than ever. She paid for the stranger's funeral, but didn't go to it.

There are some fine homes in the hills which separate Hollywood from the San Fernando Valley, and they give an illusion of country living. Near the highest point I glimpsed a wide commanding view north and south, across the valley shielded by gritty mountains from the dry Mojave desert, across the city sloping down to the Pacific in an envelope of dusk. Tall trees were silhouetted against the sky, and a blue jay flew above the driveway marked PRIVATE which led off the canyon road. This driveway passed a swimming pool with an adobe guest house overlooking it, and wound through a eucalyptus grove to a mansion built round three sides of a courtyard, like a Spanish mission. In the centre a fountain played, and at the far end marble steps led up to a front door inlaid with blue and white tiles.

A butler in tails opened the door and said in a near-English accent: 'Miss Forbes would like you to wait in the living-room.' I followed him through a bare rectangular hall without windows, only soft concealed lighting on oyster-pink walls. No furniture, except for a scarlet and white chess set standing on a table, foot-high pieces arranged as if a game were in progress but would somehow never be finished.

The L-shaped living-room bore no traces of living. Everything about it was an abstraction of comfort and elegance. The walls were white except for a strip of filigreed black and gold wallpaper above the pseudo-antique fireplace, at right angles to which stood two long low black couches. Pressed flowers lay under the glass tops of white marble coffee tables. A plaster-cast pink and blue angel floated above the grand piano, suspended on a gold wire from the ceiling. There were cigarettes in little glass bowls and book matches in gold leaf covers, each one with a facsimile signature, *Julie Forbes*. The only painting was of Julie Forbes, a pastel blur about five feet tall in a frame overlaid with black velvet.

The butler asked if I'd like a drink and I ordered Scotch. As he left the room, I went to look at the painting more closely. Almost at once a voice said:

'What do you think of it?'

I turned and saw a stocky, rather bull-necked woman, thick white hair brushed back smooth and straight from her forehead, standing by the window. She must have come in from the garden.

'I painted it,' she said before I could answer, and held out a blunt hand which enclosed mine in a naturally powerful grip. 'I'm Mrs. Lynch. You didn't come with Mr. Harriston?'

'No, but he should be along any moment.'

Mrs. Lynch gave a little nod and smoothed the starched cuffs of her blouse. 'I understand you've already worked with Mr. Harriston?' She cleared her throat loudly. It was the first move in an interview, not conversation.

'Yes, on a picture that's just finished. He thought he'd like me to be on this one, if he does it.'

'*If?*' Frowning, Mrs. Lynch sat down on one of the couches. 'I think you'll find that everything's set.'

'I don't know,' I said. 'All Cliff told me was that Miss Forbes had a story she wanted him to do.'

He had told me a little more, but not much. Yesterday on the telephone. 'Can you have dinner with Julie Forbes tomorrow night?' I said I didn't know her. 'She wants me to direct a picture for her.'

'Are you serious?' 'I'm broke.' 'Where do I come in, exactly?' 'Maybe on the script.' 'Does she have one already?' 'I'm afraid so.'

Naturally I said nothing of this to Mrs. Lynch. I had already decided she was a sinister bodyguard-figure, and relations with her should be strictly formal. I went over to the french windows and admired the view.

'It's the best in the canyon,' she said as the butler came in with my drink. She ordered vodka on the rocks with a beer chaser, then asked if I'd ever met Miss Forbes. I shook my head. 'In my opinion, she is one of the truly outstanding personalities of our time.' Mrs. Lynch made a deep clearing sound in her throat again. 'And with all of that, so—so . . .' She searched for a word. 'So lovely. Why don't you sit down?'

She patted the cushion beside her. I sat on the opposite couch.

'It should be a great chance for you, working with Miss Forbes. She's a perfectionist, you know. Sometimes I think she'll wear herself out. But she's got more energy than a man.' There was an undertone of contempt in the last word. 'Have you seen *The Crime of Hannah Kingdom*?'

'Not yet,' I said.

'It's great.' She spoke in a flat businesslike voice. 'Simply great. No other word will do. She gets under the skin of things, you know. Sometimes it's . . . uncanny.'

'Have you been with Miss Forbes for long?' I asked.

'Since *For Pity's Sake*. That's nine years. She's more than an employer to me, she's a friend.'

'You live here?' I was pumping Mrs. Lynch now, and trying to appear casual.

She nodded. 'Miss Forbes offered me a suite after—after the accident. She didn't want to live alone.'

'I thought she had a son?'

'Timmy's only thirteen. That's not quite the same thing, is it?' Smoothing her hospital nurse's cuffs again, she looked up sharply at me. I realized she had given this information very deliberately, to establish her position. Now her tone changed. Regaining the offensive, she became almost inquisitorial. 'In your opinion, is Mr. Harriston truly interested in this project?'

Her methods were less subtle than mine, and probably more effective. For a moment I was taken aback. 'I'm sure he is. Otherwise he wouldn't be coming here to talk about it.'

Mrs. Lynch appeared not to have heard this. She regarded her shoes, which were heavy black brogues. 'He's a very talented director, don't you agree?'

'Very.'

'At the studio they say, "he's good but you have to watch him." ' She gave a rather bleak smile. 'Miss Forbes told me that.'

'They watch him too much, that's the trouble. He doesn't often get a chance to do what he wants.'

'I didn't mean that.' Mrs. Lynch became brusquely matter-of-fact. 'He once socked a producer in the jaw.'

I laughed. 'A friend of yours?'

'I don't know the man in question.' Her mouth tightened with disapproval. 'But it was dislocated.'

'And he couldn't speak for a week.' I nodded. 'It probably saved the picture.'

I met her small, pitiless eyes. 'He was drunk when he did it.'

'I know nothing about that,' I said.

'I'm sure you must.' It was a statement, not an opinion. 'I understand you're one of his closest friends. We also have a report from the producer of his last picture. They used to find bottles of Scotch in his desk. Of course——'

She broke off as the butler came back with her drink. 'Would you like another?' she asked me.

'Please. I drink too—or don't you have a report on me?'

She took this quite seriously. 'That would hardly be necessary.'

'If Miss Forbes is so doubtful about Cliff,' I said when the butler left the room, 'why does she want to work with him?'

'But she has no doubts at all! How could I have given you that impression?' Mrs. Lynch leaned forward and patted my knee. 'All this is just routine. As a matter of fact, she agrees with you entirely. "All that man needs is a good picture, and I'm going to give it to him." I quote her very words.'

The front door bell rang.

'That must be Mr. Harriston.' Mrs. Lynch swallowed her chaser. 'I hope you'll regard this as a friendly private talk.'

'I'm sure we both will.'

A sound of voices came from the hall. Mrs. Lynch stood up smartly, as if going on parade. 'Miss Forbes has opened the door herself, I think.'

A moment later she came into the room. The first thing I noticed was her dress: deep, flaring crimson. Like everything else about her it had a bright perfect glitter. The diamond choker round her neck. The silver sandals with jewelled toes. From the smooth legendary face, beautiful luminous cat's eyes stared out. Cut short, her blonde hair gleamed. Her skin was golden, her figure trim and pliant as a young girl's. She had been created a moment ago. There was no childhood, no past, nothing. I thought of a joke about the mortuaries in California; they supply human ashes to cannibals in the South Seas, who make them flesh by adding water. Instant people, like instant coffee. Julie Forbes, I decided, was an instant person. That must be her secret. Every few years she was reduced to ashes, then reconstituted in a new form. Different. Shining. Instant.

'So lovely,' breathed Mrs. Lynch. 'So very lovely.'

Julie acknowledged this by raising her hand. A tender smile cracked Mrs. Lynch's face, she became like a loyal subject rewarded by her sovereign after waiting below the palace balcony for hours.

Behind Julie walked a tiny black Pekinese puppy, and then Cliff with his handsome leonine head, tall, broad-shouldered, almost lumbering. She scooped up the Pekinese in her arms and held it out to us. 'This is Chen, I just bought her today. Did you know there are only six bitches of the original strain left in the world?'

Cliff didn't answer. He let Mrs. Lynch wring his hand and sprawled into a chair. Massiveness made all his moods seem heroic. When he glanced round the room, it shrank to a wretched little cage. He gave me a wink, which Mrs. Lynch noticed.

'We hear your last picture is just wonderful,' she said.

'It's just lousy.' Cliff gave the wry discontented smile that so often crept over his face, and at other times haunted it.

'That's not at all what they say at the studio,' said Mrs. Lynch.

'Cliff's an artist!' There was a slight throb in Julie's voice. She sat on the end of the couch, near his chair. 'He has tremendously high standards. I understand that so well.'

'Nobody works harder than Julie,' said Mrs. Lynch.

The butler came back. 'Get Timmy,' ordered Julie, then turned to Cliff. 'I want you to meet my son. He's a wonderful kid.'

'How old is he?' Cliff asked.

'Thirteen.' She smiled. 'Age is one thing I never lie about. I'm forty-nine.' Hands stroked her neat, perfect hips. 'I was nineteen when I made my first picture, *Look Out, Sister!* You know we ran it at the studio the other night?'

'How did it look?'

'Great.' She gave a flicker of surprise. 'A lot of those early musicals were great. Have you seen *Hannah* yet?'

Cliff nodded.

'Well?' She was fingering her choker.

'You ought to be ashamed of yourself.'

Her face showed no reaction. 'Go on.'

'It's your usual shoddy work-out of the glamorous life-wrecker who gets it all her own way till the last reel.' Cliff lay back in the chair, closed his eyes for a moment. 'I didn't find it interesting at all.'

Mrs. Lynch gasped, but Julie only picked a black puppy hair from the sleeve of her dress. 'What kind of movies interest you, Cliff?'

'Something with a bit of truth.'

She considered this, frowning slightly. 'Of course you're an artist. A very fine artist in my opinion. Frankly I don't get all this talk about truth, but then I left school in Atlantic City when I was fourteen, and that's all the formal education I had.'

'It's not a question of education.' Cliff sighed. 'If you have any idea of truth, it comes from the kind of human being you are.'

'Well, I'm a doll. Just a doll.' She found another puppy hair. 'And speaking as a human being, I believe *Hannah* has truth. Women like that exist, all over this country.'

'But you admire them, Julie. That's why your picture hasn't any truth. That's why it's repulsive.'

'Now that's a very strong word,' said Mrs. Lynch.

With a rustle of silk, Julie got up and stood by the mantelpiece, looking down at us. 'You think I admire Hannah? You must have slept through that picture. Have you forgotten the things my daughter says to me when she accuses me of snatching her boy-friend away? And what about the fire, when I lose the only man I ever really cared about—and all my property?'

'You feel sorry for her then,' Cliff said. 'You go noble. You make it like a crucifixion.'

'Don't talk that way, Cliff.' Her voice was soft and low. 'I *understand* her, don't you see? That woman has the driving force inside every woman—she wants to be loved. But she's rejected. That turns her bad. Poisons her. She gets jealous of other people who find love, and she wants to destroy *them*. The beautiful original drive in every woman is twisted in Hannah Kingdom by bitterness. It makes her hate. And it makes her very lonely.' Her eyes glistened. 'It's lonely to hate. And it's even lonelier to be hated. I believe——'

A tall, rather pale boy in a grey suit came into the room.

'Timmy!' she said. 'I want you to meet some lovely new friends of mine.'

The boy walked slowly towards us. He looked unfriendly and intelligent. The only point of resemblance to Julie lay in the eyes, dark and lustrous. He shook hands and said very formally: 'Hello, sir. Hello, sir.'

'Tell us what you've been doing today,' his mother said. 'It's vacation time,' she added, looking sharply at him. 'You can sit down, Timmy.'

He perched stiffly on the edge of a chair and pressed his lips together. 'Did you ride, Timmy?'

'Yes, I rode.'

'We have our own stables here,' Julie said. 'Timmy loves riding. What else did you do, Timmy?'

He glanced furtively at us, then stared at the floor.

'You must be able to give an account of your day, Timmy. These friends of mine are extremely interested in what you've been doing.'

'So is your mother, in case you've forgotten,' Mrs. Lynch said in a hard tone.

He didn't look at either of them. The tension was automatic; from the moment Timmy entered the room the three of them had seemed caught up in it. After a pause he said: 'I read a book.'

'What book?'

'*The Scarlet Letter*,' he answered in a mechanical tone, then looked as if he wished he hadn't.

'Did you finish it?'

'No.'

'How long did you read it for?'

'Couple of hours, I guess.'

'That's not very long. There's still most of the afternoon to account for. Did you swim?'

'Yes.'

'Can you turn somersaults in the water better now?'

'I'm improving.'

'That's good, Timmy.' His mother frowned. 'They made a movie of *The Scarlet Letter*, didn't they? What's it about?'

He looked at the floor again.

'Tell us what it's about,' said Mrs. Lynch.

Timmy drummed his fingers on his knees. 'It's by Nathaniel Hawthorne. It's about a girl in New England.'

'Go on.' Julie's voice sounded remorseless, almost vengeful. Mrs. Lynch shook out a cuff. 'Your mother wants to hear about the book, Timmy.'

'The girl gets into trouble.' He shifted in his chair. 'A priest helps her.'

'What kind of trouble does the girl get into?'

170

He hesitated. 'Steals money.'

'Why?'

'Um—she's poor and her child's starving.'

Julie gave us an anxious smile. 'You think Timmy should be reading books like that?'

'It's a classic,' I said.

'So's *Peyton Place*.' She looked grim. 'Timmy, I'd like to see that book you're reading.'

He didn't answer this, but got up. 'Nice to have met you, sir. Very pleased to have met you, sir.'

He started to leave the room. Watching him go, Julie called as he reached the door: 'I'll be up later!' He nodded over his shoulder and disappeared into the hall.

After a silence, Julie leaned towards us. 'What should I do with a kid that lies?'

Nobody answered.

'I know all about *The Scarlet Letter*. I saw the movie.'

'So did I,' said Mrs. Lynch.

'That girl gets laid by a priest. Timmy shouldn't be reading stories like that and he shouldn't be lying about it. Don't you agree, Cliff?'

'He was embarrassed because we were here. What are you after that kid for, Julie?'

'I thought you believed in truth?' She didn't give him time to answer. 'I've done a lot for Timmy. I've wanted him to have a lot of things I didn't have, like formal education. But I don't like him using education to try and make a fool out of me.'

I said: 'I think I read *The Scarlet Letter* when I was thirteen.'

'But I want to protect Timmy.' She looked steadily at me. 'I don't let him see my movies.'

'None of them?'

'I don't think it's right for Timmy to—to see me doing some of the things I do in my movies.' Her voice trembled. 'Kids are very imaginative. He might confuse me with the characters I play.'

The butler announced dinner. Julie led us round the corner of the L, through an interior tropical garden with dwarf palms and cacti and a floodlit fountain. At the far end, a door led into the dining-room. We sat on tall high-backed chairs at a long antique table. A circle had been cut in the centre, underneath the glass that covered it a single water lily floated.

Mysteriously the butler had arrived before us through another door, and stood waiting with a napkin over his arm. We ate off thick silver platters, with the hors-d'oeuvre we drank champagne and with the Beef Stroganoff claret out of blue crystal goblets. Julie beat a small Chinese gong to recall the butler as each course was finished. When we reached dessert, a tray of pears in flaming brandy, she got up. 'Excuse me, I must go and see Timmy.' Cliff and I were left alone with Mrs. Lynch, who slowly crunched a pear, then beamed with satisfaction.

She said: 'It's really great to spend an evening just shooting the breeze.'

Cliff gave her a fairly hostile look. 'Why doesn't Julie like her son?'

'She adores that boy,' Mrs. Lynch answered promptly, with no sign of surprise. 'If she seems a little strict, it's only because she's so anxious for Timmy to grow up fine and honest.'

From upstairs, we heard a door slam. I thought Julie shouted something.

'She believes the general trend of modern education is over-permissive,' Mrs. Lynch continued. 'And how can you say she's wrong, with delinquency flooding our country? We must get back to the old-fashioned methods. In my opinion they're our only hope. Did you take the book away from him?' she asked as Julie returned to the room.

Julie nodded. She sat in her chair at the head of the table and said immediately: 'You know, in June nineteen twenty-seven a train stopped at down-town L.A., and out stepped a girl called Julie Katzander. She'd had her first bit in a Broadway show which folded after two months, but there was a talent scout in the audience one night and he got her a movie contract. There wasn't anyone from the studio to meet her at the station, and she didn't know a soul in the whole mad town. When she called the studio, no one had ever heard of her. She told them she had a contract, and they'd be paying her a hundred dollars a week from now on, so they'd better take some interest. Then she took a room in a hostel, and for three months just sat there drawing her pay cheque and telling the talent scout she wasn't going to let him lay her. Whenever she called the studio, they'd say not to worry and she'd be hearing from them soon. You know, that was a pretty hard time for a nineteen-year-old salesman's daughter from Atlantic City.'

'You weren't so green,' Cliff said. 'You were a hatcheck girl in Chicago when you were sixteen, or is that just publicity?'

'Certainly not. All my publicity is true and I check it before it goes out. Furthermore, when I was seventeen I had my first pair of fishnet tights and toured the Middle West in a vaudeville show.'

She tapped the gong. Light caught a cluster of diamonds on her choker. 'I've kept those tights,' she said, 'and I'll tell you something. *I can still get into them.* Anyway, one day in September the studio sent for me and took a lot of leg pictures, and a producer liked them and Julia Katzander became Julie Forbes.'

'The rest is history,' said Mrs. Lynch.

'What else did you do in those three months while you sat around and waited?' I asked.

'That's a sixty-four dollar question. I made a mistake, boy. I got married.' Mrs. Lynch guffawed. 'He was a pianist in some bar on the Strip, and we thought we were terribly in love. Kid stuff, you know. His name was Jeff Storm, he's a famous bandleader now.' She glanced at Cliff. 'How many times have you been married?'

'Three,' he said.

She put a hand on his arm. 'We're even. If I ever marry again, it's got to be for real. Not that I regret anything—I've always got a kick out of marriage somehow, whether it's just plain old Experience or little Timmy—but after a time the whole business starts to sicken you. Do you still believe in marriage, Cliff?'

He shrugged. 'I don't believe in women.'

Her hand slid down to his wrist and held it for a moment. 'We're even again. I don't believe in men.'

After dinner, there was a good deal more conversation of this kind. If anyone ever organised a talking marathon, like the dancing and eating marathons, I am sure Julie would win it. She not only loves talking, but has an alert photographic memory that supplies her with plenty to talk about. Mainly about herself, for there is no single event of her life that she has forgotten. If she leaves something out, it is because she doesn't want to tell you. She has an extraordinary talent for remembering facts like the plots of movies and books, even the names of their characters, just as she learns the name of every technician on her set the first day of shooting, and never forgets any of them. Cliff didn't talk much, but drank steadily and listened with a kind of ironic inattention. Behind anything he said was always an implied contempt for Julie's films and Julie's talent. She responded like a piece of highly tensile steel, you could stretch it indefinitely and yet it still held brightly together. I began to wonder just how far you could bend this delicate steel.

Mrs. Lynch sat like an umpire at a tennis match, eyes switching from Julie to Cliff and back again, occasionally calling out the score with a laugh or a jocular protest. About every twenty minutes the butler silently appeared and put another drink in our hands.

It must have been three o'clock when Julie suddenly lifted the sleeping Chen from her basket and settled her on her knees. Fondling the little black head, she began to talk about her next film. 'It's time I did something new. Of course when you're a big success in Hollywood, everyone wants you to go on doing the thing that made you a success. But I've always believed in looking ahead. If you don't there comes a moment—bingo!—when Joe Public looks you in the face and says Stop Boring The Hell Out Of Me. And you're on your way out. So last week I had lunch with J.B.,' she referred to the head of the studio, 'and I told him I'd bought a fabulous story for myself and I'd like to bring it to the studio and produce it. J.B.'s crazy about the idea naturally.'

'So you're going to be an actor-manager.' Cliff slumped in his chair. 'That's a mistake, stars should never produce themselves.'

'It's only making official something that's been unofficial for years.' She watched him for a moment, eyes glittering and soft. 'Cliff, would you like to do this picture with me?' He didn't answer. 'You're a great director, Cliff. And I need you for this one.'

'What's the story?' he asked, very casual.

'You can tell it in two words.' In a low important voice, she articulated them clearly: 'Lydia Thompson.'

He looked at her with weary disgust. 'Another woman with a twisted driving force?'

'No, Cliff. Oh no.' She paused. 'Lydia Thompson is absolutely *not* Hannah Kingdom.'

She got up, walked over to the fireplace and stood with her back to it, stretching out her arms to rest them on the mantel. 'I take it you've never heard of Lydia Thompson?' She glanced at each of us in turn. We shook our heads. 'Strange,' she said. 'Lydia Thompson was a very great woman. She brought burlesque to America.'

'And vice versa,' said Mrs. Lynch.

Julie nodded. 'A hundred years ago, this woman pioneered a troupe of strippers from coast to coast. At one time,' she gave me a reproachful smile, 'the act was known as Lydia Thompson and her British Blondes.'

'No, really?' I said.

'It's authenticated. Some of the first strippers were British girls from nice Victorian families.'

'That starts to be interesting.' Cliff sat up. 'A lot of strippers are very respectable girls who get shocked by the morals of the theatre. I've met some.'

'I'll bet you have, but the important character in this story is Lydia Thompson, and not her Blondes.'

Mrs. Lynch cleared her throat. 'You know why Julie wants to play Lydia Thompson? To pay off a debt of gratitude.' I had the impression she'd been preparing this speech. 'Lydia created the great vaudeville tradition out of which Julie came herself. One pioneer wants to salute another.'

'Are you handling publicity?' Cliff asked.

If she was aware of his irony, she didn't show it. 'I handle a good deal of Julie's personal publicity. And there's another thing. Julie will sing and dance again, and show off one of the greatest figures in the country.'

Cliff yawned and stood up. 'I'm tired, Julie. We'll talk tomorrow.'

'Good idea,' Julie said, with no trace of surprise or disappointment. 'Sleep on it and call me in the morning.'

As we went into the hall, she smiled. 'I want to show you something I designed myself.' Standing by the wall, she pressed a button. Part of the wall slid away, revealing a closet behind it. A light went on automatically.

The closet was like a small room. It contained an armchair and a low table inlaid with mother-of-pearl. In the chair sat a dressmaker's dummy, without limbs or head. Hung on it was a starched evening dress shirt and a bow-tie. A white silk top hat and a pair of dancing shoes stood in a glass case on the table. Against the back wall was pinned a pair of fishnet tights.

'Memories,' she said quietly. 'Don't touch them please. They're my costume from the chorus line in nineteen twenty-seven.'

She pressed the button again, the panel slid back. When she pressed another, a second panel opened in the centre of the wall. This time the closet had a black ceiling with silver paper stars. A gold statuette glittered on the top of a broken marble column.

'My Oscar.' She looked gravely at us and closed the panel.

'What's behind the third one?' Cliff asked. 'Your husbands?'

She laughed. 'I like your sense of humour, I really do. In fact, you're one of the most interesting men I've ever met.'

'Have you ever thought of this?' Mrs. Lynch said to me in an undertone. 'It takes just a few seconds to get from the first closet to the second. Just a few seconds. But it took Julie twenty-five years. She always wanted an Oscar. She worked and waited, waited and worked. Every year she'd see it go to someone else. But she never gave up.' Her voice sank even lower. 'And when *The Big Angel* came along, Julie *knew*. She said to me, This Is It. And It Was. She can be so patient, you know—provided she gets what she wants in the end.'

I nodded and smiled at Mrs. Lynch, but felt myself shiver.

Outside, it was cool and crickets were singing everywhere.

'Well, goodnight,' I said to Cliff.

There was a stubborn, hopeful yet disconsolate look on his face. 'Let's meet back at my place,' he said. He walked slowly towards his car, shoulders sagging with tiredness.

I followed him, driving through the courtyard where the fountain still played, past the swimming pool with a streak of moonlight on the water, out of the gateway where the PRIVATE sign glimmered in phosphorescent letters. Below the twisting canyon road ranged the city, lights endlessly blinking.

Cliff rented a second-floor apartment in an eccentric Hollywood block built during the twenties in the style of a Chinese temple. It had a black tower shaped like a pyramid, and the patio was planted with pagoda trees. Now, one window framed a solitary square of light. When I came in, Cliff was lying half-asleep on the couch. On the wall behind him hung a Paul Klee.

Before he opened his eyes and said anything, I knew he'd decided to make the film with Julie. He'd want me to be the voice of his conscience, to protest. Then he could say: 'It's the last time. It's got to be. One more bad picture and I'll die . . .' We usually had this conversation in the small hours, sitting in a kind of electric disorder: Cliff on the couch with the Klee, the Kirchner, the Derain and the Ben Shahn looking down on him, myself in a chair, the books spilling over from their shelves on to tables and floor, the cigarettes and the Scotch, the unread scripts lying around everywhere. Finally a gleam of dawn appeared low in the sky, and I went home.

When Cliff first came to Hollywood after working as an actor and a director in the New York theatre, he made a very honest realistic film about the everyday life of a young couple living in Brooklyn. It was a setting he knew well, since he grew up in it. The film was praised, but failed to show a profit. He made more films, not so interesting but commercially successful. He had three quick marriages, with a night club singer, a fashion model and an Italian girl studying anthropology at the University of Southern California. By the night club singer, he had a son. After the divorce she went to live in New York, taking the child with her. Cliff hadn't seen either of them for

176

twelve years. 'Somehow the time just slipped by. I'd like to know my son—but what do I say to him?'

When I first met Cliff in Europe, he was planning to leave Hollywood for ever; but the film he hoped to make in Italy didn't materialise, and he went back. He had an affair with an actress, made another film and bought the Derain. A year later I met him again in California. He seemed full of contradictions. He disliked the company of women but had a morose sexual appetite. He talked about the next film he was going to make, which would give him a chance to return to his favourite subject, young married life. (Later I saw the film; it had an unusual, subtle tenderness. No doubt of it, he could be a fine artist.) He mentioned that he had started going to a psychoanalyst, then changed his mind. I asked why. 'My only real problem,' he said, 'is Hollywood. If I can get out of this place, I'll be all right.' Yet I thought that, in spite of himself, Cliff had been in Hollywood long enough to become part of it. There was nowhere else he really knew. He wasn't resigned to making films in which he didn't believe, but went at them in a state of feverish anger. To many people in Hollywood, especially the young and struggling, he was generous. 'I feel responsible to them,' he used to say. The analyst had told him he was acting out guilt at neglecting his son.

In the end, with a taste for self-punishment that was sometimes theatrical, sometimes despairingly real, he always seemed to trap himself. To earn money, he had to make 'bad pictures'; as soon as he earned it, he spent it, and the struggle started over again.

'Of course, I'd rather have Monroe for this one.' He had opened his eyes, got up, and started for the kitchen to get a drink.

'Or a bit of truth?'

'Maybe I can give her that.'

One up to Julie, I thought. She has made Cliff see himself in a role, the director who will give her 'truth'. He had been an actor himself; a trace of the actor's egotism was showing through. 'She doesn't want truth,' I said. 'She wants to sing and dance. She wants to put across a new, salty Julie Forbes with a sense of humour.'

'If I thought there'd be nothing more in it than that, I'd walk out now.' He sounded indignant.

'Can you really think anything else?' The discussion was under way now. 'After years and years, you know how to look a straight-forward commercial picture in the face.'

Frowning, he came out of the kitchen with a glass of Scotch. 'After years and years, I refuse ever to recognise that I'm making just another picture. I've an obligation to go beyond that.'

'Then don't work for Julie Forbes.'

'And don't be so smugly idealistic. I can't start out by telling myself this is going to be another bad picture. I have to say, I'll try and do something with it, against all the odds I'm going to make it real.'

'But why give yourself such odds?'

'I've a contract to work out.' Cliff lay down on the couch again. 'The studio wants me to make a picture about a baseball player who becomes a priest. I'll take Julie Forbes.'

'Well, if that's the only choice——'

'I don't know how it happens. Every time I make a picture, I get eighty thousand dollars. I've never bought a house since I lived out here, but I'm always owing back taxes and payments to my son . . .' He sighed. 'I guess the less satisfied you are in this place, the more you spend. I made two pictures just to be able to divorce my wives.'

'You haven't got a wife now.'

'I have to keep her divorced.'

The door from the bedroom opened and a girl came out, wearing a striped pyjama coat. She had a pretty, oval face, tousled fair hair and a sleepy smile.

'This is Tina,' said Cliff.

'Hello, nice to meet you,' I said.

'Hi.' She yawned. 'I'll make some coffee, would you like some coffee?'

Cliff watched her for a moment, then said: 'She's a very talented girl. You ought to hear her sing.' He closed his eyes again. When Tina came back with the coffee, he'd fallen asleep.

'Don't wake him,' she whispered. 'He's got to see his agent in about three hours, though he doesn't know it yet. Canning called while you were up at the palace.'

'What did he want?'

Tina shrugged. 'It was just another pitch for Julie Forbes. How important it is for Cliff to direct a really big star, and all that sort of thing. What's she *like*, anyway?'

'Oh,' I said. 'Well. In a word, she's . . . dogged.'

'I get it.'

'Of course, Canning Wallace is Julie's agent, too,' I said. Through the window I could see dawn coming up.

At the studio, the wardrobe department is a line of separate huts.

Outside each one hangs a sign with the title of a film in production. *Queen Burleycue*, said the most freshly-painted sign. *Producer, J. Forbes. Director, C. Harriston.*

In the main building they had given us offices. 202, Cliff. 294, Julie. 296, Carmen Lynch. I was back in 298, with the heavy faded curtains and the set designer's sketches on the wall. Cliff had offered me the job rewriting the script with him and working as his assistant during the shooting; I said I was delighted to accept, being as broke as he in a more modest way. (And we hoped to work together, one day, on a film we really wanted to do.) Julie established Mrs. Lynch as Assistant to the Producer, and would later import the hairdresser, make-up artist, costume supervisor and cameraman who had served on all her films during the last ten years. She redecorated her office, installing a television set and a small bar with an ice-box. In the ante-room, her secretary sat under a framed scroll on the wall, certifying that *The Crime of Hannah Kingdom* had been voted Picture of the Month by *Screentime* magazine.

The original script of *Queen Burleycue* was slightly better than either Cliff or I had expected. Of course it was dedicated to Julie, who appeared in almost every scene and performed a fantastic variety of musical numbers, from Lydia's famous *Sinbad the Sailor*, which outraged Chicago, to a *danse du ventre* in Dodge City. The main problem was that Lydia lived to the age of seventy-two and her last twenty years were unadventurous. To contract this stretch of time, the writer had used a very old device: as an old lady in London, Lydia tells the story of her life to a young girl who has just got a job in a burlesque troupe going to America. The reminiscences were mainly of the men she had loved, and who had loved her. A romance was invented with Willie Edouin, the English comedian with whom Lydia went into partnership. He toured America with the Blondes and actually married one of them, called Ada. All the Blondes had respectable English names like Ada and Pauline. Lydia never really got over being rejected by Willie. She nobly concealed her love, was a bridesmaid at his wedding, toasted the happy pair, but afterwards she broke down and said she could never fall in love again. I did some research on Willie Edouin and found that he was ten years younger than Lydia, a grotesque little pantomimist whose greatest success was as Wishee-Washee in *Bluebeard*. It was decided to ignore this.

After Willie's marriage, Lydia thought only of her career. She swept the Blondes from triumph to triumph, and offers came in from all over the world. They toured India, where Lydia was seriously tempted by a maharajah. On the Australian tour, a young cattlehand fell desperately in love with her. She remained true to her secret sorrow and never married. At the end we came back to Lydia as an old lady, and discovered that the young girl was the daughter of Willie and Ada, both long since dead. .... In the intervals of all this, Lydia acted and sang with her troupe, and skirmished with the puritans. An elderly female dramatist denounced her in San Francisco. Lydia easily drew the crowds away from her play and closed it after two nights. In Chicago, the editor of the *Times* printed a headline, BAWDS AT THE OPERA HOUSE! Lydia waited in the street outside his office, then publicly thrashed him with a riding whip.

'There should be more comedy,' I said to Cliff. 'With English girls doing the hootchy-kootchy in the old West, there should be more comedy. And the old lady has to go.'

We went into Julie's office. She was sitting behind an enormous desk, looking at publicity photographs of herself. One of them showed her in tights and low-cut blouse, cracking a whip.

'How's that, Cliff?'

He glanced at it. 'Pretty good.'

'Really?' She looked at him very intently, lips parted. 'You really mean it?'

'Sure. You look great.'

She gave him a radiant smile. 'Thank you, Cliff. I thought we might use it for the posters.' She pressed a buzzer. A moment later, Mrs. Lynch entered.

'The boys are coming up with some changes,' Julie said.

Mrs. Lynch gave a nod and seated herself squarely on the couch. They listened to our suggestions. When we had finished, Julie tapped a pencil on the desk.

'Well, Carmen, what do you think?'

'I like the old lady.' Mrs. Lynch cleared her throat. 'I think it's a good idea to start off the story with the audience not knowing this sweet old girl is a retired burlesque queen.'

'They'll know it anyway,' Cliff said impatiently. 'They'll know what the film's about.'

Still tapping the pencil, Julie considered this. Then she said: 'I was looking forward to playing the old lady. I've never played an old lady. But you're an artist, Cliff, and if you're against it, that's good enough for me.'

'I'm totally against it,' Cliff said, with a glance at Mrs. Lynch. 'It was always a stupid idea.'

'Then how do we end the show?' She looked at her shoes. 'There's no ending any more.'

'With Lydia's farewell performance,' I suggested.

Julie frowned. 'What makes her give up?'

'She's getting to . . .' I broke off. 'She decides to try something new,' I said. 'She breaks into the legitimate theatre.'

There was a silence.

'And we leave her on the brink of a great dramatic career.'

'Well, Carmen, what do you think?'

'It's not bad,' Mrs. Lynch said. 'But I'd like to *see* you as a great dramatic actress. Suppose we end it, not with the farewell performance, but with the opening night of you in *Camille* or something?'

'I like that, Carmen. But not *Camille*. We'll make the situation in the play just like the situation in real life with Willie. And all the critics will say Lydia played it from the heart.' She glanced at her watch, got up. 'I'm late for a fitting.' In the doorway she turned back. 'Oh, Cliff! I've got a table at the Grove tonight, will you be my date?'

Julie's white Lincoln was parked outside the main building. As I went out, I saw Timmy sitting in the front seat. He waved to me.

'Hello,' I said. 'What are you doing here?'

'Carmen picked me up from school, but she had to come back because my mother's got an interview with some magazine, and she wanted Carmen to help her give out the stuff.'

'And then she's going out,' I said. 'To the Coconut Grove.'

'I know. I'll be having dinner with Carmen.'

'Mrs. Lynch is almost like one of the family, isn't she?'

He smiled faintly. 'Crazy sort of family.' Then, with no change of expression: 'Have they told you about my running away yet?' I shook my head. 'They usually like to tell people about my running away, and that kind of thing. Anything *bad*.' Impassive, he gazed out of the windshield.

'Your mother said you were a wonderful kid.'

'Oh, sometimes she says that first.' His eyes flickered. 'But she'd better be careful.'

'What do you mean, Timmy?'

He turned to look at me. A flat, terrible hatred came into his voice. 'She'd better be careful, that's all.' I didn't know what to say, but then he smiled again and touched my arm. 'But you could be my friend if you wanted to.'

'I'd like to.'

'I can get away and we can talk somewhere.'

'All right.'

He stretched out his hand. 'Shake.'

We shook hands.

'I'll tell you about the last time I ran away. I went down-town and stayed there all night, just wandering around the streets. Then a cop picked me up and took me home. I wanted her to feel worried and think maybe I was dead, but she was just angry and told me how ungrateful I was. If she could just admit. . . .' He trembled slightly. 'Well, if she could only just admit . . . You know, one day she took me to see a movie she'd made. It was the only time. In the middle of it she pulled my arm and yanked me out of the theatre, because there was a scene coming up she thought I shouldn't see.' He contorted his face into an impression of Julie anxious and unhappy. 'My Timmy must never see anything bad happen to me,' he said in a hard falsetto voice. 'He mustn't think I'm bad or I get killed.' A cold, thoughtful pause. 'But I know the kind of thing she does. I know who she takes to The Pool House. I can see her car come back at night from my bedroom window.'

He glanced into the driving mirror, and his eyes flickered. 'Carmen's coming. I'll call you.'

While Julie and Cliff were at the Coconut Grove that night, and Timmy was having dinner with Mrs. Lynch at the long antique table, I went to see *The Crime of Hannah Kingdom*.

I thought Julie must have found it a satisfying farewell to the period she now considered over. Near the end of the story, Hannah remarked: 'I came from nothing and now I own this lousy town.' She meant that she owned the factory which employed most of its inhabitants. In the last reel her jealous daughter set fire to it, her lover was burned to death and Hannah walked through blackened ruins in a fur coat. Smoke enfolded her distant figure as the great chimney with KINGDOM painted on it crumbled and fell.

Coming out of the theatre into Hollywood Boulevard, I saw the usual groups of adolescents who stand on the side-walks or sit on the bus company's benches in twos and threes, mysteriously waiting in the small hours. Tonight, with their eager but unfriendly eyes, several of them reminded me of Timmy. They chewed gum and put their thumbs over the hip pockets of their jeans, posture to challenge boredom and impatience. They stared long and hard at every car that passed, and didn't want to go home.

182

In the corridor outside my office next morning, I met Mrs. Lynch. She nodded and walked past me, then turned back.

'Excuse me . . .'

She'd never said that before. I looked at her in surprise.

'There's something I should warn you about.'

We were at the door to my office. I unlocked it, and she followed me inside.

'Yes?'

'Timmy. I saw you talking to him in the car yesterday. He's a wonderful kid, you know, but he has his problems. One of them is telling the truth.' Noticing that the date on the leaf of my desk calendar was two weeks old, she gave a genial smile. 'You're a little behind the times, my boy.' But her eyes were still beady as she began to tear off fourteen leaves, very deliberately, one by one. 'If Timmy said anything about his mother, it probably wasn't true.'

'He only said one thing. He said it twice, as a matter of fact.' I paused. *'She'd better be careful.'*

I watched Mrs. Lynch. As she tore each leaf from the calendar, she crumpled it into a little ball and dropped it in the wastebasket. After I spoke, her hand hesitated for a moment in mid-air, then threw away another ball of paper.

'Oh, is that all? I expect you guessed Timmy says that when he's feeling neglected. It means he'll try and run away again if he doesn't get more attention. He thinks his mother's the most lovely person in the world, but he's terribly jealous of all the time she has to give to other people.' Mrs. Lynch tore off the last leaf. 'There. Now you're up to date.'

Every Sunday, twenty or thirty people came round to Cliff's apartment. They started arriving at about three o'clock and some of them stayed until the small hours. They were not celebrities, but mainly unknown young actors, writers and musicians. They came to talk about life and art and the movies, sometimes to perform a work they'd written, and to play records: Bach, Beethoven, twelve-tone, jazz. Cliff lay back in a chair with a glass of Scotch in his hand and talked about Hollywood. He advised everyone to get out of it. Meanwhile, he would do what he could to help these young people get jobs. He was a combination of judge, unofficial agent and father-confessor to them all. Much of the advice he gave them was good, but when he talked about himself, the melancholy smile came over his face.

Some of the married couples brought their children. They played games and looked at television in the bedroom. When they grew tired, they would stretch out on the double bed, or on piles of cushions on the floor, and sleep right through Schoenberg and Count Basie. During the evening, Tina cooked spaghetti or chicken.

Cliff called it his 'Sundays'. After we'd been working on the script for nearly a month, he invited Julie to one of them. She arrived about five o'clock, with Timmy. Silence fell as they came into the room. She wore a dress of brilliant emerald taffeta. Among jeans and sweat shirts she sat on a couch, and somebody put a Beethoven quartet on the record-player. Ignoring the other children, who were younger than he, Timmy smiled faintly at me and then wandered out to the veranda. With his back to us all he sat in a wicker chair, looking down at the view of the city.

During the first movement of the quartet, Julie watched the people in the room. She was like a tiger waiting, with infinite patience, to spring. Reconnoitred Tina. Fastened her brilliant eyes on Cliff. Granted me a fixed gracious smile. At such moments she could be almost enigmatic. Coming here, I supposed, was all part of the 'new' Julie Forbes with her desire to change, to adapt herself. When she went to New York to watch classes at the Actors' Studio, declining to do an improvisation but saying it was all fascinating, it must have been rather like this. You couldn't believe in Julie changing. She was immutable. Playing a new character was only like putting on a new set of clothes, hand-tailored and immaculately fitted; skirts grew longer and shorter as Julie moved from comedy to melodrama and back again.

When the second movement started, Tina went into the kitchen. Julie moved to sit on the arm of Cliff's chair. 'That's a very pretty little girl. Can she act?' Cliff nodded. 'Someone told me she can sing and dance, too.' Cliff nodded again. 'Maybe she could play one of the Blondes?'

Cliff sat up. 'I was going to talk to you about that.'

'I knew you were.' Her eyes glittered. 'She's too young for Ada, of course, but,' looking across at me, 'don't you think she's right for Pauline?'

'Yes,' I said, thinking this was really quite clever of her.

'Then let's have her up for a reading next week.'

Cliff shook his head. 'I never cast an actor from a reading.'

'Well, if you can convince me some other way——'

'Just talk to her. Get an idea of her personaility. You can take my word on her talent.'

Smiling, she laid her hand on his arm. 'For what, boy?'

184

Cliff didn't answer, but closed his eyes. He said: 'This slow movement is the greatest part of the whole quartet. Just listen to it, Julie.'

'Yeah, it's beautiful. Is Beethoven your favourite?'

'One of them.'

'Mine, too.' She appeared to listen for a moment. 'But if you want her to play that part, Cliff, I think she ought to give a reading.'

He sighed. 'When they put you in *Look Out, Sister!*, was that on account of a reading?'

'No, but they'd seen me in New York.'

'Then we'll run a picture in which Tina does a bit.'

Julie got up from the arm of the chair. 'I swear he's the most darned obstinate guy in the whole world,' she said to me on her way back to the couch.

The third movement began. I noticed Timmy signalling to me from the veranda.

'Like me to tell you something?' he asked with a crooked smile. 'It's important.'

'Then go ahead, Timmy.'

He looked mysterious. 'There's a friend of yours mixed up in it.'

'Who?'

'Mr. Harriston.' He paused. 'She's stuck on him.'

'I don't believe you,' I said automatically.

'It's true. She's real stuck on him, but she's not getting anywhere.' He sounded satisfied.

I glanced back into the room. Cliff was listening to the scherzo. Smoking a cigarette, Julie rested her head against the back of the couch.

'How do you know?' I said.

'I've seen things.'

'What?'

'Last week she invited him over to the pool. I hid in the guest-house and watched them all afternoon. She was always—always touching him, you know, and then she tried to play games in the water.'

'Is that all?'

'No. I heard her talking to Carmen. She said something about him holding out on her. And Carmen told her about the girl—you know, Tina. She hadn't heard about Tina.' He giggled. 'And she didn't like it.'

'Well, maybe,' I said, not sounding interested and knowing it was true. The first time Julie had asked Cliff to take her to a night-club, she said: 'I like to get to know my directors as human beings. That's tremendously important for people working together.' I had assumed that Julie was exercising her public charm and Cliff, with his need for eighty thousand dollars and his bitter conscience, was struggling to be charmed. But she asked him out too often. In the pictures of them together, there was something too eager and submissive in the way Julie kept her hand on Cliff's arm or smiled up at him with her welcoming mouth. This afternoon, her pretence of interest in Tina must have been a deliberate public gesture, making it clear they were just two professionals, keeping their minds on work.

'It's nice of you to take such an interest in Timmy.'

Her voice startled me. She was standing at the entrance to the veranda.

'He's an interesting boy,' I said.

'Imaginative, too. Come along, Timmy, we're going home.'

On her way out, she said to Tina: 'We're going to run your picture tomorrow, dear.'

'I don't know how much it'll tell you,' Tina said. 'I'm only on the screen three minutes.'

'Well, Cliff believes in you. And I believe in Cliff.' Her hand rested on Timmy's shoulder. 'He's such a wonderful person. You can imagine how important this partnership is going to be for both of us.'

Tina's eyes flickered, then she smiled. 'Yes, that's just what Canning Wallace said.'

We saw Tina's film next afternoon. She played a brief scene and sang a light romantic duet with the leading man.

'She's good,' Julie said. 'Pretty good, Cliff.'

Mrs. Lynch cleared her throat. 'Pretty good figure, too. Though maybe a little *modern*. You think she can carry off the costumes?'

'That's an interesting point. What do you think, Cliff?'

He looked at Mrs. Lynch. 'Would you describe to me exactly how women's figures have changed since eighteen sixty-four?'

'They used to be fuller.' Mrs. Lynch sounded rather nostalgic.

'Julie, you'll have to put on weight.'

She laughed. 'He's got you there, Carmen.'

'It's not just physical.' Mrs. Lynch was unruffled. 'She's got a modern quality about her altogether.'

'Well, I'll talk it over with J.B.,' Julie said quickly. 'I'd like to use Tina, but between ourselves, *he's* got a candidate for Pauline. Some little chick he's discovered and is going to sign up.'

'When did he tell you this?' Cliff asked.

'About a week ago.'

'Why didn't you tell me?'

She looked surprised. 'I didn't think it was important. The girl's no good. And remember what you told me once, Cliff?' She paused. 'A producer shouldn't bother the director with that kind of front-office battle. A producer should take it off the director's shoulders and leave him free to *create*.'

'You see how thoughtful she is,' said Mrs. Lynch.

Julie nodded. 'I'll tell J.B., maybe we can find a spot for his chick somewhere else. And talking of J.B., he called me in just before we went over to look at Tina's picture. The studio wants us to start shooting a week earlier. I told him we could—subject to your approval, of course, Cliff. We can start with the location scenes in Missouri.'

'That's okay,' Cliff said.

'I fought another battle for you there. I told J.B. how important the location scenes were going to be, and I got you a couple of extra shooting days for them.'

'Fabulous,' said Mrs. Lynch.

The script of *Queen Burleycue* lay on Julie's desk. She drummed her fingers on the red cover. 'I went through it very carefully last night,' she said. 'Carmen read Willie, and we tried out some of the scenes together. Everything's great, except for one scene—when I horsewhip that editor in Chicago.' She got up, began pacing the room in front of us. 'That moment is very important to me, Cliff, and I think we should give it a little more.'

'She's got a wonderful idea for this,' said Mrs. Lynch.

Julie stopped pacing the room and stood directly in front of Cliff. 'I see this editor as more than a guy who hated sex. He hated it,' she paused, 'because he couldn't get it.'

Cliff stared at her. 'Why couldn't he get it?'

'He was ugly,' she answered at once. 'He was really attracted to Lydia, but he couldn't admit it to himself— maybe he'd been rejected before by a beautiful woman, he was frightened of rejection, so he twisted this attraction into hate.'

'It was his only way of getting even with a beautiful woman,' said Mrs. Lynch.

There was a silence.

'In that case, he probably enjoyed being whipped by Lydia,' I suggested.

'No, that's perverted,' said Mrs. Lynch.

'And'll never get past the censor.' Julie chuckled. 'It's a pity. But we can do it this way. We can show this editor, while I'm doing *Sinbad the Sailor*, never taking his eyes off me, trying to get a better look, licking his lips and all that kind of thing. So when he attacks me in the paper, we know he's a hypocrite.'

'Do we have to be so obvious?' Cliff asked.

'Well, it needs something. Let's have dinner tonight and talk it over.'

He shook his head. 'I'm busy tonight.'

Julie gave a little shrug of annoyance. 'This is important, Cliff.'

'We'll work something out.'

'But I want to talk about it.' There was a sharp edge on her voice. 'Can't you change your plans?'

'Can't we have a conference here tomorrow?'

'I'm busy tomorrow. I'm busy every day this week.' She softened. 'You know how it is, when you get near the shooting date.'

After a pause, Cliff said: 'All right.'

She smiled. 'Eight o'clock?' As Cliff nodded and started to go out of the room, she said suddenly: 'Oh, I almost forgot something!' Opening a drawer in her desk, she took out a record album. Her voice throbbed slightly. 'I wanted to thank you for yesterday afternoon, Cliff.'

She put the album in his hands. It was a complete set of Beethoven's symphonies.

Next morning I came to the studio about half an hour late. Cliff hadn't arrived, and Julie wasn't in her office. Cliff's secretary told me that Tina had telephoned to say he wasn't feeling well but would come in during the afternoon. At that moment, Mrs. Lynch entered the office with an envelope in her hand. Her greeting to me was extremely cold. She gave the envelope to Cliff's secretary and went out again. It was marked, *memo from Julie Forbes*.

The secretary wondered if she should let Cliff know about this, but decided not. Tina had said he was sleeping and didn't want to be disturbed.

I went into my office, swivelled in my chair, and felt uneasy. Something wasn't right. The atmosphere was lifeless but menacing, as before a storm.

'Where's Miss Forbes?' I asked Julie's secretary.

'In conference with J.B. She'll be tied up most of the day.'

There was nothing for me to do. I read the papers, and wrote a letter. Towards lunchtime, Cliff's secretary received another envelope containing a memorandum. This time it was delivered by an office messenger boy. I wanted to open it, but Cliff's secretary wouldn't let me. However, she telephoned Cliff again and said when Tina answered: 'I thought Mr. Harriston would like to know there are two memos from Miss Forbes waiting for him.' Tina repeated that he was sleeping, and she didn't want to disturb him.

Julie didn't appear in the commissary for lunch. Neither did Mrs. Lynch. From my office window, I saw them both coming back together at about two o'clock. But Julie didn't go to her office. Her secretary said she'd gone back into conference with J.B.

Shortly afterwards, another memorandum arrived for Cliff.

By now I was fairly nervous, and went for a walk. I drank half a bottle of Coca-Cola, then went to the barber's shop and had my hair cut.

Walking back to my office, I stopped to buy another newspaper at the rack. The cop said:

'Did you see about Canning Wallace's son?'

I shook my head.

'It's in all the late editions. That crazy kid's in trouble again, crashed his car, some girl with him got hurt.'

'Oh,' I said.

'Mr. Wallace gave that boy every advantage. Do you know Mr. Wallace?'

'No,' I said.

'He's a fine man.' The cop yawned. 'They should give that boy the cat.'

Maybe, I thought, there was an augury in the stars of just how bad today was going to be. Back in my office, I turned to the horoscope page. Under my sign, it advised: *If you concentrate, you can improve your professional standing. P.M. good for romance.*

The door opened and Mrs. Lynch came in. 'Here's the rewrite of that scene with the editor watching Lydia's act in Chicago.' She laid some sheets of paper on my desk.

I stared at her. 'What rewrite?'

'A rewrite the way Julie wants it.' Mrs. Lynch sounded calmly matter-of-fact.

'Who wrote it?'

She backed towards the door. 'It was written this morning.'

'Does Cliff know about it?'

'There's a copy on his desk.' She went out, closing the door behind her.

I telephoned Cliff. He'd just left for the studio, Tina said. Waiting, I scanned the newspaper story on Canning Wallace's son. There was a photograph of him, dishevelled and weeping, between two police officers.

Ten minutes later Cliff came in, looking almost as desperate as Wallace in the photograph. He held out the three memos with a trembling hand. The first said, Tina was unsuitable for the part of Pauline, and the young actress recommended by J.B. had been engaged for it. The second said, all location shooting on the film had been cancelled. The third said, 'You are requested to observe the official studio hours, which are from 9 a.m. to 5.30 p.m.' All were signed, *Julie Forbes*.

'Have you talked to her?' I said.

Cliff's face was grey. 'Not since last night. She's still with J.B.'

'What on earth's going on?'

Before he could answer, my telephone rang. 'Is Mr. Harriston in your office?' It was Julie's secretary.

'Yes,' I said.

'Miss Forbes is back now. She'd like to see you both immediately.'

Cliff rushed into her office ahead of me. Towering over her, he slammed the memos on her desk. She was reading the new scene that Mrs. Lynch had distributed, and didn't look up. 'Carmen, this is perfect.' Mrs. Lynch gave a gratified nod from the couch.

'What does this mean?' Cliff's fist hit the desk again.

Julie looked up slowly, her face steely bright. 'Exactly what it says.'

For a moment I thought Cliff would hit her. He took a step nearer her, then seized the telephone.

'And J.B.'s with me all the way,' Julie said. As he put it down, she jerked her thumb towards the bar. 'Better get yourself a drink, boy.'

As Cliff did so, Julie exchanged a glance with Mrs. Lynch, then leaned back in her chair. 'When I produce my own picture, Cliff, I have to take a very hard decision as a human being.' She lit a cigarette and blew smoke towards the ceiling. 'I have a little-girl-head, you see, which is my love-head, and I have a little-boy-head which is my money-head. I have to take off my little-girl-head now. I have to put it in a safe deposit box until the picture's over. And I have to put on my little-boy-head, which is always telling me to think about a certain important investment called Lydia Thompson.' She paused. 'My little-boy-head is very tough.'

'Both your heads are tough,' said Cliff from the bar.

'But you don't want me to put my little-girl-head back on, do you, Cliff?'

He shook his head almost convulsively. 'You just keep your mind on the picture, and tell me why your little-boy-head cancelled the locations.'

'We have to cut down on the budget.'

'Why didn't you consult me first?'

'I decided to take J.B.'s advice. You may be an artist, Cliff, but J.B.'s the businessman around here. Anyway, people won't come to see this picture for Cliff Harriston's location work. They'll come to see *me*, and they'll see me on the back lot and they won't know the difference.'

Thunderous, Cliff advanced on her. 'I cannot make a picture under these conditions! I'm handed actors I've never even seen, the script is rewritten without consulting me——'

'You want to try and get out of it?' Julie cut in sharply. 'Then talk to J.B. and find out how much it'll cost you.' With a sudden sinuous movement she leaned forward in her chair, arching her back like a snake. 'And here's something else. Your last picture hasn't turned out so well. Everyone, J.B. included, thinks it's a dog. The studio's worried about you, Cliff. Now I hate to hear everyone talking this way, because I believe in you. Maybe I'm taking a risk, but I want to help you.' She gave a little smile. 'And believe me, you need my help.'

He didn't say anything, but swallowed his drink. The ice rattled in the glass. Then Mrs. Lynch stood up. 'Julie, we should have been in the music department twenty minutes ago, hearing your theme song!'

We were sitting in a bar, a long dark tunnel with booths and heavily shaded table lamps, and I knew we were going to get drunk.

'Cliff,' I said, 'for God's sake tell me what happened last night.'

He looked very tired. Hands were clasped together in his lap, shoulders massively hunched. 'You know those hurricanes that usually come in from the Florida coast? The radio gives out a bulletin on them every hour—Hurricane Hannah is heading for Tennessee, Hurricane Hannah switches course, she's going to hit Kentucky . . .' He signalled to the waiter for another round of drinks. 'Sooner or later, I knew Julie was going to hit me. I thought I could steer her off, I took her seriously as an actress, tried to make her see where

191

she was dishonest and phoney . . . And she played along with it, you saw her do that.'

I nodded. 'But she was only playing.'

'Of course. Last night I tried to talk about the script, but she didn't want to. For six hours she explained she was lonely. She pitied herself, she pitied me, she cursed the whole wide world. We drank a lot. Around four in the morning she wanted to swim in the pool'.

'Storm warning,' I said.

The waiter brought our drinks. Cliff ordered another round. 'I told her I was going home. That did it. She begged, she shouted, she put her arms round me, she slapped me. I told her she had a compulsive desire to get her directors into the bedroom. I asked, was it power?—or vanity?—or what? She slapped me again. Then I made a crack about the pool probably being empty, anyway. She told me to get out.'

'Where was the palace eunuch all this time?' I asked.

'Carmen? Confined to quarters, I guess.'

'And Timmy probably watching from his bedroom window,' I said. 'It's like an oriental court, you know, with everybody spying on everybody else.'

'Make them all doubles now!' Cliff called to the waiter. 'When I was driving home,' he went on, 'I thought it was like Hannah Kingdom. I'd twisted her beautiful original drive.'

'The more it's twisted, the stronger it gets.'

He gave a long sigh. 'It'll ruin the picture.'

'Oh no,' I said. 'She'll give the picture everything it needs from her point of view, just as she's always done. All she wants to ruin is you.'

We drank in silence, then Cliff got up. 'I'm going to call Canning Wallace.'

'Well, he has his problems too.' Watching Cliff disappear down the tunnel, I thought: *P.M. good for getting drunk, and nothing else.* He was away for a long time. I had another Scotch, and began to feel euphoric. Down the tunnel, a Negro started to play silky blues on a piano I could hardly see.

'First of all, I got Canning's wife.' Cliff had come back. 'She was crying, and said what had they done to deserve it. Then I got Canning, who talked like Julie. I've got to make a success of this picture, I need it. Can't I play along? I told him to come right out and admit he was backing his more important client. He said I sounded drunk, and I hung up.'

'It feels like the whole town's falling down tonight,' I remarked in a strangely contented voice. 'Like Hannah Kingdom's blasted chimney.'

Outside the stage on the day we began shooting *Every Inch a Lady*, as the story of Lydia Thompson was now called, a sign announced CLOSED SET. POSITIVELY NO VISITORS. The studio doesn't often close a set; but sometimes a star or director insists he cannot work in the presence of strangers, sometimes the publicity department decides that a cloak of secrecy is the best way to arouse interest in a new film. No reason was given for closing this set, though a columnist wrote that when he asked for one, the reply came in a word: *Personal:*
Shooting was scheduled for forty days. Eight weeks. Nearly four hundred hours, when you counted the overtime. In prospect the routine looked unbearable. In practice it had a soothing, almost anaesthetising effect. Partly this was due to Julie. Regulated as time itself, she was a source of power, energy, habitual purpose. When she entered the brightly-lit set, it was as if somebody stepped up the current. From every side the lights glared white-hot.
I had never watched her work before. Most of it was galvanic concentration, for she had very little natural talent. The imaginative stroke, the sudden passionate instinct, were never hers. Acting was hard labour, like coal-mining or road-mending. After thirty years, she still found it difficult to remember lines. She went over and over them with Mrs. Lynch in a half-dark corner of the stage. Before each take she looked tense and grim, paced up and down in front of the camera, snapping her fingers with a sound as hard as castanets. When Cliff called 'Action!' it was like an electric shock. In a second all tension disappeared; she was precise, confident, and extraordinarily young.
When she fluffed a line in the middle of a take, she stopped at once and cursed loudly. Then she paced up and down a few steps, snapped her fingers and glittered into action once more. Watching her, I found dialogue and movements became ritual abstractions, stripped of meaning. Sometimes the machine worked perfectly, sometimes it stopped.
LYDIA (after a pause): *You're in love with Ada, aren't you?*
WILLIE: *How did you know?*
LYDIA: *The night they threw that party for us in New York. You didn't dance with anyone except Ada. Didn't look at anyone. When I spoke to you, you heard what I was saying——*

'Damn!' Julie waves at the camera, as if rubbing out a line of chalk on a blackboard. ' "You *hardly* heard what I was saying." ' Cliff calls, 'Cut it!' Lights are switched off. Out of the darkness surrounding the set, Mrs. Lynch appears with a script. ' "You *hardly* heard what I was saying . . ." ' The fingers snap. Her make-up man runs up with a powder puff and mirror.

The lights come on again. 'Ready, Julie?' She scans herself in the mirror, nods. 'It's a very difficult line,' Mrs. Lynch says. The cameraman glances at her. 'Be a good girl, Carmen, and take your shadow away.'

LYDIA (after a pause): *You're in love with Ada, aren't you? . . .*

Portable dressing-rooms stood at the side of the stage. Cliff's and Julie's were next to each other, the door to Cliff's was usually closed but Julie liked to keep her door open. Waiting between scenes, she often played records. *You Make Me Feel so Young* and *I Get a Kick Out of You*, her favourite tunes, drifted across the murk of different sets and photographic backings, up to the high scaffolding of lights.

The technicians adored her. She knew all their names, of course. 'Good morning, Chuck—how's your lovely wife?' She told dirty jokes to the camera crew and sometimes played poker with them. With Cliff, she was quietly professional, listened intently to his suggestions, always thanked him. 'That's really very helpful.' 'I was worried about that, Cliff, but now you've set me straight.' The dramas occurred in her portable dressing-room, and then the phonograph was silent and the door closed. 'We have to do something about that scene, Julie. Every time I look at those new lines, I want to throw up.' She gives a regretful smile. 'J.B.'s approved them you know.' 'I'll talk to him.' 'You can talk to him all you want, but if I tell him I want those lines to stay, they'll stay . . .'

They stayed. Occasionally, signs of conflict came out into the open. One morning a note was pinned to the door of Cliff's dressing-room:

> Dear Cliff, you should be more attentive to Wardrobe Dept. I asked you to okay Diane's new costume because I was too busy. But when we started shooting yesterday, we wasted nearly an hour because it was too bright in relation to mine. *This is important.* Please concentrate more on your work, like.
>
> JULIE FORBES.

Two outsiders were admitted to the closed set. One day I saw a tall thin-faced man with cropped grey hair talking to Julie outside her dressing-room. He wore a dark suit with protruding white cuffs, white silk shirt, silk tie and diamond clasp, black suede shoes. Cliff came over and they shook hands. Standing between them, Julie linked an arm with each of theirs, and a stills man took a photograph. 'I hear J.B.'s crazy about the dailies,' the visitor said. Julie nodded. 'Everything's just great now.' He turned to Cliff. 'You happy too?' 'As a sandboy, Canning.'

About half-way through shooting, a rather stout middle-aged man in spectacles came to see Julie for the first time. After that, he came almost every day. Cliff and I were introduced to him, but we spoke very little. He was a vitamin manufacturer called Dave Roeling II. He had a nervous blink and a genial smile. Whenever he saw Cliff, he said, 'Hi, D. W. Griffith?' and laughed.

A columnist predicted that Julie would marry him.

A Monday morning. Outside the offices of the Chicago *Times*, a carriage draws up. Lydia opens the door, steps down to the sidewalk. She is draped in a long rich crimson cloak. You can just see the toes of her little yellow boots. She waits. Some passers-by recognise her. A crowd forms. Behind the crowd, another crowd: Cliff in a sweat shirt near the camera, the silent crew, Mrs. Lynch and Dave Roeling II on the sidelines. The editor, plump and rather dandified, comes out into the street. Cliff makes a rapid signal, the camera moves forward. Throwing back her cloak, Lydia confronts him. She wears her theatre costume, tights, a middy blouse, high-heeled cross-laced yellow boots, and carries a long embroidered whip. The crowd gasps. The editor takes a step back, but she brings down the whip on his shoulders. He starts to run. Lydia follows, cracking him across the buttocks. He falls into the gutter. Suddenly whistles are blowing, a squad of police breaks through the crowd. They seize Lydia . . .

The cameraman shakes his head. 'When he fell in the gutter, we lost him. He has to fall at least two feet earlier.'

'Okay, give him another mark and let's go again.'

Two hours later, Cliff and I had gone off the lot for lunch and were sitting in a bar. He ordered another Scotch and said: 'I was going through some papers at home yesterday and I found a poem. Poem by Cliff Harriston aged fourteen, very lonely and Thomas Wolfey, not really any good but it had a sort of private reality.' The wry smile crept over his face. 'I wanted to find that reality again, and I tried to look back down a long long time. All I saw was a line that got thinner and thinner. I couldn't get back to fourteen, I could hardly get back further than the day I came to this place. When I tried, it didn't mean anything. Somehow, it . . .' His eye narrowed, as if he were trying to read a sign from a great distance, then he shook his head. '*It wasn't as real as Julie Forbes.*'

He finished his drink, put down the glass with a thud on the table. The barman came over with a faint, hateful smile. 'Same again, Mr. Harriston?'

Cliff nodded. 'I took off in the car, drove down to the ocean, then along the highway, turned into the mountains, said to myself all the way—*trees. Look, the ocean. Sky. They're still here, why aren't you?* It began to sound like a poem aged fourteen. I turned back, stopped at a bar, had a few drinks, then called up some friends and they came over for cards.' The barman brought his drink. 'I lost three hundred dollars.'

A few minutes before lunchtime next day, I passed Julie's dressing-room. She was sitting on the steps in tights and blouse and a pair of soft slippers instead of the boots examining photographs of herself.

'Hello!' She seemed in a very good humour. 'You busy?'

'No,' I said. 'They're just doing a close-up of the editor getting thwacked.'

'Come inside for a moment.'

Dave Roeling II sat on the couch. He blinked nervously behind spectacles, sweat pricked out his forehead. He had undone the top button of his shirt and a spotted red and white bow-tie hung down the front.

Pulling at one end of the bow-tie, Julie perched on his knee. 'Shall I tell him?'

'Why him?' asked Roeling.

She gave the tie another pull. Her eyes gleamed. 'I just want to tell somebody.'

'Well, I guess it's no secret.' He tried to pull the tie away.

Julie held on to it. 'Dave's asked me to marry him. Do you think I should?'

'Oh, honey,' he protested.

'Do you want to?' I asked.

'Sure. I'm crazy about him.' She got the tie away and started twisting it round her fingers. 'And he's very rich.'

'Aren't *you*?' I said.

Roeling blinked. 'She's just making a joke of it, to disguise her real emotions. But I think,' he put his hand on her thigh, 'she ought to come right out and say she loves me.'

'Vitamin king, I love you.' Julie touched his cheek. 'Let me tie your tie.'

'I don't know what's gotten into her this morning,' Roeling said. 'She's as full of mischief as a child. People always ask me how I stand her temperament. I tell them it's not temperament, it's just her mask to the world. Hi, D. W. Griffith!' he said as Cliff came up.

Julie put her arms round Roeling's neck and began to knot his tie. 'Oh Cliff, I looked at those dailies again with J.B. this morning, and he agrees we need that extra close-up of me.' Her voice was briskly professional, like her hands with the tie. 'I told him you didn't think it was necessary, and he couldn't understand why. Hold still,' she said to Roeling. 'So let's shoot it tomorrow morning, shall we?'

Cliff nodded and turned to me. 'Let's get some lunch.'

'Why don't we all get some lunch together?' With a brilliant smile, she pulled Roeling to his feet, slipped one hand through his arm and one through Cliff's. 'Do you realize, Cliff, we've never had lunch together since the picture started? I think that's simply terrible.'

'Honey, you're not going over to the commissary like that?' Roeling pointed to her tights. 'I guess it might be distracting,' Julie said, and put on a long green robe. 'I don't know what's gotten into her this morning,' Roeling said.

We walked over to his Cadillac. Julie tightened her hand on Cliff's arm. 'Dave's asked me to marry him.'

Cliff looked straight ahead. 'It couldn't happen to two nicer people.'

'Thank you very much,' said Roeling.

She pulled Cliff with her into the back of the Cadillac. 'You look tired,' she told him, then chuckled. 'Maybe you need vitamins, boy.'

As we entered the commissary, a small old man came out through the swing doors. He had a tanned but emaciated face and pale callous eyes. 'Isn't she great?' He held Julie by the shoulders. 'I don't believe she's more than twenty-five.'

'I've got news for you, J.B. I'm twenty-six.' She kissed him on the forehead. 'I told Cliff you agreed about that close-up.'

The old man took a monogrammed handkerchief from his breast pocket and mopped his face with a delicate, fussy gesture. 'Julie's right,' he said to Cliff. 'Shoot it.'

'He'll shoot it in the morning,' Julie said.

'Fine.' J.B. folded the handerchief and put it back in his pocket with the monogram showing. Then he tapped Cliff on the chest with his knuckles. 'Happy?'

'As a sandboy, J.B.'

On the last day of shooting, Julie gave a party. She'd sung and danced *Sinbad the Sailor* nineteen times all the way through, while the camera covered her from different angles. 'Well, that's it, boys!' Cliff said after the final shot. Julie doffed her sailor hat. 'Now let everybody get drunk, I've ordered enough liquor to keep us here through next week.' She walked off the set, not at all breathless.

Lights were turned out. The stage of the Chicago Opera House went dark. A long, hollow silence broken only by the echo of footsteps as we picked our way across cables to the New York ballroom set, brilliant with chandeliers. Under powerful arcs from the gantry, circled by darkness, it looked like an island suddenly risen out of the sea. At one end, a flight of stairs swept down from nowhere. Footmen in period costume had been brought in to serve drinks from a buffet. I saw Roeling and Timmy standing together under a tall bay window; and Mrs. Lynch toasting two of the Blondes, who wore tight-waisted dresses with flounced skirts, ostrich plumes waving above their heads.

Then, piped at full strength through a loudspeaker, came Julie's voice singing the theme tune:

> *I'm every inch a Lady,*
> *I've got everything to prove it.*
> *The basis of my act is*
> *To show how true this fact is . . .*

A footman came up to Cliff and myself with a tray of glasses.

'How do you think it's turned out?' Cliff asked. He looked grimy and exhausted.

'Like a Julie Forbes picture,' I said quietly.

He made a grimace. 'Is that all?'

'I'm afraid so.'

He nodded. 'Yeah, I'm afraid so.' He walked slowly away and stood looking out of a window, at a long perspective of darkness.

Julie hadn't come back. 'Where is she?' I asked Timmy as he came up to me, neat in a dark blue suit and his hair freshly brilliantined.

He shrugged. 'Who cares? I can go on drinking vodka as long as she doesn't come.'

'Vodka, is that vodka in your glass, Timmy?' Roeling had joined us. He blinked.

'I'm developing a taste for it,' Timmy said gravely.

'I don't know what your mother will say.'

'She won't say anything unless you tell her.'

'Well,' said Roeling in a genial voice, and blinked again. 'I guess I can keep your secret for you. You're a pretty bright kid, you know.' He clapped him on the shoulder.

Timmy looked coldly at him. 'It says in the paper there's a slump in vitamins. What's that going to mean for you?'

'Now Timmy.' Roeling began to clean his spectacles. 'Not everything you read in the papers is true.'

He moved away to join Mrs. Lynch and the Blondes. As a footman passed us with a tray, Timmy took another vodka and tonic. He came closer to me, and gave a peculiar smile. '*Not everything you read in the papers is true,*' he said.

'What do you mean by that?'

'I've told you. I've seen things.' He was pale with excitement.

'What things?'

'Oh . . .' He swayed a little on his feet. His voice dropped to a whisper. 'Once I saw a man fall into an empty pool.'

'Timmy, you'd better not have any more vodka.'

'It's true!'

His eyes, slightly bloodshot, searched my face. With an insistent pleading movement, he stroked my arm. 'I swear it's true.'

I said: 'What happened when the man fell?'

Timmy didn't answer at once. Then: 'I guess he died.' He smiled again. 'She didn't push him, if that's what you're thinking. All the same . . .' He broke off. 'You'll never tell anyone, will you?'

'No.'

'Swear it.'

'I swear it.'

'All the same,' he said, looking thoughtful, 'she could have called a doctor. Nobody called a doctor.'

'I thought he died at once.'

'She could have called a doctor,' he repeated, 'instead of leaving him there. And he cried out. And he tried to get up. And she wouldn't take any notice.'

The loudspeaker stopped, leaving a well of silence. Then the murmur of voices began again.

'What about Carmen?' I said. 'And Canning? Did you ever say anything to them?'

'They said I'm a liar. They said I have fantasies.'

'And why are you telling me?'

He frowned. 'I don't know. I sort of feel you hate her as much as I do.'

'No, I don't,' I said. 'Really I don't. I used to think I did. But she's too—too extraordinary, if you know what I mean.'

'Well,' Timmy said. He gave me a long look. 'Don't feel sorry. You don't have to feel sorry for me. She knows what I saw, and . . .' I saw he was smiling in the prematurely old, crooked way that chilled me. 'I can get anything I want for my birthday. Christmas, too. So it's——'

The studio lights flickered and dimmed. From the gantry, an arc swung round to the staircase. Ragtime, very quiet and strict, came through the loudspeaker. A girl walked down the stairs into the spotlight. She wore fishnet tights, man's evening shirt, bow-tie and white top hat.

When she came nearer, everyone realised it was Julie. There were gasps of admiration. For a moment, we were all in the twenties. Serious, unsmiling, she advanced to the centre of the ballroom. The columnists rushed forward, making a semicircle round her.

Then she winked. Pulled the hat down at a jaunty angle over her eyes. Hips swayed to the ragtime, feet tapped a few steps. A photographer's bulb flashed. She tipped her hat. The tap of her feet echoed across the darkened stage.

Applause. The ragtime stopped. She held out her arms. 'Nineteen twenty-seven,' she said. 'I wore this in nineteen twenty-seven.' She extended one leg, then the other. 'You'll notice it's still a perfect fit.'

J.B. pushed through the columnists and kissed her. He was trembling. 'Julie, I'm proud of you.'

'No one but you, Julie,' said Roeling.

'An experience I shall never forget,' said Mrs. Lynch.

Julie laughed. 'So give the old-timer a drink.' She glanced across the ballroom to Cliff, who was still standing by the window. Then she made a little speech. She thanked the crew and all the actors for being so wonderful to her. She thanked J.B. for his faith. 'And I want to say a special word about Cliff Harriston.' She paused. 'Working with Cliff has been one of the most stimulating experiences of my life. He's—well, you don't need me to tell you what Cliff Harriston is.'

'Why did you close the set?' a columnist asked.

'We both felt the need for terrific concentration. This picture was very hard for both of us.' Julie turned away quickly, went over to Timmy and ruffled his hair. 'Timmy darling, this is your mother. What do you think of her?'

'Oh, you're the greatest,' he said.

'Isn't that the truth?' Roeling agreed. 'Timmy, I'm glad you realise your mother is just about the most fabulous woman in the world.'

'I do, I do realise it.' He giggled. 'But I think I'm drunk.'

Julie took the glass from his hand and sniffed it. 'Dave, did you know the kid's been drinking vodka?'

Sweat broke out on Roeling's forehead. 'Guess it's more tonic than vodka.'

She took a sip. 'More vodka than tonic.'

'I'll get him home,' Mrs. Lynch said, and took Timmy's arm. He followed her without a word.

Julie watched them leave, then tipped her hat to the back of her head and went over to Cliff. They were alone by the window.

'It's a very nice custom,' she said quietly, 'to give presents at the end of a picture. I mean, the way stars and directors usually do.'

He nodded. 'I usually give presents.'

'But not this time?'

'I've got a present for you,' Cliff said rather slowly. 'I give you this movie, Julie. I'd give you all your movies if I had them.'

'I think that's a very nice present.'

'You know what you can do with it.'

She smiled. 'I'm so glad you got me a present, because I got you one too.' Still holding Timmy's glass, she looked over her shoulder. Then she threw the vodka in Cliff's face and slapped him on the mouth with the back of her hand. The force of the blow nearly sent him through the window.

Straightening her hat, she walked away. As she reached the door a spotlight was trained on her and a voice called from the gantry:

'Hi, Julie!'

An electrician with a creased veteran's face and a cigar in his mouth was up there, holding the light. He gave a wide admiring grin, keeping the cigar between his teeth.

'Good luck, Julie. It's been a pleasure every moment.'

Her hat glittered. She put her hands on her hips. 'And God bless you, Louie!'

He waved and held the spotlight on her till the door closed.

The empty stage like an enormous grotto, dark and deep under the ground. At the far end, outside Julie's dressing-room, one light was burning. My footsteps echoed monstrously.

'Who's there?'

As I reached the dressing-room steps, I saw that she had taken off her make-up. Her skin looked fresh and smooth, only a little pale. She was wrapped in the vivid green robe. Behind her, the dressmaker's dummy stood like a totem pole, hung with shirt and bow-tie, festooned with the sacred tights.

'What do you want?' She spoke through gritted teeth.

'Somewhere here,' I said, 'I left a book.'

'A *book*?'

'Yes. I was reading it between takes.'

'You'll never find it in all this dark.'

'I think I know where it is,' I said, and turned away.

Her voice called me back. 'Enjoy the party?'

I turned round. 'Very much. It was fun.'

'Yeah, it was fun . . .' She sat down on the steps, folded her arms and gazed at the vacant stage with an expression of disgust.

I started to turn away again, but she beckoned me to come closer with a quick, irritated gesture.

'Do you want something?' I asked.

'What should I want, boy?'

'I don't know. But you look . . .' I broke off.

'What?'

'Is it the after-the-picture-blues?'

She gave a short bitter laugh. 'I never get them. And the picture's fine. Great. I pulled it through. It'll make a lot of money.' She lit a cigarette. 'I'll buy Timmy that yacht.'

'He wants a yacht?' Julie nodded. 'Isn't he too young to handle it?'

'He'll learn fast,' she said. 'Timmy's very advanced for his age.' Smoke from her cigarette twisted towards the darkness. She watched it, then shrugged. 'Dave's waiting, but for some reason I feel like sitting here, in this barn. Sometimes I get a feeling. I feel . . .'

A curious thing happened. It seemed to me that the light went out of her eyes. They became like empty lakes. 'I feel that I'm in the middle of a purposeless, hostile universe.'

Her voice rasped across the shadows, the rows of heavy lamps, the dark outlines of painted flats.

'Isn't that strange?' Her eyes grew bright again. She got up, yawned and stretched her arms.

'Well, maybe,' I said, 'maybe you *are*.'

I haven't seen Julie again. Nearly three months have passed and tonight is the première of *Every Inch a Lady*. As they say at the studio, 'the word's gone round it'll be the money-spinner of the year.' J.B. is said to be convinced. A record of Julie singing the theme tune is already on the list of best-sellers, and goes into the nation's juke-boxes next week.

Cliff told me he wasn't going to the première. He is working on a new story, and is very excited about it. 'This one's going to be really good.' It will be for a different studio, as J.B. didn't renew his contract. Cliff looks better now than at the end of shooting *Every Inch a Lady*, but I always find a deep and almost fearful tiredness in his face. When he talks, he often looks away from you; his eyes are gazing out of a window, through an open door. I suppose they see a thin line stretching away, growing thinner.

Timmy has telephoned once. Julie and Dave Roeling II had a honeymoon in Tahiti, then Roeling flew to Brazil to promote his vitamins. Next time, Julie plans to accompany him on a business tour. A columnist says she intends to take an active interest in her husband's work. Timmy says she still uses The Pool House. He expects his yacht in about a week.

Outside the theatre in Hollywood is a papiermâché figure that looks even bigger than the skeleton of the imperial mastodon unearthed near Wilshire Boulevard before the new insurance company building went up. It is Julie as Lydia Thompson. She brandishes a glittering whip.

The ceremonies won't begin for another two hours, but already a crowd is massing. Police prepare cordons. People eat popcorn or peanuts and chew gum while they wait. They don't say much. A quiet middle-aged woman remarks: 'She's still the greatest.' A man nods: 'And she'll be the last to go.' The crowd grows more dense and impatient as there comes a light surprising shower of rain and dusk falls.

JOHN NORMANTON

(b. 1918)

Stars in an Oldie

They are all dead. These are vestiges
Remaining a little while longer
Of their existence.

Those who were their lovers and mistresses,
Do they want to know about
Such poor travesties?

Voices and certain tricks of speech
Yes. Mannerisms beloved of many
Perhaps. But the character each

Is playing only spoils the memorable
Smile, Adulterates the pure
Bogie or Gable.

Still—something's recorded of them
Though it may not comfort
Any who loved them.

These are the stars, who are assured
Of a re-run when the time is ripe.
But we don't repeat our show.

Only a few traces last.
Impressions left lying about.
Or at a wedding breakfast

On a home-movie. Or holiday slide—
All fixed enjoyment and bosom
And grinning sky.

But fading like the after-image on
Your retina. If anything does linger
That's God's pigeon.

Just what's been drawn to His attention.
Old drama re-enacted. Goodies and baddies
Raising up dead passion.

Is it merely casual cruelty
That those who see ghosts from armchairs
May suffer more fully

In the gratuitous and random habit
Of this famous world, so loved,
As they roll the credits?

Please do not repeat me yet.
Anyway not too loud or
Bang, bang, I shall be dead.

BARRY N. MALZBERG

(b. 1935)

Barry N. Malzberg is one of the new generation of .American writers who—by way of science fiction and erotica—measures the ambitions and possible bankruptcy of the West. His images are compelling, his adjudication exact. Movies, for Malzberg, are a metaphor which matches the hopes and the frustrations of his readers. The hero of Screen *(1969) is a recluse whose life, is literally, a projection of his dreams. They offer scant hope, but all the hope there is.*

Screen

I could have told her—if only I could have told her—that it had begun a long time ago; that I had been doing it since I was thirteen years old, first in loss and then in doubt but that now, finally, I was not doing it those ways but rather in affirmation: that what it came down to, simply enough, was that the stars had more reality than this girl herself and that what I did with them mattered infinitely more than anything which could pass from my turgid genitals and into her. I could have given her bits of sociology, pieces of old data wrung from the sentimentality of scholarship: I could have told her, then, that a broken home, a loveless childhood, wandering existence must always find either a kind of affirmation or a most definite kind of death and I had found the former and forsaken the latter as the most important of all that most tentative series of choices which I had been compelled to make; which all of us had been compelled to make. I could have told her that not very long ago, a decade, or maybe less than that— and a decade meant nothing to the bleak, spinning universe—I had come to the understanding that I would either have to find a certain justification for what was going on or I would die, and although death, in the stretch of years, was an abstraction it was also something so final that life, perhaps, was all that we could know anyway; life was perhaps an absolute as timeless as death if you could only see that way. I wanted to tell her that I had made my choice then, for life, and it was a question of how I could best find it and I had found it within the pathway of my own skull, the best place, the only place, the place where all beginning had begun, and that within that I had found a balance and a righteousness where I could find them no place else. I could have told this foolish girl with the bare arms and with the breasts still pointlessly, mechanically upthrust towards her neckline, the breasts that had no significance whatsoever because she was simply incapable of acknowledging what they were—as I had acknowledged what I was—and proceeding to make the point with one finger and a good deal of intensity that I was perfectly content with what I was doing; that there was absolutely nothing wrong with what I was doing; that all the trouble—if trouble there were—came not from me but from what the world would have made of what I had become and so from that peripety—because I was a sane man, sane enough to entertain not only peripeties but epiphanies themselves, those tiny orgasms of the psyche—had come a kind of accommodation and everything that I had built up around me. I could have told her all of that just, as in so many embraces, I had whispered the same to Sophia, Brigitte, Elizabeth, Ann, Jane, Marilyn, Jayne, Angela, Judith, Rhonda. They had understood—even, at the very beginning, Sophia had understood the best of all—and she, perhaps could have been led to understand this as well; if I only had been able to make her understand then there might be a beginning to our relationship and even a kind of outcome waiting for us at its termination but I couldn't say any of it to her. I couldn't say any of it to her at all. Because if I had said it to her I would have been mad and I wasn't mad; not in the least mad, I was sane, sane, sane, locked in coldness, locked at last in the finality of what I had glimpsed in my room pumping her. So I only talked then about the Welfare Department and replied to what she said with intelligences of my own and that is the way we made it through dinner. For her, I must have been a very proper escort; locked into that small, equivocal security in the restaurant we must have, for her, created a small, real exile of need and cunning, possibility and inference, because, towards the end of the dinner she took to stroking my hand and bidding me hello with her lips and I let her; I let her because none of it made any difference. I could do it with this girl. I could handle it with her. Because there was no alternative and because now I saw how it would all end before me; the path slammed down in my mind by my gallery as I had fucked her was clear and final and all doubt was lost. Nothing was a mystery any more except what was happening inside and that would be settled inside, inside, Everything would come to its final asking, eventually.

'Well,' she said, when I paid the check. 'That was very nice. I enjoyed that.'

'A movie,' I said. 'Now we'll go to a movie.'

'You really like the movies, don't you, Martin? You really can't get over that urge to go to a movie, can you?'

'Is there any need to? You said you'd give the enemy equal time, remember that?'

'I don't think you're the enemy.'

'I didn't mean it that way. What do you want to see? You have any preference?'

'Not really.'

'Foreign or American?'

'I guess foreign.'

'I guess not. There's a retrospective over at the Bijou right in the neighbourhood here. They're showing PILLOW TALK with Rock Hudson and Doris Day.'

'That was awful, wasn't it?'

'It was a big hit in its year.'

'Well, that doesn't make it good. Most big hits are awful. What do you want to see Doris Day for anyway? She's about 45 years old, isn't she? And awful looking.'

'It's a comedy. It's a light comedy.'

She went for the packet of cigarettes again, lit one with such a flourish and urgency that I thought she wouldn't be satisfied; would dive for another. But she only smoked it with a drawing kind of intensity; the same intensity that I had shown against her nipples. 'Oh, what the hell,' she said. 'If you want to see it, we'll see it. It's not going to prove a thing to me, though. I'll probably absolutely hate it and make the rest of the evening miserable for you.' She smiled.

'I can risk it.'

'You really like to see Hollywood films, don't you? Hollywood is something special for you.'

'No, I see a lot of foreign films too,' I said. 'There's nothing wrong with foreign films; they can be great sometimes. It all depends.' I stood, feeling the table sway under me as I put palms flatly against it; she rose with me, putting out the cigarette in the ashtray. I put down a tip and paid the clerk at the register—he eyed me with the numb Saturday-hostility with which, transmuted, I would dountless greet my clients Monday—and we went out into the hot spaces of the street touching, hands together. She ran a finger through my palm, put her head against my shoulder, then withdrew it as two dangerous-looking youths passed murmuring obscenities to one another, then put it back again. I let it rest there. I had nothing to lose. It didn't matter.

'Right down the block,' I said.

'I see it. It's kind of an old theatre, isn't it?'

'There are newer.'

'Sometimes I think a movie theatre is the most depressing place in the world. More depressing even than a bar-and-grill. They must be the worst places going.'

'It all depends,' I said. 'It all depends.' I put an arm around her and guided her to the window. The price signs were up, the old lady behind the window was slumped down, there was nobody anywhere around us. I paid while she stood in that half-elusive, half-protected slump which girls always seem to assume while waiting for their escorts to pay their way in—and then put the arm around her and guided her through the doors, into the blasts of air piling out of the house. I was affectionate, careful, graceful. It was the first time I had ever taken a girl to the movies. I gave the doorman our tickets and got us into the lobby—the creased, blotched lobby of a theatre on a decline so slow and yet so tumultuous that nothing short of a bombing would stop it before the walls themselves began to fester and clambered in against one another—and asked her if she wanted anything. She said she would have a candy bar and I bought her one; then, after thinking it over, decided to have some popcorn because it was important to do everything as if I were alone; if not, it would be fraudulent, it would come to nothing. We went inside—once again the place was almost empty; I had had my usual luck—and went into a middle aisle and she sat against me. The short subject was on, something dealing with Oregon and the sawing down of trees in that pointless state and I let her subside against me, her head a slight, almost inconsequential pressure against my shoulder, her hand chastely dipping toward but not cupping my genitals as she slipped it back and forth on my thigh, then dropped it to my knee. I could hear the paper of the candy bar crackle and a chewing sound.

'So what?' she said.

'The feature hasn't started yet.'

'What's the difference? Feature, short, they're all the same. There have to be better places in the world to spend an evening.'

'You're just afraid,' I said to her then. 'You're just afraid to be in the movies. You're afraid because you might find out that they're better than the life you're leading and then you'd have to take a good, long look at this life you're leading and you wouldn't be able to stand it. That's all. Why don't you give it a chance?'

She took her hand off my knee, I could see it reach like a bird in the darkness towards her face. 'You're wrong,' she said, 'and there's no need to say that. No need at all.'

'There are people around us who want to see the picture. Let's not talk; it bothers them.'

'Nobody's around us. We're all alone here. Why did you say that? It isn't fair, it isn't right.'

'But it's true, Barbara,' I said, gently. 'It's true and you know it's true and now the short subject is off and we're going to watch the movie. So just relax and let the movie come on.'

'I like my life. I like being with you. I don't mind anything that's happening to me. What's wrong with life anyway? How do you have the right to say that, Martin?'

'Because it's the truth and because you never listen to me so I have to tell you. Hush, now, we'll miss the picture.'

'That's a terrible thing to say.'

'No it isn't. It's the truth and the truth is never terrible. We're here tonight, Barbara; the two of us are together tonight because it's true and because for you at least there's no one better to be with. Now fact's facts, so face them.'

I could feel her hands clawing at me now. 'No,' she said. 'No, no, no, don't say that to me.'

'I won't say anything to you. I want to watch the picture.' The curtains swung closed, lights going on greenish behind them for an instant and then they cut open again. The titles started. 'I said that I wanted to watch this picture.'

'I should leave.'

'No you shouldn't. And you won't. Just stay.'

'I could get up and walk out on you, Martin; I tell you, I could get up and leave you. I don't need this. I don't need to sit and listen to this. I should get away from you.'

'Don't do it,' I said. 'You won't do it anyway because I'm your last hope. But believe me, Barbara, even if you did, I would hardly know the difference. Not here. Not now. Just sit and watch the picture.'

And then, not knowing whether she has heard this or not; not knowing whether she has stayed or not, I watch the colours of the screen brighten and, posed with a piece of popcorn in my hand like an arrow I feel myself once again being drawn, being drawn utterly, and everything outside in the totality of its discovered abstraction vanishes for I am here, I am back, I have returned. There is nothing but space and tension and I can feel the waters drawing, drawing; drawing me back to that first and most ultimate of all resolutions.

PHILIP OAKES

(b. 1928)

The Midnight Movie

Garland dances, Peck and Heston fight
To a draw in a moon-washed meadow.
Late night movies pit
Our substance against their shadow.

The heroes have not changed. Bogart still wears
His trench coat, Dooley Wilson plays
As Time Goes By. Their spent years
Go more slowly than our days.

Between us and them
There's no closing up; the distance is
The same before and after the programme,
We never meet face to face.

It's just as well. Those lovers kissing now
Lie deep in Forest Lawn, their profiles
Mangier than twenty years ago
When we admired them from the stalls.

The television set is haunted:
Not by the tenants, but the hosts.
We turn the reels of what we wanted,
Watched by our own ghosts.